D0442149

Mr. BOSTON

Official Bartender's and Party Guide

Edited by Anthony Giglio
Photography by Steven McDonald

WILEY
John Wiley & Sons, Inc.

Published by John Wiley & Sons, Inc., Hoboken, New Jersey
Published simultaneously in Canada

For general information about our other products and services, please contact our Customer Care Department within the United States at (800) 762-2974, outside the United States at (317) 572-3993 or fax (317) 572-4002.

Wiley also publishes its books in a variety of electronic formats. Some content that appears in print may not be available in electronic books. For more information about Wiley products, visit our Web site at www.wiley.com.

Library of Congress Cataloging-in-Publication Data:

Mr. Boston Official bartender's and party guide /
edited by Anthony Giglio;
photography by Steven McDonald.
  p. cm.
  Includes index.
  ISBN-13: 978-0-7645-9732-9 (cloth)
  ISBN-10: 0-7645-9732-9 (cloth)
  1. Bartending. 2. Cocktails. I. Giglio, Anthony.

TX951.O334 2005
641.8'74—dc22

    2005010216

Printed in China

10 9 8 7 6 5 4 3 2

Cover design by Paul DiNovo
Cover illustration by Howard Roberts

Book design and text composition by HRoberts Design

CONTENTS

INTRODUCTION

Welcome! You are holding in your hands the all-new, definitive guide to mixing perfect drinks. *Mr. Boston Official Bartender's and Party Guide* has been endorsed, consulted, and considered a basic tool for bartenders since it was first published in 1935. In fact, over 11 million copies have been in print since it first appeared shortly after the repeal of prohibition.

This edition also marks the 70th anniversary of the very first printing of what was then called *Old Mr. Boston Deluxe Official Bartenders Guide*. That rare, hard-to-find first edition was compiled and edited by Leo Cotton, a purchasing agent for the Mr. Boston liquor brand, who was as meticulous about his work as he was passionate about cocktails. His foreword in the original book still reads timeless:

> With repeal came the inevitable avalanche of cocktail books, most of them published without regard to accuracy or completeness. A survey proved the need for a cocktail book that would be *authentic* and *accurate*. The task of compiling this OFFICIAL BARTENDERS GUIDE was thereupon undertaken and now after almost one year of tedious work it is presented to the thousands of bartenders throughout the country and to that portion of the American public who desire a truly official source of information for home mixing.
>
> The OFFICIAL BARTENDERS GUIDE was compiled and edited in collaboration with four old time Boston

Bartenders whose background and experience make them authorities on the correct ingredients to be used and the proper manner of serving cocktails. This experience plus the fact that every cocktail has been *actually tested* makes this truly an OFFICIAL BARTENDERS GUIDE.

Leo Cotton's enthusiasm was such that his editing side-job became a near-full time vocation; he updated the OFFICIAL BARTENDERS GUIDE through its 49th edition, until he retired in 1970.

Though Leo Cotton died in 1990, his spirit lives on in this latest edition—perhaps more than in any since his retirement. The current cocktail renaissance, which began in the early 1990s, has brought with it a return to classicism in the art of cocktail making. That means that you won't find prefabricated mixers in this edition that didn't exist when this book was first published. You won't find references to "sour mix," "daiquiri mix," or "collins mix." We also eliminated all mentions of powdered sugar—which actually were in the original—because today's powdered sugar contains cornstarch to keep it soft. Instead, many recipes call for Simple Syrup (sugar water) and citrus juices to achieve a superior substitute to the quick-fix mixes.

Therefore, this edition has been completely overhauled, with all the recipes retested for accuracy, the format revised for both ease and beauty, and the categories—with recipes listed by primary liquor—restored to their historical places. For example, you'll find a Manhattan listed under rye instead of blended whiskey. In fact, we've sorted out all the whiskey references to more accurately suggest which type of whiskey to use, instead of simply saying "blended."

The myriad details of the overall subtle changes that went into rebuilding this book might be lost on the novice or first-time reader of this guide. But our hope is that professional or veteran *Mr. Boston* readers will be pleasantly surprised by this latest incarnation. We'd like to think that Leo Cotton would be pleased to see how much of this book reflects the spirit of his original edition (which, by the way, didn't contain a single vodka cocktail).

Before you continue reading, however, please take a moment to think about both the responsible use and serving of alcoholic drinks. The consumption of alcohol dates back many centuries, and, in many cultures throughout the world, is part of social rituals associated with significant occasions and celebrations. Most adults who choose to drink do not abuse alcohol and are aware that responsible drinking is key to their own enjoyment, health, and safety, as well as that of others, particularly when driving. Be a responsible drinker, and, if you're under the legal drinking age, our nonalchoholic drinks chapter is the *only* one for you.

So, congratulations! You're well on your way to enhancing your expertise as a professional bartender or a properly prepared host. Let's raise a proverbial glass in honor of Mr. Boston, as he was introduced in his 1935 debut:

Sirs—May we now present to you Old Mr. Boston in permanent form. We know you are going to like him. He is a jolly fellow, one of those rare individuals, everlastingly young, a distinct personality and famous throughout the land for his sterling qualities and genuine good fellowship. His friends number in the millions those who are great and those who are near great even as you and I. He is jovial and ever ready to accept the difficult role of "Life of the Party," a sympathetic friend who may be relied upon in any emergency. Follow his advice and there will be many pleasant times in store for you.

Gentlemen, Old Mr. Boston.

COCKTAIL EXPERTS
WHO CONTRIBUTED TO THIS EDITION

Tony Abou Ganim
Ed Allen
Ektoras Bini
Sean Bigley
Eric Buxton
Dorothy Colquhoun
Francisco Fabara
Dale DeGroff
Marco Dionysis
Chris Drumm
Dorrie Lynn Faulkner
Eli Feldman
Kevin Felker
Elizabeth Fraser
Nelson Flores-Giacometto
Mia Germano
John Gertsen
Christopher Golub
Jordan Goncharoff
Chris Goodhart
Mardee Haidin Regan
David Haley
Tim Hardin
Paul Harrington
Robert Hess

Ray Isle
Erik Johnson
Bill Koenig
Livio Lauro
Thomas Lavin
Roberta Lewis
Jeffery Lindenmuth
David Lynch
Lolly Mason
Ryan McGrale
Jim Meehan
Patty Murray
Sal Nardone
Chuck O'Connor
Mark Osgood
Leo Ramirez
Heather Regan
Gary Regan
Julie Reiner
Audrey Saunders
Willy Shine
Monica L. Smith
Ronald Sperry
Tara Thomas
Paul Zappoli

ACKNOWLEDGMENTS

The editor would like to officially acknowledge the following people behind Mr. Boston's all-new *Official Bartender's and Party Guide:*

Editor extraordinaire Pamela Chirls and her team at John Wiley & Sons, Inc., including Christine DiComo, Rachel Bartlett, and Shannon Egan, for grace under fire.

The keen eyes of fabulous photographers Steven McDonald, assistants Brian Reilly and Matt Bansuch, and stylists Joe Maer, Steven McDonald, Alicia Warner, and Kelly McKaig for making the drinks look sexy and beautiful; and Maximilian Riedel, for the beautiful Riedel glassware.

The steadfast vision of Jason Dyke at Barton Brands, for keeping us on message.

The brilliant resourcefulness and generous spirit of cocktail professionals Robert Hess, Audrey Saunders, Gary Regan, Dale DeGroff, Tony Abou Ganim, and Jeffery Lindenmuth.

The thoughtful Bonnie Berman, Leo Cotton's daughter, for reminding us how passionate her dad was about editing the first 49 editions of this book—and never receiving a penny in royalties!

And to my wife, Antonia LoPresti Giglio, who was pregnant with our second child throughout much of the editing of this book, for putting up with my absence.

Can and bottle openers

Easy-to-use corkscrew

Waiter's corkscrew

Small, sharp stainless-steel paring knife for cutting fruit or for shearing off rind

Glass stirring rod or long spoon

Coil-rimmed bar strainer

Tall, heavy-duty mixing glass or shaker

Wooden muddler or the back of a large wooden spoon for mashing herbs, fruit, etc.

Fruit juice extractor

Large pitcher

Set of measuring spoons

A jigger measure with easy-to-read ½- and ¼-ounce measures

Ice bucket and ice tongs

Mr. BOSTON

Official Bartender's
and
Party Guide

BAR BASICS

EQUIPMENT

The right tools make mixing drinks easier, but some tasks simply can't be done without the right gizmo.

- **Boston Shaker:** Two-piece set comprised of a mixing glass and a slightly larger metal container that acts as a cover for the mixing glass for shaking cocktails. The mixing glass can be used alone for stirring drinks that aren't shaken.
- **Barspoon:** Long-handled, shallow spoon with a twisted handle used for stirring drinks.
- **Hawthorne Strainer:** Perforated metal top for the metal half of a Boston shaker, held in place by a wire coil. Serves as a strainer.
- **Julep Strainer:** Perforated, spoon-shaped strainer used in conjunction with a mixing glass.
- **Cocktail Shaker:** Metal pitcher with a tight-fitting lid, under which sits a strainer. While styles vary widely, the popular retro-style pitcher has a handle as well as a spout that's sealed with a twist-off cap.
- **Electric Blender:** Absolutely necessary to make frozen drinks, puree fruit, and even crush ice for certain recipes.
- **Cutting Board:** Either wood or plastic, it is used to cut fruit upon for garnishes.
- **Paring Knife:** Small, sharp knife to prepare fruit for garnishes.
- **Muddler:** Looks like a wooden pestle, the flat end of which is used to crush and combine ingredients in a serving glass or mixing glass.
- **Grater:** Useful for zesting fruit or grating nutmeg.
- **Bottle Opener:** Essential for opening bottles that aren't twist-off.
- **Church Key:** Usually metal, it is pointed at one end to punch holes in the tops of cans, while the other end is used to open bottles.

• **Corkscrew:** There are a myriad of styles from which to choose: Professionals use the "Waiter's Corkscrew," which looks like a pen-knife, the "Screw-Pull," or the "Rabbit Corkscrew." The "Winged Corkscrew," found in most homes, is considered easiest to use but often destroys the cork.

• **Citrus Reamer:** Essential for juicing fruit, it comes in two styles: either the strainer bowl with the pointed cone on top, or the wooden handle with the cone attached, which must be used with a strainer.

• **Jigger:** Helpful for precise measuring (though professionals just count out the ounces in seconds silently), it is usually two v-shaped metal cups conjoined at the narrow end, one end measuring 1 ounce, the other 1½ ounces.

• **Ice Bucket with Scoop and Tongs:** A bar without ice is like a car without gas. Use the scoop—never the glass—to gather ice in a mixing glass or shaker and tongs to add single cubes to a prepared drink.

• **Miscellaneous Accoutrements:** Sipsticks or stirrers, straws, cocktail napkins, coasters, and cocktail picks.

GLASSWARE

Clean, polished glasses show off good drinks to great advantage. The best glasses should be thin-lipped, transparent, and sound off in high registers when "pinged." In practice, these five glasses could be used to make most of the mixed drinks and cocktails found in this book:

• **Cocktail Glass** (also known as Martini Glass): Typically 4 to 8 ounces, but lately much larger.

• **Collins Glass:** Tall and narrow, typically 8 to 12 ounces.

• **Highball Glass:** Shorter Collins Glass, typically 8 to 10 ounces.

• **Hurricane Glass:** Short-stem, hour-glass-shaped, typically 14 to 20 ounces.

• **Old-Fashioned Glass:** Wide and squat, typically 6 to 8 ounces.

A complete inventory of glassware, however, would include the following:

• Shot Glass
• Beer Mug
• Beer/Pilsner Glass
• Irish Coffee Glass
• Pousse Café Glass

• Parfait Glass
• Red Wine Glass
• White Wine Glass
• Sherry Glass

• Champagne Flute
• Brandy Snifter
• Cordial or Pony Glass
• Whiskey Sour Glass

Collins   Shot   Highball   Old-Fashioned

Beer Mug   Beer Pilsner   Irish Coffee Glass   Pousse Café

Red Wine   White Wine   Sherry   Champagne Flute   Parfait

Brandy Snifter   Cocktail   Cordial or Pony   Whiskey Sour

TAKING STOCK

Nobody ever said stocking a home bar is easy or inexpensive, which is probably why so few people bother to do it. However, if you're above the fray, feeling inspired by this book, and make the reasonable rationalization about the money you'll spend stocking your bar versus the money you'll save on buying drinks at bars, here's what you'll need to do it right:

Bitters
- Angostura Bitters
- Peychaud's Bitters
- Orange Bitters

Fruit Juices
- Lime Juice
- Lemon Juice
- Cranberry Juice
- Pineapple Juice
- Other juices and nectars

Savory Ingredients
- Tomato Juice
- Clam Juice
- Horseradish
- Hot Sauces
- Worcestershire Sauce

Sweetening Ingredients
- Simple Syrup (equal parts water and granulated sugar, heated over a flame, and then cooled and stored in refrigerator until needed)
- Superfine Sugar
- Granulated Sugar
- Coconut Cream
- Various Fruit Syrups (Orgeat, Elderflour)
- Grenadine

Dairy/Egg Ingredients
- Milk
- Cream (Heavy, Half-and-Half)
- Butter
- Eggs

Sodas
- Seltzer/Club Soda
- Quinine/Tonic Water
- Various: Cola, Lemon/Lime, etc.

Garnishes
- Lemon Wedges
- Lime Wedges
- Assorted Fruit Wheels
- Pineapple Chunks
- Maraschino Cherries
- Olives
- Celery
- Fresh Herbs (Mint, Basil, etc.)

TECHNIQUES

How to Chill a Glass

Always chill before you fill. There are two ways to make a cocktail glass cold:

1. Put the glasses in the refrigerator or freezer a couple of hours before using them.
2. Fill the glasses with ice and water, stir, and then discard when drink is ready.

How to Frost a Glass

There are two types of "frosted" glasses. For "frosted" drinks, glasses should be stored in a refrigerator or buried in shaved ice long enough to give each glass a white, frosted, ice-cold look and feel.

For a "sugar-frosted" glass, moisten the rim of a pre-chilled glass with a slice of lime or lemon and then dip the rim into powdered sugar.

For Margaritas, rub the rim of the glass with a lime, invert the glass, and dip it into coarse salt.

How to Muddle

Muddling is a simple mashing technique for grinding herbs, such as mint, smooth in the bottom of a glass. You can buy a wooden muddler in a bar-supply store. It crushes the herbs, much as the blunt handle of a wooden spoon might, without scarring your glassware.

To Stir or Not to Stir

Pitchers of cocktails need at least 10 seconds of stirring to mix properly. Carbonated mixers in drinks do much of their own stirring just by naturally bubbling. Two stirs will complete the job.

When to Shake

Shake any drink made with juices, sugar, or cream, or use an electric blender. Strain cocktails from shaker or blender to a glass through a coil-rimmed strainer.

Pouring

Pour drinks as soon as you make them or they will wilt. Leftovers should be discarded or they will be too diluted by the time you get to seconds.

When making a batch of drinks at once, set up the glasses in a row. Pour until each glass is half-full, and then backtrack until the shaker is empty. That way everyone gets the same amount, thoroughly mixed.

Floating Liqueurs

Creating a rainbow effect in a glass with different-colored cordials requires a special pouring technique. Simply pour each liqueur slowly over an inverted teaspoon (rounded side up) into a glass. Start with the heaviest liqueur first. (Recipes will give proper order.) Pour *slowly*. The rounded surface of the spoon will spread each liqueur over the one beneath without mixing them. You can accomplish the same trick using a glass rod. Pour slowly down the rod.

The Secret of Flaming

The secret of setting brandy (or other high-alcohol spirits) aflame is first to warm it and its glass until almost hot. You can warm a glass by holding it by its stem above the flame or electric coil on your stove until the glass feels warm. (Avoid touching the glass to the flame or coil, which could char or crack it.)

Next, heat 2 to 4 ounces of brandy in a saucepan above the flame (or in a cooking pan). When the brandy is hot, ignite it with a match.

If it's hot enough, it will flame instantly. Pour the flaming liquid carefully into the other brandy you want flamed. If all the liquid is warm enough, it will ignite.

Warning: Flames can shoot high suddenly. Look up and be sure there's nothing en route that can ignite. That includes your hair. Have an open box of baking soda handy in case of accidents. Pour it over flames to extinguish them. Use pot holders to protect your hands from the hot glass, spoon, or pan.

Using Fruit and Fruit Juices

Whenever possible, use only *fresh* fruit. Wash the outside peel before using. Fruit can be cut in wedges or in slices. If slices are used, they should be cut about ¼-inch thick and slit toward the center to fix slice on rim of glass. Make sure garnishes are fresh and cold.

When mixing drinks containing fruit juices, always pour the liquor last. Squeeze and strain fruit juices just before using to ensure freshness and good taste. Avoid artificial, concentrated substitutes.

When recipes call for a twist of lemon peel, rub a narrow strip or peel around the rim of the glass to deposit the oil on it. Then twist the peel so that the oil (usually one small drop) will drop into the drink. Then drop in the peel. The lemon oil gives added character to the cocktail, which many prefer.

Opening Champagne or Sparkling Wine

When the bottle is well chilled, wrap it in a clean towel and undo the wire around the cork. Pointing the bottle away from people and priceless objects, hold the cork with one hand, grasp the bottle by the indentation on the bottom, and slowly turn the bottle (not the cork!) until the cork comes free with a pop! Pour slowly into the center of the glass.

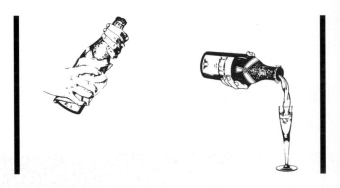

Opening Wine

Cut the seal neatly around the neck with a sharp knife just below the top. Peel off, exposing the cork. Wipe off the cork and bottle lip. Insert the corkscrew and turn until the corkscrew is completely inside the cork. With a steady pull, remove the cork. If the cork crumbles or breaks, pour the wine through a tea strainer into another container for serving. The host or hostess should taste the wine to check its quality before offering it to guests.

SERVING A CROWD

Whether you're hosting an intimate dinner party or throwing a bash for a crowd, the buying guide charts in this section can make it easy for you to determine how much liquor and wine you'll need.

HOW MANY DRINKS TO PLAN

	For 4 People	For 6 People	For 10 People
Lunch	6 cocktails/wine	10 cocktails/wine	15 cocktails/wine
	6 glasses wine with lunch	10 glasses wine with lunch	15 glasses wine with lunch
	4 liqueurs	6 liqueurs	10 liqueurs
Cocktails	8 cocktails or	12 cocktails or	20 cocktails or
	8 glasses wine first 2 hours	12 glasses wine first 2 hours	20 glasses wine first 2 hours
	6 drinks an hour thereafter	9 drinks an hour thereafter	15 drinks an hour thereafter
Dinner	8 cocktails/wine	12 cocktails/wine	20 cocktails/wine
	8 glasses wine with dinner	12 glasses wine with dinner	20 glasses wine with dinner
	4 liqueurs	6 liqueurs	10 liqueurs
	4 drinks an hour after dinner	6 drinks an hour after dinner	10 drinks an hour after dinner
Evening	16 cocktails/wine	24 cocktails/wine	40 cocktails/wine

HOW MANY BOTTLES OF WINE FOR DINNER

Table Wines, Champagnes, Sparkling Wines
(average 2 servings, 5 ounces each, per person)

People	4	6	8	10	12	20
750 ml	2	2+	3+	4	5	8
1.5 Liter	1	1+	2	2	2+	4

Generally, bottle quantities recommended provide some small overages of wine from 10-ounces-per-guest formula; "+" indicates somewhat less formula, and you may desire to have an additional bottle on hand.

HOW MANY DRINKS PER BOTTLE

Cocktails, Mixed Drinks
(1.5-ounce liquor servings)

Bottles	1	2	4	6	8	10	12
750 ml	16	33	67	101	135	169	203
Liter	22	45	90	135	180	225	270
1.5 Liter	39	78	157	236	315	394	473

Table Wines, Champagnes, Sparkling Wines
(5-ounce wine servings)

Bottles	1	2	4	6	8	10	12
750 ml	5	10	20	30	40	50	60
Liter	6	13	27	40	54	67	81
1.5 Liter	10	20	40	60	81	101	121
3 Liter	20	40	80	121	161	202	242
4 Liter	27	54	108	162	216	270	324

PARTY
PLANNING

A well-made libation can elevate even the humblest of gatherings from simple to swanky with little more effort than mixing up one of this book's 1,500 recipes. Crafting an entire party around cocktails, then, is itself an occasion, and one that already carries recognition that goes beyond the simple term "party." Indeed, a "cocktail party" promises something better than just a beer-wine-soda get-together; it connotes sophistication and craftsmanship, even if the recipes are simple-but-sublime (think of a properly made Martini, for example). The very fact that drinks are shaken, stirred, or "built," makes them special, and those to whom they are proffered will recognize a drink's pedigree not only by sight, but also by taste.

Mixed drinks and cocktails can also play a supporting role in parties that are themed, either by relating to the overall scheme of the party, or just by being respectable refreshments in the background. While our foremost concern is to help you plan a fabulous party employing one or more of our cocktails as the stars, we'll also give you some ideas around which to build a themed party.

While we will admit up front that planning and throwing a party involves some very serious considerations, we believe that we've got you covered enough to make pulling off a successful shindig more fun than frustrating. All it takes is a little planning, organization, and imagination.

PARTY ESSENTIALS

The Home Bar/Bar Table

Whether you're hosting an elegant cocktail party, a formal dinner party, or a no-holds-barred costume extravaganza, you need to have a designated bar station where all of the drinks can be made, preferably away from the heat and hubbub of the kitchen. Unless you happen to live in a former speakeasy, having your own 40-foot mahogany Art Deco bar in the basement is probably not an option, but all you really need is a sturdy, 6-foot table. Having a dedicated bar table set up and stocked before the party is paramount to a successful party.

Where you set up the bar is as important as what you serve at it. The bar should be located in the main room of the party—the living room, for instance—in an area with room for flow. Remember that wherever you situate the bar, it will become a gathering place for guests waiting for drinks as well as those socializing (because that's what always happens at bars, right?). If you have the space, place the bar table so that it's accessible from three sides—ideally with a bartender behind it on the fourth side, or at the head if the table is against the wall. If you don't have a bartender, make sure the bar is prepped with plenty of ice and even a few handmade signs encouraging a special drink du jour or cocktail that fits the theme (if any).

Set up all the spirits and drink ingredients in the center of the table, and put glassware at each end (consider stocking martini glasses, rocks glasses, highball glasses, all-purpose wine glasses, and, if you're serving Champagne, flutes). Most important of all are filled ice buckets—with tongs—placed at each end of the table, because ice—or lack of it—is one of the most underestimated party-killers in the history of entertaining. Cocktail shakers and/or mixing pitchers are also necessary, as well as fun.

A Drink in Every Hand

If first impressions are the proverbial *everything,* then a consummate host makes a guest's arrival at a party memorable by placing a drink in his or her hand as soon as possible. This makes the guest feel immediately comfortable, and it helps the host move on to greet other guests and socialize. To do this, consider making the first drink, perhaps a light aperitif, in advance and in bulk. Then, as guests arrive, the drinks can be quickly dispensed in glassware according to the recipe. Though it might seem anachronistic—or at least retro—never underestimate the power of a punch. It takes all the pressure off the host to mix drinks all night (if you don't have a bartender), and it takes pressure off the guests to have to create their own concoctions.

PARTY THEMES

A little advance planning can turn a special occasion or holiday into an especially memorable endeavor. Are you a movie buff? How about a *Gone with the Wind* gala, with participants dressed up like their favorite characters? Or a *Casablanca* cocktail hour to which guests come dressed in 1940s black-and-white elegance—with period piano music in the background? Period parties are fun, too, and more open to creative interpretation. A trove of trivia can make for hours of fun, paired, of course, with drinks from each era. Equally fun are ethnocentric parties commemorating feasts, folklore, and family traditions. While a Halloween party is quite common, you could also have your own New York–style San Gennaro feast with Italian wine cocktails to accompany pasta and delicious pastries; celebrate Oktoberfest with German beer and hearty sausages; and toast a new year the Russian way with vodka and caviar. There are as many party ideas as there are cocktails. To get you started, here are a few ideas that are evergreen:

Political Party

Whether you're toasting a winner or looking forward to trying again the next time, an election-night party is sure to draw support from your own circle of constituents. Even if voting day is months away, why wait? Bring out the buttons and placards, the favorite foods of your candidate, and a batch of El Presidente cocktails. For those who don't support your candidate, provide a Double Standard Sour, Incider Cocktail, or Journalist Cocktail—or even a shooter like the International Incident.

Hawaiian Luau

While Trader Vic's of the San Francisco establishment of the same name lays claim to originating the Mai Tai, this popular drink has long been associated with the soft winds and perfect beaches of Hawaii. To set the mood, ask each guest to wear a flowered shirt and present each one with a paper lei upon arrival. For outdoor gatherings, light store-bought torches and serve up pineapple, melons, bananas, and other tropical fruits on platters decorated with flowers. Barbecue chicken, fish, and pork and sit down at flower-covered tables to eat. Perfect drink choices include the Waikiki Beachcomber, the Blue Hawaiian, the Pineapple Fizz, or the nonalcoholic Banana Punch.

Just Desserts

Guests with a sweet tooth will appreciate liquid confections like the Chocolate-Covered Strawberry, Raspberry Cheesecake, Peach Melba, Pineapple Upside-Down Cake, Banana Foster, Death by Chocolate, and nonalcoholic Creamy Creamsicle. Often featuring ice cream, these drinks make perfect adult birthday-party treats. Fresh fruit, cookies, petit fours, and candy-coated nuts make the party extra-delicious.

Murder Mystery

On a dark and stormy night, invite eight guests to play a board game that provides the clues. Draw the curtains and place candles throughout the house. Have each person dress the part, from the ingénue in peril to the tweedy English detective. Lower the lights before serving red wine, Bloody Marys, and, of course, shooters. Serve finger food like crustless sandwiches, a cheese board and crackers, and assorted nuts.

Of course, every day can be a holiday; it's not up to Congress to declare one. Here are some of our favorites:

NEW YEAR'S DAY: Brunch Punch or a Mimosa will bring out the flavor of eggs Florentine, an assortment of breads and muffins, and various preserves. Wear slippers: This is a day for quiet.

MARDI GRAS/CARNIVAL: Oysters, crayfish, and fabulous desserts are the right fare to have with a Hurricane (a specialty of Pat O'Brien's in New Orleans), a New Orleans Buck, or a Basin Street Daiquiri.

VALENTINE'S DAY: A kiss is still a kiss, so wear your heart on your sleeve and offer up a Red-Hot Passion, an Amber Amour, a Kiss on the Lips, or a nonalcoholic Innocent Passion. Whatever you choose for dinner, make sure you have a decadent chocolate dessert. With after-dinner coffee or cappuccino, offer a classic romantic liqueur, Amaretto.

SAINT PATRICK'S DAY: Corned beef and cabbage and boiled potatoes are a must, as are an Emerald Isle Cocktail, an Irish Shillelagh, or an Irish Flag. And beer, of course.

CINCO DE MAYO (THE FIFTH OF MAY): Celebrate Mexico's holiday with mariachi music, chicken in mole sauce, a piñata, and a Margarita, a Chapala, or a Purple Pancho.

INDEPENDENCE DAY: Barbecue your favorites, set up a dessert buffet with strawberry and vanilla ice cream topped with blueberries and assorted toppings, and serve an Americana, a Fourth of July Tooter, or a Stars and Stripes.

BASTILLE DAY (JULY 14): A Champs Élysées Cocktail is the beverage of choice to accompany French bread, pâté, and (why not?) Napoleons.

NATIONAL BOURBON MONTH (SEPTEMBER): Kentucky Derby Day isn't the only time to savor this native American drink. Have a salad with the dressing of choice, a baked potato, and a steak along with a Bull and Bear, a Thoroughbred Cooler, or a Southern Lady.

HALLOWEEN: Bob for apples, pass the candy corn, and have a Nightmare, a Frisky Witch, or a Zombie.

THANKSGIVING: Turkey with all the trimmings has its particular drink: A Thanksgiving Special.

REPEAL OF PROHIBITION (DECEMBER 5): If you really need an excuse to have a party, this is the day. Don Roaring Twenties attire and roll up the rug to dance the Charleston (or play the soundtrack from *The Sting*). Mix pitchers of gin cocktails kept cool in a bathtub filled with ice, and celebrate the end of the dry spell with your own speakeasy.

CHRISTMAS: Bake a ham, roast a goose, and serve up a Christmas Yule Eggnog.

NEW YEAR'S EVE: Serve Champagne Punch with your favorite elegant foods, a lovely way to ring in a new year.

BRANDY

Brandy takes its name from the Dutch phrase *bran-dewijn,* or "burned wine," which refers to the process of heating the wine during distillation. Brandy as a category embodies a dizzying number of subcategories, including fruit brandy, grappa, marc, pomace, and eau-de-vie, to name only a few. The most generic definition for this spirit is that it is distilled from fermented fruit; it is sometimes aged in oak casks or barrels; and it usually clocks in at around 80-proof. While it is often considered an after-dinner sipping spirit, brandy is also widely used in cocktails.

Generally, fruit brandies and eau-de-vie can legally be made from practically any fruit, including apples, pears, apricots, blackberries, and cherries. At the high end of the brandy spectrum, you'll find Calvados from the north of France, Cognac and Armagnac from southwest France, and Solera Gran Reservas under the Brandy de Jerez—or sherry—imprimatur from the south of Spain. Artisanal brandies are also being made here in the United States, but not from any specific region, though the best hail from California and Oregon.

In cocktails, dry sherry is sometimes employed in place of vermouth, while Cognac plays a leading role in a number of recipes dating back to the birth of the cocktail in Antoine Peychaud's Apothecary shop in New Orleans. Indeed, the original juleps were made with Cognac, as were many of the early Pousse Café recipes. Armagnac, Cognac's rustic cousin, has a distinctly stronger flavor than Cognac, and is employed as such a substitute to enhance the brandy presence in a cocktail. Calvados, made with apples, is naturally used to ratchet up the quality of any cocktail calling for mere fruit or apple brandy.

THE "23"

2½ oz. Armagnac
½ oz. Sweet Vermouth
½ oz. Lemon Juice
2 dashes Bitters

Shake with ice and strain into chilled, sugar-rimmed cocktail glass. Garnish with a twist of lemon peel.

AFTER-DINNER COCKTAIL

1 oz. Apricot-flavored
    Brandy
1 oz. Triple Sec
1 oz. Lime Juice

Shake with ice and strain into chilled cocktail glass. Leave lime in glass.

ALABAZAM

2 oz. Armagnac
¾ oz. Lemon Juice
½ oz. Orange Curaçao
½ oz. Superfine Sugar (or
    Simple Syrup)
2 dashes Angostura Bitters
2 dashes Peychaud's Bitters

Shake with ice and strain into ice-filled rocks glass. Garnish with a flamed orange peel.

ALEXANDER COCKTAIL NO. 2

1 oz. Crème de Cacao
    (White)
1 oz. Brandy
1 oz. Light Cream

Shake with ice and strain into chilled cocktail glass. Garnish with fresh-grated nutmeg on top.

AMERICAN BEAUTY COCKTAIL

½ oz. Orange Juice
½ oz. Grenadine
½ oz. Dry Vermouth
½ oz. Brandy
¼ tsp. Crème de Menthe
    (White)
1 dash Port

Shake first five ingredients with ice and strain into chilled cocktail glass. Top with a dash of Port.

APPLE BRANDY COCKTAIL

1½ oz. Apple Brandy
1 tsp. Grenadine
1 tsp. Lemon Juice

Shake with ice and strain into chilled cocktail glass.

APPLE BRANDY HIGHBALL

2 oz. Apple Brandy
Ginger Ale or Club Soda

Pour brandy into ice-filled highball glass. Fill with ginger ale or club soda. Add a twist of lemon peel, if desired, and stir.

APPLE BRANDY RICKEY

½ oz. Lime Juice
1½ oz. Apple Brandy
Club Soda

Pour lime juice and brandy into ice-filled highball glass. Fill with club soda and stir. Garnish with a wedge of lime.

APPLE BRANDY SOUR

1 oz. Lemon Juice
1/2 tsp. Superfine Sugar (or
    Simple Syrup)
2 oz. Apple Brandy

Shake with ice and strain into
chilled sour glass. Garnish
with a half-slice of lemon and
a maraschino cherry.

APRICOT BRANDY RICKEY

1/2 oz. Lime Juice
2 oz. Apricot-flavored
    Brandy
Club Soda

Pour lime juice and brandy
into ice-filled highball glass.
Fill with club soda and stir.
Garnish with a wedge of
lime.

APRICOT COCKTAIL

1/2 oz. Lemon Juice
1 oz. Orange Juice
1 1/2 oz. Apricot-flavored
    Brandy
1 tsp. Gin

Shake with ice and strain into
chilled cocktail glass.

APRICOT COOLER

1/2 tsp. Superfine Sugar (or
    Simple Syrup)
2 oz. Club Soda or Ginger Ale
2 oz. Apricot-flavored
    Brandy

In collins glass, dissolve
sugar/syrup and club soda.
Stir and fill glass with ice and
add brandy. Add club soda or
ginger ale and stir again.
Insert a spiral of orange or
lemon peel (or both) and
dangle end over rim of glass.

APRICOT FIZZ

1 oz. Lemon Juice
1/2 oz. Lime Juice
1 tsp. Superfine Sugar (or
    Simple Syrup)
2 oz. Apricot-flavored
    Brandy
Club Soda

Shake juices, sugar/syrup,
and brandy with ice and
strain into ice-filled highball
glass. Fill with club soda and
stir.

B & B

1/2 oz. Benedictine
1/2 oz. Brandy

Use cordial glass and carefully float the brandy on top
of the Benedictine.

BRANDY

BABBIE'S SPECIAL COCKTAIL

½ oz. Light Cream
1½ oz. Apricot-flavored
   Brandy
¼ tsp. Gin

Shake with ice and strain into
chilled cocktail glass.

BEE STINGER

½ oz. Crème de Menthe
   (White)
1½ oz. Blackberry Brandy

Shake with ice and strain into
chilled cocktail glass.

BETSY ROSS

1½ oz. Brandy
1½ oz. Port
1 dash Triple Sec

Stir with ice and strain into
chilled cocktail glass.

BISTRO SIDECAR

1½ oz. Brandy
½ oz. Tuaca
½ oz. Frangelico
¼ oz. Lemon Juice
¼ oz. Superfine Sugar (or
   Simple Syrup)
1 wedge Tangerine,
   squeezed

Shake with ice. Strain into
chilled, sugar-rimmed cocktail glass. Garnish with a
roasted hazelnut.

BLACK FEATHER

2 oz. Brandy
1 oz. Dry Vermouth
½ oz. Triple Sec
1 dash Bitters

Stir with ice and strain into
chilled cocktail glass. Garnish
with a twist of lemon peel.

BOMBAY COCKTAIL

½ oz. Dry Vermouth
½ oz. Sweet Vermouth
1 oz. Brandy
¼ tsp. Anisette
½ tsp. Triple Sec

Stir with ice and strain into
chilled cocktail glass.

BOSOM CARESSER

1 oz. Brandy
1 oz. Madeira
½ oz. Triple Sec

Stir with ice and strain into
chilled cocktail glass.

BRANDIED MADEIRA

1 oz. Brandy
1 oz. Madeira
½ oz. Dry Vermouth

Stir with ice and strain into
ice-filled old-fashioned glass.
Add a twist of lemon peel.

BRANDIED PORT

1 oz. Brandy
1 oz. Tawny Port
1/2 oz. Lemon Juice
1 tsp. Maraschino Liqueur

Shake all ingredients and strain into ice-filled old-fashioned glass. Add a slice of orange.

BRANDY ALEXANDER

1/2 oz. Crème de Cacao (Brown)
1/2 oz. Brandy
1/2 oz. Heavy Cream

Shake well with ice and strain into chilled cocktail glass.

BRANDY CASSIS

1 1/2 oz. Brandy
1 oz. Lemon Juice
1 dash Crème de Cassis

Shake with ice and strain into chilled cocktail glass. Add a twist of lemon peel.

BRANDY COBBLER

1 tsp. Superfine Sugar (or Simple Syrup)
2 oz. Club Soda
2 oz. Brandy

Dissolve sugar/syrup in club soda. Fill 10-oz. goblet with shaved ice. Add brandy. Stir well and garnish with fruits in season. Serve with straws.

BRANDY COCKTAIL

2 oz. Brandy
1/4 tsp. Superfine Sugar (or Simple Syrup)
2 dashes Bitters

Stir ingredients with ice and strain into chilled cocktail glass. Add a twist of lemon peel.

BRANDY COLLINS

1 oz. Lemon Juice
1 tsp. Superfine Sugar (or Simple Syrup)
2 oz. Brandy
Club Soda

Shake lemon juice, sugar/syrup, and brandy with ice and strain into ice-filled collins glass. Fill with club soda and stir. Garnish with a slice of orange or lemon and a maraschino cherry. Serve with straws.

BRANDY CURSTA COCKTAIL

1 tsp. Maraschino Liqueur
1 dash Bitters
1 tsp. Lemon Juice
1/2 oz. Triple Sec
2 oz. Brandy

Moisten the edge of a cocktail glass with lemon and dip into sugar. Cut the rind of half a lemon into a spiral and place in glass. Stir above ingredients with ice and strain into chilled, sugar-rimmed glass. Add a slice of orange.

BRANDY DAISY

1 oz. Lemon Juice
½ tsp. Superfine Sugar (or Simple Syrup)
1 tsp. Raspberry Syrup or Grenadine
2 oz. Brandy

Shake with ice and strain into stein or 8-oz. metal cup. Add cubes of ice and garnish with fruit.

BRANDY FIX

1 oz. Lemon Juice
1 tsp. Superfine Sugar (or Simple Syrup)
1 tsp. Water
2½ oz. Brandy

Mix lemon juice, sugar/syrup, and water in highball glass. Stir. Then fill glass with shaved ice and brandy. Stir, add a slice of lemon. Serve with straws.

BRANDY FIZZ

1 oz. Lemon Juice
1 tsp. Superfine Sugar (or Simple Syrup)
2 oz. Brandy
Club Soda

Shake lemon juice, sugar/syrup, and brandy with ice and strain into ice-filled highball glass. Fill with club soda and stir.

BRANDY GUMP COCKTAIL

1½ oz. Brandy
1 oz. Lemon Juice
½ tsp. Grenadine

Shake with ice and strain into chilled cocktail glass.

BRANDY HIGHBALL

2 oz. Brandy
Ginger Ale or Club Soda

Pour brandy into ice-filled highball glass. Fill with ginger ale or club soda. Add a twist of lemon peel and stir gently.

BRANDY JULEP

5–6 Mint Leaves
1 tsp. Superfine Sugar (or Simple Syrup)
2½ oz. Brandy

Put sugar/syrup, mint leaves, and brandy into collins glass. Fill glass with finely shaved ice and stir until mint rises to top, being careful not to bruise leaves. (Do not hold glass while stirring.) Garnish with a slice of pineapple, orange, or lemon, and a maraschino cherry. Serve with straws.

BRANDY SANGAREE

½ tsp. Superfine Sugar (or Simple Syrup)
1 tsp. Water
2 oz. Brandy
Club Soda
½ oz. Port

Dissolve sugar/syrup in water and add brandy. Pour into ice-filled highball glass. Fill with club soda and stir. Float Port on top and garnish with fresh-grated nutmeg.

BRANDY SLING

1 tsp. Superfine Sugar (or Simple Syrup)
1 tsp. Water
1 oz. Lemon Juice
2 oz. Brandy

Dissolve sugar/syrup in water and lemon juice in old-fashioned glass. Fill with ice, add brandy, and stir. Garnish with a twist of lemon peel.

BRANDY SMASH

1 cube Sugar
1 oz. Club Soda
4 sprigs Mint
2 oz. Brandy

Muddle cube of sugar with club soda and mint in old-fashioned glass. Add brandy and ice. Stir and garnish with a slice of orange and a maraschino cherry. Add a twist of lemon peel on top.

BRANDY AND SODA

2 oz. Brandy
Club Soda

Pour brandy into ice-filled collins glass. Fill with club soda.

BRANDY SOUR

1 oz. Lemon Juice
½ tsp. Superfine Sugar (or Simple Syrup)
2 oz. Brandy

Shake with ice and strain into chilled sour glass. Garnish with a half-slice of lemon and a maraschino cherry.

BRANDY SQUIRT

1½ oz. Brandy
1 tbsp. Superfine Sugar (or Simple Syrup)
1 tsp. Grenadine
Club Soda

Shake with ice and strain into chilled highball glass and fill with club soda. Garnish with stick of pineapple and strawberries.

BRANDY SWIZZLE

1 oz. Lime Juice
1 tsp. Superfine Sugar (or
    Simple Syrup)
2 oz. Club Soda
2 dashes Bitters
2 oz. Brandy

Dissolve the sugar/syrup in
lime juice and club soda in
collins glass. Fill glass with
ice and stir. Add bitters and
brandy. Add club soda and
serve with a swizzle stick.

BRANDY TODDY

1/2 tsp. Superfine Sugar (or
    Simple Syrup)
1 tsp. Water
2 oz. Brandy
1 Ice Cube

Dissolve the sugar/syrup and
water in old-fashioned glass.
Add the brandy and the ice
cube. Stir and add a twist of
lemon peel on top.

BRANDY VERMOUTH COCKTAIL

1/2 oz. Sweet Vermouth
2 oz. Brandy
1 dash Bitters

Stir with ice and strain into
chilled cocktail glass.

BRANTINI

1 1/2 oz. Brandy
1 oz. Gin
1 dash Dry Vermouth

Stir with ice and strain into
ice-filled old-fashioned glass.
Add a twist of lemon peel.

BULLDOG COCKTAIL

1 1/2 oz. Cherry-flavored
    Brandy
3/4 oz. Gin
1/2 oz. Lime Juice

Shake with ice and strain into
chilled cocktail glass

BULL'S EYE

1 oz. Brandy
2 oz. Hard Cider
Ginger Ale

Pour brandy and hard cider
into ice-filled highball glass
and fill with ginger ale. Stir.

BULL'S MILK

1 tsp. Superfine Sugar (or
    Simple Syrup)
1 oz. Light Rum
1 1/2 oz. Brandy
1 cup Milk

Shake with ice and strain into
chilled, collins glass. Garnish
with fresh-grated nutmeg and
a pinch of cinnamon on top.

BUTTON HOOK COCKTAIL

½ oz. Crème de Menthe (White)
½ oz. Apricot-flavored Brandy
½ oz. Anisette
½ oz. Brandy

Shake with ice and strain into chilled cocktail glass.

CADIZ

¼ oz. Dry Sherry
¼ oz. Blackberry-flavored Brandy
½ oz. Triple Sec
½ oz. Light Cream

Shake with ice and strain into ice-filled old-fashioned glass.

CALVADOS COCKTAIL

1½ oz. Calvados (Apple Brandy)
1½ oz. Orange Juice
¾ oz. Triple Sec
¾ oz. Orange Bitters

Shake with ice and strain into chilled cocktail glass.

CARA SPOSA

1 oz. Coffee-flavored Brandy
1 oz. Triple Sec
½ oz. Light Cream

Shake with ice and strain into chilled cocktail glass.

CARROL COCKTAIL

1½ oz. Brandy
¾ oz. Sweet Vermouth

Stir with ice and strain into chilled cocktail glass. Garnish with a maraschino cherry.

CHAMPS ÉLYSÉES COCKTAIL

1 oz. Brandy
½ oz. Chartreuse (Yellow)
½ oz. Lemon Juice
½ tsp. Superfine Sugar (or Simple Syrup)
1 dash Bitters

Shake with ice and strain into chilled cocktail glass.

CHARLES COCKTAIL

1½ oz. Sweet Vermouth
1½ oz. Brandy
1 dash Bitters

Stir with ice and strain into chilled cocktail glass.

CHERRY BLOSSOM

1½ oz. Brandy
½ oz. Cherry-flavored Brandy
1½ tsps. Triple Sec
1½ tsps. Grenadine
2 tsps. Lemon Juice

Prepare chilled cocktail glass by dipping rim in cherry brandy and then superfine sugar. Shake ingredients with ice and strain into prepared glass. Add a maraschino cherry.

CHERRY FIZZ

1 oz. Lemon Juice
2 oz. Cherry-flavored Brandy
Club Soda

Shake with ice and strain into ice-filled highball glass. Fill with club soda and garnish with a maraschino cherry.

CHERRY SLING

2 oz. Cherry-flavored
   Brandy
1 oz. Lemon Juice

Serve in ice-filled old-fashioned
glass and stir. Add a twist of
lemon peel.

CHICAGO COCKTAIL

2 oz. Brandy
1 dash Bitters
1/4 tsp. Triple Sec

Prepare chilled old-fashioned
glass by rubbing slice of
lemon around rim and then
dipping into sugar. Stir ingredients with ice and strain
into prepared glass.

CLASSIC COCKTAIL

1/2 oz. Lemon Juice
1 1/2 tsps. Curaçao
1 1/2 tsps. Maraschino
   Liqueur
1 oz. Brandy

Prepare rim of chilled old-
fashioned glass by rubbing
with lemon and dipping into
superfine sugar. Shake ingredients with ice and strain
into prepared glass.

COFFEE GRASSHOPPER

3/4 oz. Coffee-flavored
   Brandy
3/4 oz. Crème de Menthe
   (White)
3/4 oz. Light Cream

Shake with ice and strain into
ice-filled old-fashioned glass.

COGNAC HIGHBALL

2 oz. Cognac
Ginger Ale or Club Soda

Pour Cognac into ice-filled
highball glass and fill with
ginger ale or club soda. Add
a twist of lemon peel, if
desired, and stir.

COLD DECK COCKTAIL

1/2 tsp. Crème de Menthe
   (White)
1/2 oz. Sweet Vermouth
1 oz. Brandy

Stir with ice and strain into
chilled cocktail glass.

CRÈME DE CAFÉ

1 oz. Coffee-flavored
   Brandy
1/2 oz. Rum
1/2 oz. Anisette
1 oz. Light Cream

Shake with ice and strain into
chilled old-fashioned glass.

CUBAN COCKTAIL NO. 2

1/2 oz Lime Juice
1/2 oz. Apricot-flavored
   Brandy
1 1/2 oz. Brandy
1 tsp. Light Rum

Shake with ice and strain into
chilled cocktail glass.

D'ARTAGNAN

½ tsp. Armagnac
½ tsp. Grand Marnier
3 tsp. Orange Juice
½ tsp. Simple Syrup
3 oz. Champagne, Chilled
Orange Peel, cut into thin
strips

Chill first four ingredients in
mixing glass and strain into
Champagne flute. Top with
Champagne and add strips of
orange peel so they extend
the length of the glass.

DEAUVILLE COCKTAIL

½ oz. Lemon Juice
½ oz. Brandy
½ oz. Apple Brandy
½ oz. Triple Sec

Shake with ice and strain into
chilled cocktail glass.

DEPTH BOMB

1 oz. Apple Brandy
1 oz. Brandy
1 dash Lemon Juice
1 dash Grenadine

Shake with ice and strain into
ice-filled old-fashioned glass.

DREAM COCKTAIL

¾ oz. Triple Sec
1½ oz. Brandy
¼ tsp. Anisette

Shake with ice and strain into
chilled cocktail glass.

EAST INDIA COCKTAIL NO. 1

1½ oz. Brandy
½ tsp. Pineapple Juice
½ tsp. Triple Sec
1 tsp. Jamaica Rum
1 dash Bitters

Shake with ice and strain into
chilled cocktail glass. Add a
twist of lemon peel and a
maraschino cherry.

ETHEL DUFFY COCKTAIL

¾ oz. Apricot-flavored
Brandy
¾ oz. Crème de Menthe
(White)
¾ oz. Triple Sec

Shake with ice and strain into
chilled cocktail glass.

FALLEN LEAVES

¾ oz. Calvados (Apple
Brandy)
¾ oz. Sweet Vermouth
¼ oz. Dry Vermouth
1 dash Brandy
1 squeeze Lemon Peel

Stir with ice and strain into
chilled cocktail glass.
Squeeze lemon twist into
drink, and use as garnish.

FANCY BRANDY

2 oz. Brandy
1 dash Bitters
¼ tsp. Triple Sec
¼ tsp. Superfine Sugar (or
Simple Syrup)

Shake with ice and strain into
chilled cocktail glass. Add a
twist of lemon peel.

BRANDY

FANTASIO COCKTAIL

1 tsp. Crème de Menthe
    (White)
1 tsp. Maraschino Liqueur
1 oz. Brandy
3/4 oz. Dry Vermouth

Stir with ice and strain into
chilled cocktail glass.

FONTAINEBLEAU SPECIAL

1 oz. Brandy
1 oz. Anisette
1/2 oz. Dry Vermouth

Shake with ice and strain into
chilled cocktail glass.

FRENCH QUARTER

2 1/2 oz. Brandy
3/4 oz. Lillet Blonde

Stir with ice and strain into
chilled cocktail glass. Garnish
with a thin quarter wheel of
lemon.

FROUPE COCKTAIL

1 1/2 oz. Sweet Vermouth
1 1/2 oz. Brandy
1 tsp. Benedictine

Stir with ice and strain into
chilled cocktail glass.

GEORGIA MINT JULEP

2 sprigs Mint
1 tsp. Superfine Sugar (or
    Simple Syrup)
1 splash Water
1 1/2 oz. Brandy
1 oz. Peach-flavored Brandy

Put mint, sugar/syrup, and splash
of water into collins glass and
muddle. Fill with ice, and then
add brandy and peach liqueur.
Garnish with mint leaves.

GILROY COCKTAIL

1/2 oz. Lemon Juice
1/2 oz. Dry Vermouth
3/4 oz. Cherry-flavored
    Brandy
3/4 oz. Gin
1 dash Orange Bitters

Shake with ice and strain into
chilled cocktail glass.

GOAT'S DELIGHT

1 3/4 oz. Kirschwasser
1 3/4 oz. Brandy
1/4 oz. Orgeat Syrup
    (Almond Syrup)
1/4 oz. Cream
1/4 oz. Pastis (Pernod or
    other absinthe substi-
    tute)

Shake with ice and strain into
chilled cocktail glass.

GOLDEN DAWN

1 oz. Apple Brandy
1/2 oz. Apricot-flavored
    Brandy
1/2 oz. Gin
1 oz. Orange Juice
1 tsp. Grenadine

Shake all ingredients except
grenadine with ice and strain
into ice-filled old-fashioned
glass. Add grenadine.

GOTHAM

1/2 tsp. Pernod (or Absinthe Substitute)
3 dashes Peach Bitters
3 oz. Brandy

Coat a chilled old-fashioned glass with Pernod (or Absinthe substitute), and then add the peach bitters and brandy. Garnish with a twist of lemon peel.

HARVARD COCKTAIL

1 1/2 oz. Brandy
3/4 oz. Sweet Vermouth
1 dash Bitters
1 tsp. Grenadine
2 tsps. Lemon Juice

Shake with ice and strain into chilled cocktail glass.

HARVARD COOLER

1/2 tsp. Superfine Sugar (or Simple Syrup)
2 oz. Club Soda or Ginger Ale
2 oz. Apple Brandy

In collins glass, stir sugar/syrup into club soda. Add ice cubes and apple brandy. Fill with club soda or ginger ale and stir again. Insert a spiral of orange or lemon peel (or both) and dangle end over rim of glass.

HONEYMOON COCKTAIL

3/4 oz. Benedictine
3/4 oz. Apple Brandy
1 oz. Lemon Juice
1 tsp. Triple Sec

Shake with ice and strain into chilled cocktail glass.

JACK-IN-THE-BOX

1 oz. Apple Brandy
1 oz. Pineapple Juice
1 dash Bitters

Shake with ice and strain into chilled cocktail glass.

JACK ROSE COCKTAIL

1 1/2 oz. Apple Brandy
1/2 oz. Lime Juice
1 tsp. Grenadine

Shake with ice and strain into chilled cocktail glass.

JAMAICA GRANITO

1 small scoop Lemon or Orange Sherbet
1 1/2 oz. Brandy
1 oz. Triple Sec
Club Soda

Combine in collins glass and stir. Garnish with fresh-grated nutmeg on top.

JAMAICA HOP

1 oz. Coffee-flavored Brandy
1 oz. Crème de Cacao (White)
1 oz. Light Cream

Shake well with ice and strain into chilled cocktail glass.

JAPANESE

2 oz. Brandy
1/2 oz. Orgeat Syrup (Almond Syrup)
2 dashes Angostura Bitters

Stir with ice and strain into chilled cocktail glass. Garnish with a twist of lemon peel.

JERSEY LIGHTNING

1½ oz. Apple Brandy
½ oz. Sweet Vermouth
1 oz. Lime Juice

Shake with ice and strain into chilled cocktail glass.

LADY BE GOOD

1½ oz. Brandy
½ oz. Crème de Menthe (White)
½ oz. Sweet Vermouth

Shake with ice and strain into chilled cocktail glass.

LA JOLLA

1½ oz. Brandy
½ oz. Crème de Banana
1 tsp. Orange Juice
2 tsps. Lemon Juice

Shake with ice and strain into chilled cocktail glass.

LIBERTY COCKTAIL

¾ oz. Light Rum
1½ oz. Apple Brandy
¼ tsp. Superfine Sugar (or Simple Syrup)

Stir with ice and strain into chilled cocktail glass.

LUGGER

1 oz. Brandy
1 oz. Apple Brandy
1 dash Apricot-flavored Brandy

Shake with ice and strain into chilled cocktail glass.

LUXURY COCKTAIL

3 oz. Brandy
2 dashes Orange Bitters
3 oz. Well-chilled Champagne

Stir and pour into Champagne flute.

MERRY WIDOW COCKTAIL NO. 2

1¼ oz. Maraschino Liqueur
1¼ oz. Cherry-flavored Brandy

Stir with ice and strain into chilled cocktail glass. Garnish with a maraschino cherry.

METROPOLE

1½ oz. Brandy
1½ oz. Dry Vermouth
2 dashes Orange Bitters
1 dash Peychaud's Bitters

Stir with ice and strain into chilled cocktail glass. Garnish with a maraschino cherry.

METROPOLITAN COCKTAIL

1¼ oz. Brandy
1¼ oz. Sweet Vermouth
½ tsp. Superfine Sugar (or Simple Syrup)
1 dash Bitters

Stir with ice and strain into chilled cocktail glass.

MIDNIGHT COCKTAIL

1 oz. Apricot-flavored Brandy
½ oz. Triple Sec
½ oz. Lemon Juice

Shake with ice and strain into chilled cocktail glass.

MIKADO COCKTAIL

1 oz. Brandy
1 dash Triple Sec
1 dash Grenadine
1 dash Crème de Noyaux
1 dash Bitters

Stir in old-fashioned glass over ice cubes.

MONTANA

1½ oz. Brandy
1 oz. Port
½ oz. Dry Vermouth

Stir in ice-filled old-fashioned glass.

MOONLIGHT

2 oz. Apple Brandy
1 oz. Lemon Juice
1 tsp. Superfine Sugar (or Simple Syrup)

Shake with ice and strain into ice-filled old-fashioned glass.

MORNING COCKTAIL

1 oz. Brandy
1 oz. Dry Vermouth
¼ tsp. Triple Sec
¼ tsp. Maraschino Liqueur
¼ tsp. Anisette
2 dashes Orange Bitters

Stir with ice and strain into chilled cocktail glass. Garnish with a maraschino cherry.

NETHERLAND

1 oz. Brandy
1 oz. Triple Sec
1 dash Orange Bitters

Stir in ice-filled old-fashioned glass.

NICKY FINN

1 oz. Brandy
1 oz. Triple Sec
1 oz. Lemon Juice
1 dash Pernod (or Absinthe Substitute)

Shake with ice and strain into chilled cocktail glass. Garnish with a maraschino cherry or a lemon zest.

THE NORMANDY

1½ oz. Calvados (Pere Magloire or Apple Brandy)
1½ oz. Dubonnet Rouge
1 oz. Fresh Apple Cider
¼ oz. Lime Juice

Shake with ice and strain into chilled cocktail glass. Garnish with a slice of red apple.

OLYMPIC COCKTAIL

¾ oz. Orange Juice
¾ oz. Triple Sec
¾ oz. Brandy

Shake with ice and strain into chilled cocktail glass.

PARADISE COCKTAIL

1 oz. Apricot-flavored Brandy
¾ oz. Gin
1 oz. Orange Juice

Shake with ice and strain into chilled cocktail glass.

BRANDY

PEACH SANGAREE

1 oz. Peach-flavored
    Brandy
Club Soda
1 tsp. Port

Pour brandy into ice-filled
highball glass. Fill glass with
club soda. Stir and float Port
on top. Garnish with fresh-
grated nutmeg.

PISCO SOUR

2 oz. Pisco (Peruvian
    Brandy)
1 oz. Lime Juice
¼ oz. Superfine Sugar (or
    Simple Syrup)
½ Egg White
1 dash Angostura Bitters

Shake all ingredients except bitters with ice. Strain into a Champagne flute. Dash with bitters.

POLONAISE

1½ oz. Brandy
½ oz. Blackberry-flavored
    Brandy
½ oz. Dry Sherry
1 dash Lemon Juice

Shake with ice and strain into
ice-filled old-fashioned glass.

POOP DECK COCKTAIL

1 oz. Brandy
1 oz. Port
½ oz. Blackberry-flavored
    Brandy

Shake with ice and strain into
chilled cocktail glass.

PRESTO COCKTAIL

½ oz. Orange Juice
½ oz. Sweet Vermouth
1½ oz. Brandy
¼ tsp. Anisette

Shake with ice and strain into
chilled cocktail glass.

PRINCESS POUSSE CAFÉ

¾ oz. Apricot-flavored
    Brandy
1½ tsps. Light Cream

Pour cream carefully on top
of brandy, in a pousse-café
glass so that it does not mix.

RENAISSANCE

2 oz. Brandy
1⅓ oz. Sweet Vermouth
⅓ oz. Limoncello
2 dashes Peach Bitters

Stir with ice and strain into
chilled cocktail glass. Garnish
with a twist of lemon peel.

ROYAL SMILE COCKTAIL

½ oz. Lemon Juice
1 tsp. Grenadine
½ oz. Gin
1 oz. Apple Brandy

Stir with ice and strain into
chilled cocktail glass.

ST. CHARLES PUNCH

1 oz. Brandy
1/2 oz. Triple Sec
2 oz. Lemon Juice
1 tsp. Sugar
3 oz. Port

Shake all ingredients except
Port with ice. Strain into ice-
filled collins glass. Top with
Port. Add a slice of lemon
and a maraschino cherry.

SARATOGA COCKTAIL

2 oz. Brandy
2 dashes Bitters
1 tsp. Lemon Juice
1 tsp. Pineapple Juice
1/2 tsp. Maraschino Liqueur

Shake with ice and strain into
chilled cocktail glass.

SAUCY SUE COCKTAIL

1/2 tsp. Apricot-flavored Brandy
1/2 tsp. Pernod
2 oz. Apple Brandy

Stir with ice and strain into
chilled cocktail glass.

SHRINER COCKTAIL

1 1/2 oz. Brandy
1 1/2 oz. Sloe Gin
2 dashes Bitters
1/2 tsp. Superfine Sugar (or
    Simple Syrup)

Stir with ice and strain into
chilled cocktail glass. Add a
twist of lemon peel.

SIDECAR COCKTAIL

1/2 oz. Lemon Juice
1 oz. Triple Sec
1 oz. Brandy

Shake with ice and strain into
chilled cocktail glass.

SINGAPORE SLING

1 1/2 oz. Gin
1/2 oz. Cherry-flavored Brandy
1/4 oz. Triple Sec
1/4 oz. Benedictine
4 oz. Pineapple Juice
1/2 oz. Lime Juice
1/3 oz. Grenadine
1 dash Bitters

Shake with ice and strain into
ice-filled collins glass. Garnish with a maraschino
cherry and a slice of
pineapple.

As served at the Raffles Hotel, Singapore

SLOPPY JOE'S COCKTAIL NO. 2

3/4 oz. Pineapple Juice
3/4 oz. Brandy
3/4 oz. Port
1/4 tsp. Triple Sec
1/4 tsp. Grenadine

Shake with ice and strain into
chilled cocktail glass.

SOMBRERO

1 1/2 oz. Coffee-flavored
    Brandy
1 oz. Light Cream

Pour brandy into ice-filled
old-fashioned glass. Float
cream on top.

BRANDY

SOOTHER COCKTAIL

$\frac{1}{2}$ oz. Brandy
$\frac{1}{2}$ oz. Apple Brandy
$\frac{1}{2}$ oz. Triple Sec
1 oz. Lemon Juice
1 tsp. Superfine Sugar (or Simple Syrup)

Shake with ice and strain into chilled cocktail glass.

SPECIAL ROUGH COCKTAIL

$1\frac{1}{2}$ oz. Apple Brandy
$1\frac{1}{2}$ oz. Brandy
$\frac{1}{2}$ tsp. Anisette

Stir with ice and strain into chilled cocktail glass.

STAR COCKTAIL

1 oz. Apple Brandy
1 oz. Sweet Vermouth
1 dash Bitters

Stir with ice and strain into chilled cocktail glass. Add a twist of lemon peel.

STINGER

$\frac{1}{2}$ oz. Crème de Menthe (White)
$1\frac{1}{2}$ oz. Brandy

Shake with ice and strain into chilled cocktail glass.

STIRRUP CUP

1 oz. Cherry-flavored Brandy
1 oz. Brandy
1 oz. Lemon Juice
1 tsp. Sugar

Shake with ice and strain into ice-filled old-fashioned glass.

THE TANTRIS SIDECAR

1 oz. Cognac (VS)
$\frac{1}{2}$ oz. Calvados (Apple Brandy)
$\frac{1}{2}$ oz. Triple Sec
$\frac{1}{2}$ oz. Lemon Juice
$\frac{1}{2}$ oz. Superfine Sugar (or Simple Syrup)
$\frac{1}{4}$ oz. Pineapple Juice
$\frac{1}{4}$ oz. Green Chartreuse

Shake all ingredients and strain into chilled, sugar-rimmed cocktail glass. Garnish with a lemon twist.

TEMPTER COCKTAIL

1 oz. Port
1 oz. Apricot-flavored Brandy

Stir with ice and strain into chilled cocktail glass.

THANKSGIVING SPECIAL

$\frac{3}{4}$ oz. Apricot-flavored Brandy
$\frac{3}{4}$ oz. Gin
$\frac{3}{4}$ oz. Dry Vermouth
$\frac{1}{4}$ tsp. Lemon Juice

Shake with ice and strain into chilled cocktail glass. Garnish with a maraschino cherry.

TULIP COCKTAIL

1 1/2 tsps. Lemon Juice
1 1/2 tsps. Apricot-flavored
    Brandy
3/4 oz. Sweet Vermouth
3/4 oz. Apple Brandy

Shake with ice and strain into
chilled cocktail glass.

VALENCIA COCKTAIL

1/2 oz. Orange Juice
1 1/2 oz. Apricot-flavored
    Brandy
2 dashes Orange Bitters

Shake with ice and strain into
chilled cocktail glass.

VANDERBILT COCKTAIL

3/4 oz. Cherry-flavored
    Brandy
1 1/2 oz. Brandy
1 tsp. Superfine Sugar (or
    Simple Syrup)
2 dashes Bitters

Stir with ice and strain into
chilled cocktail glass.

WHIP COCKTAIL

3/4 oz. Dry Vermouth
1/2 oz. Sweet Vermouth
1 1/2 oz. Brandy
1/4 tsp. Anisette
1 tsp. Triple Sec

Stir with ice and strain into
chilled cocktail glass.

WIDOW'S KISS

2 oz. Calvados (Apple Brandy)
1 oz. Chartreuse (Yellow)
1 oz. Benedictine
1 dash Angostura Bitters

Stir with ice and strain into
chilled cocktail glass.

WINDY-CORNER COCKTAIL

2 oz. Blackberry-flavored
    Brandy

Stir brandy with ice and
strain into chilled cocktail
glass. Garnish with fresh-
grated nutmeg on top.

▶ Chicago Cocktail

► French Quarter

▶ Singapore Sling

▶ Martini

▶ The Outsider

► Red Snapper

▶ Gin Gin
  Mule

▶ Caipirinha

► Mai Tai

► Daiquiri

▶ Vacation Cocktail

GIN

Gin was created over 300 years ago by a Dutch chemist named Dr. Franciscus Sylvius in an attempt to enhance the therapeutic properties of juniper in a medicinal beverage. He called it *genièvre,* French for "juniper," a term that was anglicized by English soldiers fighting in the lowlands of the Netherlands. The soldiers also nicknamed it "Dutch courage." The popularity of gin in England became such that the "London Dry" style evolved into what is today the benchmark of quality. The clear spirit is made from a mash of cereal grain (primarily corn, rye, barley, and wheat) that is flavored with botanicals (primarily juniper), which gives it its unique taste. Other botanicals employed in top-secret recipes include coriander, lemon and orange peel, cassia root, anise, and fennel seeds, to name only a few.

Gin, like many other spirits, changed in character in the early 19th century, when advances made in distilling equipment were revolutionized. Today gin is made around the world, but "London Dry" style is considered the best. Ironically, myriad gins labeled "London Dry" exist that aren't necessarily from London, or even England, but rather made by special license agreements with British distillers. This is certainly the case with many popular domestic brands here in the United States, though some are simply made in the "London Dry" style—a technicality that doesn't warrant the licensed designation. Confused by terminology? Here's how to keep them straight:

Dutch Genièvre still exists and, because it is aged in oak casks, it probably tastes much more like the original gin than highly-rectified English gin. London Dry gins, on the other hand, are used in more crisply refreshing cocktails than any other spirit, from the classic *original* Martini to the malaria-proof Gin and Tonic.

ABBEY COCKTAIL

1½ oz. Gin
1 oz. Orange Juice
1 dash Orange Bitters

Shake with ice and strain into chilled cocktail glass. Add a maraschino cherry.

ADAM AND EVE

1 oz. Forbidden Fruit
  Liqueur
1 oz. Gin
1 oz. Brandy
1 dash Lemon Juice

Shake with ice and strain into chilled cocktail glass.

ALABAMA FIZZ

1 oz. Lemon Juice
1 tsp. Superfine Sugar (or
  Simple Syrup)
2 oz. Gin
Club Soda

Shake lemon juice, sugar/syrup, and gin with ice and strain into ice-filled highball glass. Fill with club soda. Garnish with two sprigs of fresh mint.

ALASKA COCKTAIL

2 dashes Orange Bitters
1½ oz. Gin
¾ oz. Chartreuse (Yellow)

Stir with ice and strain into chilled cocktail glass.

ALBEMARLE FIZZ

1 oz. Lemon Juice
1 tsp. Superfine Sugar (or
  Simple Syrup)
2 oz. Gin
1 tsp. Raspberry Syrup
Club Soda

Shake gin and sugar/syrup with ice and strain into ice-filled highball glass. Fill with club soda.

ALEXANDER COCKTAIL NO. 1

1 oz. Gin
1 oz. Crème de Cacao
  (White)
1 oz. Light Cream

Shake with ice and strain into chilled cocktail glass. Garnish with fresh-grated nutmeg on top.

ALEXANDER'S SISTER COCKTAIL

1 oz. Dry Gin
1 oz. Crème de Menthe
  (Green)
1 oz. Light Cream

Shake with ice and strain into chilled cocktail glass. Garnish with fresh-grated nutmeg on top.

ALLEN COCKTAIL

1½ tsps. Lemon Juice
¾ oz. Maraschino Liqueur
1½ oz. Gin

Shake with ice and strain into chilled cocktail glass.

ANGLER'S COCKTAIL

2 dashes Bitters
3 dashes Orange Bitters
1½ oz. Gin
1 dash Grenadine

Shake with ice and pour into
ice-filled old-fashioned glass.

APRICOT ANISETTE COLLINS

1½ oz. Gin
½ oz. Apricot-flavored
   Brandy
1½ tsps. Anisette
½ oz. Lemon Juice
Club Soda

Shake first four ingredients
with ice and strain into ice-
filled collins glass. Fill with
club soda and stir lightly.
Garnish with a slice of
lemon.

ARTILLERY

1½ oz. Gin
1½ tsps. Sweet Vermouth
2 dashes Bitters

Stir with ice and strain into
chilled cocktail glass.

AVIATION

2 oz. Gin
½ oz. Maraschino Liqueur
¼ oz. Lemon Juice

Shake with ice and strain into
chilled cocktail glass. Garnish
with a maraschino cherry.

BARBARY COAST

½ oz. Gin
½ oz. Rum
½ oz. White Crème de
   Cacao
½ oz. Scotch
½ oz. Light Cream

Shake with ice and strain into
chilled cocktail glass.

BARON COCKTAIL

½ oz. Dry Vermouth
1½ oz. Gin
1½ tsps. Triple Sec
½ tsp. Sweet Vermouth

Stir with ice and strain into
chilled cocktail glass. Add a
twist of lemon peel.

BEAUTY-SPOT COCKTAIL

1 tsp. Orange Juice
½ oz. Sweet Vermouth
½ oz. Dry Vermouth
1 oz. Gin
1 dash Grenadine

Shake first four ingredients
with ice and strain into
chilled cocktail glass, with a
dash of grenadine in bottom
of glass.

BELMONT COCKTAIL

2 oz. Gin
1 tsp. Raspberry Syrup
¾ oz. Light Cream

Shake with ice and strain into
chilled cocktail glass.

GIN

BENNETT COCKTAIL

½ oz. Lime Juice
1½ oz. Gin
½ tsp. Superfine Sugar (or Simple Syrup)
2 dashes Orange Bitters

Shake with ice and strain into chilled cocktail glass.

BERMUDA BOUQUET

1 oz. Orange Juice
1 oz. Lemon Juice
1 tsp. Superfine Sugar (or Simple Syrup)
1½ oz. Gin
1 oz. Apricot-flavored Brandy
1 tsp. Grenadine
½ tsp. Triple Sec

Shake with ice and strain into ice-filled highball glass.

BERMUDA HIGHBALL

¾ oz. Gin
¾ oz. Brandy
¾ oz. Dry Vermouth
Ginger Ale or Club Soda

Pour gin, brandy, and vermouth into ice-filled highball glass. Fill with ginger ale or club soda. Add a twist of lemon peel and stir.

BERMUDA ROSE

1¼ oz. Gin
1½ tsps. Apricot-flavored Brandy
1½ tsps. Grenadine

Shake with ice and strain into chilled cocktail glass.

BIJOU COCKTAIL

¾ oz. Gin
¾ oz. Chartreuse (Green)
¾ oz. Sweet Vermouth
1 dash Orange Bitters

Stir with ice and strain into chilled cocktail glass. Add a maraschino cherry on top.

BILLY TAYLOR

½ oz. Lime Juice
2 oz. Gin
Club Soda

Fill collins glass with club soda and ice. Stir in lime juice and gin.

BLOODHOUND COCKTAIL

½ oz. Dry Vermouth
½ oz. Sweet Vermouth
1 oz. Gin

Shake with ice and strain into chilled cocktail glass. Garnish with two or three crushed strawberries.

BLOOMSBURY

2 oz. Gin
½ oz. Licor 43
½ oz. Lillet Blonde
2 dashes Peychaud's Bitters

Stir with ice and strain into chilled cocktail glass. Garnish with a lemon twist.

BLUE BIRD

1 1/2 oz. Gin
1/2 oz. Triple Sec
1 dash Bitters

Stir with ice and strain into
chilled cocktail glass. Add a
twist of lemon peel and a
maraschino cherry.

BLUE CANARY

3/4 oz. Gin
3 tbsps. Grapefruit Juice
1 tbsp. Blue Curaçao

Stir all ingredients with ice.
Strain into chilled cocktail
glass filled with crushed ice.
Garnish with a mint sprig.

BLUE DEVIL COCKTAIL

1 oz. Gin
1 oz. Lemon Juice
1 tbsp. Maraschino Liqueur
1/2 tsp. Blue Curaçao

Shake with ice and strain into
chilled cocktail glass.

BLUE MOON COCKTAIL

1 1/2 oz. Gin
3/4 oz. Blue Curaçao

Stir with ice and strain into
chilled cocktail glass. Add a
twist of lemon peel.

BOBBO'S BRIDE

1 oz. Gin
1 oz. Vodka
1/3 oz. Peach Liqueur
1/6 oz. Campari

Stir with ice and strain into
chilled cocktail glass. Garnish
with a slice of fresh peach.

BOOMERANG

1 oz. Dry Vermouth
1 1/2 oz. Gin
1 dash Bitters
1 dash Maraschino Liqueur

Stir with ice cubes and strain
into chilled cocktail glass.
Add a twist of lemon peel.

BOSTON COCKTAIL

3/4 oz. Gin
3/4 oz. Apricot-flavored
    Brandy
1/2 oz. Lemon Juice
1 1/2 tsps. Grenadine

Shake with ice and strain into
chilled cocktail glass.

BRIDAL

2 oz. Gin
1 oz. Sweet Vermouth
1/4 oz. Maraschino Liqueur
1 dash Orange Bitters

Stir with ice and strain into
chilled cocktail glass. Garnish
with a maraschino cherry.

BRONX COCKTAIL

1 oz. Gin
1/2 oz. Dry Vermouth
1/2 oz. Sweet Vermouth
1 oz. Orange Juice

Shake with ice and strain into
chilled cocktail glass. Garnish
with a slice of orange.

GIN

BRONX COCKTAIL (DRY)

1 oz. Gin
1 oz. Dry Vermouth
1/2 oz. Orange Juice

Shake with ice and strain into chilled cocktail glass. Garnish with a slice of orange.

BRONX TERRACE COCKTAIL

1 1/2 oz. Gin
1 1/2 oz. Dry Vermouth
1/2 oz. Lime Juice

Shake with ice and strain into chilled cocktail glass. Add a maraschino cherry.

BROWN COCKTAIL

3/4 oz. Gin
3/4 oz. Light Rum
3/4 oz. Dry Vermouth

Stir with ice and strain into chilled cocktail glass.

BULLDOG HIGHBALL

2 oz. Orange Juice
2 oz. Gin
Ginger Ale

Pour orange juice and gin into ice-filled highball glass. Fill with ginger ale and stir.

CABARET

1 1/2 oz. Gin
2 dashes Bitters
1/2 tsp. Dry Vermouth
1/4 tsp. Benedictine

Stir with ice and strain into chilled cocktail glass. Garnish with a maraschino cherry.

THE CARICATURE COCKTAIL

1 1/2 oz. Gin
1/2 oz. Sweet Vermouth
3/4 oz. Triple Sec
1/2 oz. Campari
1/2 oz. Grapefruit Juice

Shake with ice and strain into chilled cocktail glass. Garnish with an orange twist.

CARUSO

1 1/2 oz. Gin
1 oz. Dry Vermouth
1/2 oz. Crème de Menthe (Green)

Stir with ice and strain into chilled cocktail glass.

CASINO COCKTAIL

2 dashes Orange Bitters
1/4 tsp. Maraschino Liqueur
1/4 tsp. Lemon Juice
2 oz. Gin

Shake with ice and strain into chilled cocktail glass. Garnish with a maraschino cherry.

CHELSEA SIDECAR

1/2 oz. Lemon Juice
3/4 oz. Triple Sec
3/4 oz. Gin

Shake with ice and strain into chilled cocktail glass.

CLARIDGE COCKTAIL

¾ oz. Gin
¾ oz. Dry Vermouth
1 tbsp. Apricot-flavored
   Brandy
1 tbsp. Triple Sec

Stir with ice and strain into
chilled cocktail glass.

CLOVER CLUB

1½ oz. Gin
¼ oz. Grenadine
¾ oz. Lemon Juice
1 Egg White

Shake with ice and strain into
chilled wine glass.

CLUB COCKTAIL

1½ oz. Gin
¾ oz. Sweet Vermouth

Stir with ice and strain into
chilled cocktail glass. Add a
maraschino cherry or olive.

COLONIAL COCKTAIL

½ oz. Grapefruit Juice
1 tsp. Maraschino Liqueur
1½ oz. Gin

Shake with ice and strain into
chilled cocktail glass. Garnish
with an olive.

COOPERSTOWN COCKTAIL

½ oz. Dry Vermouth
½ oz. Sweet Vermouth
1 oz. Gin

Shake with ice and strain into
chilled cocktail glass. Add a
sprig of mint.

CORPSE REVIVER

¾ oz. Gin
¾ oz. Lemon Juice
¾ oz. Triple Sec
¾ oz. Lillet Blonde
1 dash Pastis (Pernod or
   Other Absinthe Substi-
   tute)

Shake with ice and strain into
chilled cocktail glass.

COUNT CURREY

1½ oz. Gin
1 tsp. Superfine Sugar (or
   Simple Syrup)
Champagne, Chilled

Shake gin and sugar/syrup
with ice and strain into
chilled Champagne flute. Fill
with Champagne.

CREAM FIZZ

1 oz. Lemon Juice
1 tsp. Superfine Sugar (or
   Simple Syrup)
2 oz. Gin
1 tsp. Light Cream
Club Soda

Shake with ice and strain into
ice-filled highball glass. Fill
with club soda and stir.

CRIMSON COCKTAIL

1½ oz. Gin
2 tsps. Lemon Juice
1 tsp. Grenadine
¾ oz. Port

Shake first three ingredients
with ice and strain into
chilled cocktail glass. Float
the Port on top.

CRYSTAL SLIPPER COCKTAIL

½ oz. Blue Curaçao
2 dashes Orange Bitters
1½ oz. Gin

Stir with ice and strain into chilled cocktail glass.

DAMN-THE-WEATHER COCKTAIL

1 tsp. Triple Sec
1 tbsp. Orange Juice
1 tbsp. Sweet Vermouth
1 oz. Gin

Shake with ice and strain into chilled cocktail glass.

DARB COCKTAIL

1 tsp. Lemon Juice
¾ oz. Dry Vermouth
¾ oz. Gin
¾ oz. Apricot-flavored
   Brandy

Shake with ice and strain into chilled cocktail glass.

DEEP SEA COCKTAIL

1 oz. Dry Vermouth
¼ tsp. Anisette
1 dash Orange Bitters
1 oz. Gin

Stir with ice and strain into chilled cocktail glass.

DELILAH

1½ oz. Gin
¾ oz. Triple Sec
¾ oz. Lemon Juice

Shake with ice and strain into chilled cocktail glass.

DELMONICO NO. 1

¾ oz. Gin
½ oz. Dry Vermouth
½ oz. Sweet Vermouth
½ oz. Brandy

Stir with ice and strain into chilled cocktail glass. Garnish with a twist of lemon peel.

DELMONICO NO. 2

1 dash Orange Bitters
1 oz. Dry Vermouth
1½ oz. Gin

Stir with ice and strain into chilled cocktail glass. Garnish with a twist of lemon peel.

DEMPSEY COCKTAIL

1 oz. Gin
1 oz. Apple Brandy
½ tsp. Anisette
½ tsp. Grenadine

Stir with ice and strain into chilled cocktail glass.

DIAMOND FIZZ

1 oz. Lemon Juice
1 tsp. Superfine Sugar (or
   Simple Syrup)
2 oz. Gin
Champagne, Chilled

Shake first three ingredients with ice and strain into ice-filled highball glass. Fill with Champagne and stir.

DIXIE COCKTAIL

1 oz. Orange Juice
1 tbsp. Anisette
½ oz. Dry Vermouth
1 oz. Gin

Shake with ice and strain into chilled cocktail glass.

DRY MARTINI (5-TO-1)

1⅔ oz. Gin
⅓ oz. Dry Vermouth

Stir vermouth and gin with ice. Strain into chilled cocktail glass. Garnish with a twist of lemon peel or olive.

DU BARRY COCKTAIL

1 dash Bitters
¾ oz. Dry Vermouth
½ tsp. Anisette
1½ oz. Gin

Stir with ice and strain into chilled cocktail glass. Garnish with a slice of orange.

EARL GREY MAR-TEA-NI

¾ oz. Lemon Juice
1 oz. Superfine Sugar (or Simple Syrup)
1½ oz. Earl Grey Infused Gin
1 Egg White

Shake all ingredients with ice and strain into chilled, sugar-rimmed cocktail glass. Garnish with lemon zest and a lemon twist.

*To infuse gin: Combine 1 tbsp tea with 1 cup gin. Agitate and let stand for 2 hours.

EASY LIKE SUNDAY MORNING COCKTAIL

1½ oz. Gin
¾ oz. Superfine Sugar (or Simple Syrup)
½ oz. Lemon Juice
1¼ oz. Pineapple Juice
1 dash Bitters

Shake first four ingredients with ice and strain into ice-filled collins glass. Add dash of bitters and stir.

EMERALD ISLE COCKTAIL

2 oz. Gin
1 tsp. Crème de Menthe (Green)
3 dashes Bitters

Stir with ice and strain into chilled cocktail glass.

EMERSON

1½ oz. Gin
1 oz. Sweet Vermouth
½ oz. Lime Juice
1 tsp. Maraschino Liqueur

Shake with ice and strain into chilled cocktail glass.

ENGLISH HIGHBALL

¾ oz. Gin
¾ oz. Brandy
¾ oz. Sweet Vermouth
Ginger Ale or Club Soda

Pour gin, brandy, and vermouth into ice-filled highball glass. Fill with ginger ale or club soda and stir. Garnish with a twist of lemon peel.

ENGLISH ROSE COCKTAIL

1½ oz. Gin
¾ oz. Apricot-flavored
   Brandy
¾ oz. Dry Vermouth
1 tsp. Grenadine
¼ tsp. Lemon Juice
Granulated Sugar

Prepare rim of glass by rubbing with lemon and dipping in granulated sugar. Shake all ingredients with ice and strain into chilled cocktail glass. Garnish with a maraschino cherry.

FALLEN ANGEL

1 oz. Lime Juice
1½ oz. Gin
1 dash Bitters
½ tsp. Crème de Menthe
   (White)

Shake with ice and strain into chilled cocktail glass. Garnish with a maraschino cherry.

FANCY GIN

2 oz. Gin
1 dash Bitters
¼ tsp. Triple Sec
¼ tsp. Superfine Sugar (or
   Simple Syrup)

Shake with ice and strain into chilled cocktail glass. Add a twist of lemon peel.

FARE THEE WELL

1½ oz. Gin
½ oz. Dry Vermouth
1 dash Sweet Vermouth
1 dash Triple Sec

Shake with ice and strain into chilled cocktail glass.

FARMER'S COCKTAIL

1 oz. Gin
½ oz. Dry Vermouth
½ oz. Sweet Vermouth
2 dashes Bitters

Stir with ice and strain into chilled cocktail glass.

FAVORITE COCKTAIL

¾ oz. Apricot-flavored
   Brandy
¾ oz. Dry Vermouth
¾ oz. Gin
¼ tsp. Lemon Juice

Shake with ice and strain into chilled cocktail glass.

FIFTY-FIFTY COCKTAIL

1½ oz. Gin
1½ oz. Dry Vermouth

Stir with ice and strain into chilled cocktail glass.

FINE-AND-DANDY COCKTAIL

½ oz. Lemon Juice
½ oz. Triple Sec
1½ oz. Gin
1 dash Bitters

Shake with ice and strain into chilled cocktail glass. Garnish with a maraschino cherry.

FINO MARTINI

2 oz. Gin
2 tsps. Fino Sherry

Stir gin and sherry with ice in mixing glass. Strain into chilled cocktail glass. Garnish with a twist of lemon peel.

FLAMINGO COCKTAIL

1/2 oz. Lime Juice
1/2 oz. Apricot-flavored Brandy
1 1/2 oz. Gin
1 tsp. Grenadine

Shake with ice and strain into chilled cocktail glass.

FLORADORA COOLER

1 oz. Lime Juice
1/2 tsp. Superfine Sugar (or Simple Syrup)
1 tbsp. Grenadine
2 oz. Gin
2 oz. Club Soda or Ginger Ale

Stir first three ingredients in collins glass. Top with ice and add gin. Fill with club soda or ginger ale and stir again.

FLORIDA

1/2 oz. Gin
1 1/2 tsps. Kirschwasser
1 1/2 tsps. Triple Sec
1 oz. Orange Juice
1 tsp. Lemon Juice

Shake with ice and strain into chilled cocktail glass.

FLYING DUTCHMAN

2 oz. Gin
1 dash Triple Sec

Shake with ice and strain into ice-filled old-fashioned glass.

FOG HORN

1/2 oz. Lime Juice
1 1/2 oz. Gin
Ginger Ale

Pour lime juice and gin into ice-filled highball glass. Fill with ginger ale and stir. Garnish with a slice of lime.

FRANKENJACK COCKTAIL

1 oz. Gin
3/4 oz. Dry Vermouth
1/2 oz. Apricot-flavored Brandy
1 tsp. Triple Sec

Stir with ice and strain into chilled cocktail glass. Garnish with a maraschino cherry.

FREE SILVER

1/2 oz. Lemon Juice
1/2 tsp. Superfine Sugar (or Simple Syrup)
1 1/2 oz. Gin
1/2 oz. Dark Rum
1 tbsp. Milk
Club Soda

Shake first five ingredients with ice and strain into ice-filled collins glass. Fill with club soda and stir.

FRENCH "75"

2 oz. Lemon Juice
2 tsps. Superfine Sugar (or
    Simple Syrup)
2 oz. Gin
Champagne, Chilled

Stir first three ingredients in collins glass. Add ice cubes, fill with Champagne, and stir. Garnish with a slice of lemon or orange and a maraschino cherry. Serve with straws.

G-TANG

1½ oz. Gin
1½ oz. Campari
1 oz. Orange Juice
1 oz. Sweet Vermouth

Combine all ingredients in an ice-filled rocks glass. Garnish with a twist of lemon peel.

GIBSON

2½ oz. Gin
½ oz. Dry Vermouth

Stir with ice and strain into chilled cocktail glass. Garnish with a cocktail onion

GIMLET

1 oz. Lime Juice
1 tsp. Superfine Sugar (or
    Simple Syrup)
1½ oz. Gin

Shake with ice and strain into chilled cocktail glass.

GIN ALOHA

1½ oz. Gin
1½ oz. Triple Sec
1 tbsp. Unsweetened
    Pineapple Juice
1 dash Orange Bitters

Shake with ice and strain into chilled cocktail glass.

GIN AND BITTERS

½ tsp. Bitters
Gin

Pour bitters into cocktail glass and revolve the glass until it is entirely coated with the bitters. Then fill with gin. (No ice is used in this drink.)

GIN BUCK

1 oz. Lemon Juice
1½ oz. Gin
Ginger Ale

Pour lemon juice and gin into ice-filled old-fashioned glass. Fill with ginger ale and stir.

GIN COBBLER

1 tsp. Superfine Sugar (or
    Simple Syrup)
2 oz. Club Soda
2 oz. Gin

Dissolve sugar/syrup and club soda in goblet, fill with ice, and add gin. Stir and garnish with seasonal fruits. Serve with straws.

GIN COCKTAIL

2 oz. Gin
2 dashes Bitters

Stir with ice and strain into chilled cocktail glass. Garnish with a twist of lemon peel.

GIN COOLER

1/2 tsp. Superfine Sugar (or Simple Syrup)
2 oz. Club Soda
2 oz. Gin
Club Soda or Ginger Ale

In collins glass stir sugar/syrup with club soda. Fill glass with ice and add gin. Fill with club soda or ginger ale and stir again. Insert a spiral of orange or lemon peel (or both) and dangle end over rim of glass.

GIN DAISY

1 oz. Lemon Juice
1/2 tsp. Superfine Sugar (or Simple Syrup)
1 tsp. Grenadine
2 oz. Gin

Shake with ice and strain into chilled stein or metal cup. Add ice cubes and garnish with fruit.

GIN FIX

1 oz. Lemon Juice
1 tsp. Superfine Sugar (or Simple Syrup)
1 tsp. Water
2 1/2 oz. Gin

Mix lemon juice, sugar/syrup, and water in highball glass. Stir and top with ice. Add gin and stir again. Garnish with a slice of lemon. Serve with straws.

GIN FIZZ

1 oz. Lemon Juice
1 tsp. Superfine Sugar (or Simple Syrup)
2 oz. Gin
Club Soda

Shake first three ingredients with ice and strain into ice-filled highball glass. Fill with club soda and stir.

GIN GIN MULE

3/4 oz. Lime Juice
1 oz. Superfine Sugar (or Simple Syrup)
6–8 sprigs Mint
1 1/2 oz. Gin
1 oz. Ginger Beer

In a mixing glass, muddle mint with lime juice and sugar/syrup. Add gin and ice and shake well. Strain into ice-filled highball glass and fill with ginger beer.

GIN HIGHBALL

2 oz. Gin
Ginger Ale or Club Soda

Pour gin into ice-filled high-ball glass and fill with ginger ale or club soda. Stir. Garnish with a twist of lemon peel.

GIN AND IT

2 oz. Gin
1 oz. Sweet Vermouth

Stir ingredients in cocktail glass. (No ice is used in this drink.)

GIN RICKEY

1/2 oz. Lime Juice
1 1/2 oz. Gin
Club Soda

Pour lime juice and gin into ice-filled highball glass and fill with club soda. Stir. Add a wedge of lime.

GIN SANGAREE

1/2 tsp. Superfine Sugar (or Simple Syrup)
1 tsp. Water
2 oz. Gin
Club Soda
1 tbsp. Port

Dissolve sugar/syrup in water and gin in highball glass. Top with ice, and then fill with club soda and stir. Float Port on top. Garnish with fresh-grated nutmeg on top.

GIN AND SIN

1 oz. Gin
1 oz. Lemon Juice
1 tbsp. Orange Juice
1 dash Grenadine

Shake with ice and strain into chilled cocktail glass.

GIN SLING

1 tsp. Superfine Sugar (or Simple Syrup)
1 tsp. Water
1 oz. Lemon Juice
2 oz. Gin

Dissolve sugar/syrup in water and lemon juice in old-fashioned glass. Add gin. Top with ice and stir. Garnish with a twist of orange peel.

GIN SMASH

1 cube Sugar
1 oz. Club Soda
4 sprigs Mint
2 oz. Gin

Muddle sugar with club soda and mint in old-fashioned glass. Add gin, top with ice, and stir. Garnish with a slice of orange and/or a maraschino cherry and a twist of lemon peel.

GIN SOUR

1 oz. Lemon Juice
½ tsp. Superfine Sugar (or Simple Syrup)
2 oz. Gin

Shake with ice and strain into chilled sour glass. Garnish with a half-slice of lemon and a maraschino cherry.

GIN SQUIRT

1½ oz. Gin
1 tbsp. Superfine Sugar (or Simple Syrup)
1 tsp. Grenadine
Club Soda

Stir first three ingredients with ice and strain into ice-filled highball glass. Fill with club soda and stir. Garnish with cubes of pineapple and strawberries.

GIN SWIZZLE

1 oz. Lime Juice
1 tsp. Superfine Sugar (or Simple Syrup)
2 oz. Club Soda
2 dashes Bitters
2 oz. Gin

Combine first three ingredients in collins glass. Fill with ice and stir. Add bitters and gin. Serve with swizzle stick.

GIN THING

1½ oz. Gin
½ oz. Lime Juice
Ginger Ale

Pour gin and lime juice into ice-filled highball glass and fill with ginger ale.

GIN TODDY

½ tsp. Superfine Sugar (or Simple Syrup)
2 tsps. Water
2 oz. Gin

In old-fashioned glass, mix sugar/syrup and water. Add gin and one ice cube. Stir and add a twist of lemon peel.

GIN AND TONIC

2 oz. Gin
Tonic Water

Pour gin into ice-filled highball glass and fill with tonic water. Stir.

GOLDEN DAZE

1½ oz. Gin
½ oz. Peach-flavored
    Brandy
1 oz. Orange Juice

Shake with ice and strain into
chilled cocktail glass.

GOLF COCKTAIL

1½ oz. Gin
¾ oz. Dry Vermouth
2 dashes Bitters

Stir with ice and strain into
chilled cocktail glass.

GRAND ROYAL FIZZ

2 oz. Orange Juice
1 oz. Lemon Juice
1 tsp. Superfine Sugar (or
    Simple Syrup)
2 oz. Gin
½ tsp. Maraschino Liqueur
2 tsps. Light Cream
Club Soda

Shake with ice and strain into
ice-filled highball glass. Fill
with club soda and stir.

GRAPEFRUIT COCKTAIL

1 oz. Grapefruit Juice
1 oz. Gin
1 tsp. Maraschino Liqueur

Shake with ice and strain into
chilled cocktail glass. Garnish
with a maraschino cherry.

GREENBACK

1½ oz. Gin
1 oz. Crème de Menthe
    (Green)
1 oz. Lemon Juice

Shake with ice and strain into
ice-filled old-fashioned glass.

GREEN DEVIL

1½ oz. Gin
1½ oz. Crème de Menthe
    (Green)
1 tbsp. Lime Juice

Shake with ice and strain into
ice-filled old-fashioned glass.
Garnish with mint leaves.

GREEN DRAGON

1 oz. Lemon Juice
½ oz. Kümmel
½ oz. Crème de Menthe
    (Green)
1½ oz. Gin
4 dashes Orange Bitters

Shake with ice and strain into
chilled cocktail glass.

GREYHOUND

1½ oz. Gin
5 oz. Grapefruit Juice

Pour into highball glass over
ice cubes. Stir well.

GYPSY COCKTAIL

1½ oz. Sweet Vermouth
1½ oz. Gin

Stir with ice and strain into
chilled cocktail glass. Garnish
with a maraschino cherry.

HARLEM COCKTAIL

¾ oz. Pineapple Juice
1½ oz. Gin
½ tsp. Maraschino Liqueur

Shake with ice and strain into chilled cocktail glass. Garnish with two pineapple chunks.

HASTY COCKTAIL

¾ oz. Dry Vermouth
1½ oz. Gin
¼ tsp. Anisette
1 tsp. Grenadine

Stir with ice and strain into chilled cocktail glass.

HAWAIIAN COCKTAIL

2 oz. Gin
1 tbsp. Pineapple Juice
½ oz. Triple Sec

Shake with ice and strain into chilled cocktail glass.

HOFFMAN HOUSE COCKTAIL

¾ oz. Dry Vermouth
1½ oz. Gin

Stir with ice and strain into chilled cocktail glass. Garnish with an olive.

HOKKAIDO COCKTAIL

1½ oz. Gin
1 oz. Sake
½ oz. Triple Sec

Shake with ice and strain into chilled cocktail glass.

HOMESTEAD COCKTAIL

1½ oz. Gin
¾ oz. Sweet Vermouth

Stir with ice and strain into chilled cocktail glass. Garnish with a slice of orange.

HONOLULU COCKTAIL NO. 1

1 dash Bitters
¼ tsp. Orange Juice
¼ tsp. Pineapple Juice
¼ tsp. Lemon Juice
½ tsp. Superfine Sugar (or Simple Syrup)
1½ oz. Gin

Shake with ice and strain into chilled cocktail glass.

HONOLULU COCKTAIL NO. 2

¾ oz. Gin
¾ oz. Maraschino Liqueur
¾ oz. Benedictine

Stir with ice and strain into chilled cocktail glass.

HOSKINS

2 oz. Gin
¾ oz. Torani Amer
½ oz. Maraschino Liqueur
¼ oz. Triple Sec
1 dash Orange Bitters

Stir with ice and strain into chilled cocktail glass. Flame an orange peel over the drink and garnish with the peel.

H. P. W. COCKTAIL

1½ tsps. Dry Vermouth
1½ tsps. Sweet Vermouth
1½ oz. Gin

Stir with ice and strain into chilled cocktail glass. Garnish with a twist of orange peel.

HUDSON BAY

1 oz. Gin
½ oz. Cherry-flavored Brandy
1½ tsps. 151-proof Rum
1 tbsp. Orange Juice
1½ tsps. Lime Juice

Shake with ice and strain into chilled cocktail glass.

HULA-HULA COCKTAIL

¾ oz. Orange Juice
1½ oz. Gin
¼ tsp. Superfine Sugar (or Simple Syrup)

Shake with ice and strain into chilled cocktail glass.

IDEAL COCKTAIL

1 oz. Dry Vermouth
1 oz. Gin
¼ tsp. Maraschino Liqueur
½ tsp. Grapefruit or Lemon Juice

Shake with ice and strain into chilled cocktail glass. Garnish with a maraschino cherry.

IMPERIAL COCKTAIL

1½ oz. Dry Vermouth
1½ oz. Gin
½ tsp. Maraschino Liqueur
1 dash Bitters

Stir with ice and strain into chilled cocktail glass. Garnish with a maraschino cherry.

INCOME TAX COCKTAIL

1½ tsps. Dry Vermouth
1½ tsps. Sweet Vermouth
1 oz. Gin
1 dash Bitters
1 oz. Orange Juice

Shake with ice and strain into chilled cocktail glass.

JAMAICA GLOW

1 oz. Gin
1 tbsp. Claret
1 tbsp. Orange Juice
1 tsp. Jamaica Rum

Shake with ice and strain into chilled cocktail glass.

JASMINE

1½ oz. Gin
1 oz. Triple Sec
¾ oz. Campari
½ oz. Lemon Juice

Shake with ice and strain into chilled cocktail glass.

JEWEL COCKTAIL

¾ oz. Chartreuse (Green)
¾ oz. Sweet Vermouth
¾ oz. Gin
1 dash Orange Bitters

Stir with ice and strain into chilled cocktail glass. Garnish with a maraschino cherry.

JEYPLAK COCKTAIL

1½ oz. Gin
¾ oz. Sweet Vermouth
¼ tsp. Anisette

Shake with ice and strain into chilled cocktail glass. Garnish with a maraschino cherry.

JOCKEY CLUB COCKTAIL

1 dash Bitters
¼ tsp. Crème de Cacao (White)
½ oz. Lemon Juice
1½ oz. Gin

Shake with ice and strain into chilled cocktail glass.

JOULOUVILLE

1 oz. Gin
½ oz. Apple Brandy
1½ tsps. Sweet Vermouth
½ oz. Lemon Juice
2 dashes Grenadine

Shake with ice and strain into chilled cocktail glass.

JOURNALIST COCKTAIL

1½ tsps. Dry Vermouth
1½ tsps. Sweet Vermouth
1½ oz. Gin
½ tsp. Lemon Juice
½ tsp. Triple Sec
1 dash Bitters

Shake with ice and strain into chilled cocktail glass.

JUDGE JR. COCKTAIL

¾ oz. Gin
¾ oz. Light Rum
½ oz. Lemon Juice
½ tsp. Superfine Sugar (or Simple Syrup)
¼ tsp. Grenadine

Shake with ice and strain into chilled cocktail glass.

JUDGETTE COCKTAIL

¾ oz. Peach-flavored Brandy
¾ oz. Gin
¾ oz. Dry Vermouth
¼ oz. Lime Juice

Shake with ice and strain into chilled cocktail glass. Garnish with a maraschino cherry.

JUPITER

2 oz. Gin
1 oz. Dry Vermouth
1 tsp. Orange Juice
1 tsp. Parfait Amour

Shake with ice and strain into chilled cocktail glass.

GIN

KISS IN THE DARK

¾ oz. Gin
¾ oz. Cherry-flavored
   Brandy
¾ oz. Dry Vermouth

Stir with ice and strain into
chilled cocktail glass.

KNICKERBOCKER COCKTAIL

¼ tsp. Sweet Vermouth
¾ oz. Dry Vermouth
1½ oz. Gin

Stir with ice and strain into
chilled cocktail glass. Garnish
with a twist of lemon peel.

KNOCKOUT COCKTAIL

½ oz. Anisette
¾ oz. Gin
¾ oz. Dry Vermouth
1 tsp. Crème de Menthe
   (White)

Stir with ice and strain into
chilled cocktail glass. Garnish
with a maraschino cherry.

KUP'S INDISPENSABLE COCKTAIL

½ oz. Light Vermouth
½ oz. Dry Vermouth
1½ oz. Gin
1 dash Bitters

Stir with ice and strain into
chilled cocktail glass.

LADY FINGER

1 oz. Gin
½ oz. Kirschwasser
1 oz. Cherry-flavored
   Brandy

Shake with ice and strain into
chilled cocktail glass.

LAST WORD

½ oz. Gin
½ oz. Maraschino Liqueur
½ oz. Chartreuse
½ oz. Lime Juice

Shake with ice and strain into
chilled cocktail glass.

LEAP FROG HIGHBALL

1 oz. Lemon Juice
2 oz. Gin
Ginger Ale

Pour lemon juice and gin
into ice-filled highball glass
and fill with ginger ale. Stir.

LEAPYEAR

2 oz. Gin
½ oz. Sweet Vermouth
½ oz. Grand Marnier
1 dash Lemon Juice

Shake with ice and strain into
chilled cocktail glass.

LEAVE-IT-TO-ME COCKTAIL NO. 1

½ oz. Apricot-flavored
   Brandy
½ oz. Dry Vermouth
1 oz. Gin
¼ tsp. Lemon Juice
¼ tsp. Grenadine

Shake with ice and strain into
chilled cocktail glass.

LEAVE-IT-TO-ME COCKTAIL NO. 2

1 tsp. Raspberry Syrup
1 tsp. Lemon Juice
¼ tsp. Maraschino Liqueur
1½ oz. Gin

Stir with ice and strain into
chilled cocktail glass.

THE LIBATION GODESS

2 oz. Gin
¾ oz. Crème de Cacao
   (White)
½ oz. Cranberry Juice

Stir and strain into a chilled
cocktail glass. Garnish with a
lime wedge.

LONDON BUCK

2 oz. Gin
1 oz. Lemon Juice
Ginger Ale

Pour gin and lemon juice in
ice-filled highball glass. Fill
with ginger ale and stir.

LONDON COCKTAIL

2 oz. Gin
2 dashes Orange Bitters
½ tsp. Superfine Sugar (or
   Simple Syrup)
½ tsp. Maraschino Liqueur

Stir with ice and strain into
chilled cocktail glass. Add a
twist of lemon peel.

LONE TREE COCKTAIL

¾ oz. Sweet Vermouth
1½ oz. Gin

Stir with ice and strain into
chilled cocktail glass.

LONE TREE COOLER

½ tsp. Superfine Sugar (or
   Simple Syrup)
2 oz. Club Soda
2 oz. Gin
1 tbsp. Dry Vermouth
Club Soda or Ginger Ale

Stir sugar/syrup and club
soda in collins glass. Fill glass
with ice, and add gin and
vermouth. Fill with club soda
or ginger ale and stir again.
Garnish with a spiral of
orange or lemon peel (or
both) and dangle end over
rim of glass.

MAIDEN'S BLUSH COCKTAIL

¼ tsp. Lemon Juice
1 tsp. Triple Sec
1 tsp. Grenadine
1½ oz. Gin

Shake with ice and strain into
chilled cocktail glass.

MAIDEN'S PLEA

1 ½ oz. Gin
½ oz. Triple Sec
1 oz. Lemon Juice

Shake with ice and strain into chilled cocktail glass.

MAJOR BAILEY

1 ½ tsps. Lime Juice
1 ½ tsps. Lemon Juice
½ tsp. Superfine Sugar (or Simple Syrup)
12 Mint Leaves
2 oz. Gin

Muddle first four ingredients, pour into ice-filled collins glass, and add gin. Stir until glass is frosted. Garnish with sprig of mint, and serve with straws.

MAMIE'S SISTER

1 oz. Lime Juice
2 oz. Gin
Ginger Ale

Pour the lime juice and a lime twist into collins glass, and add gin. Fill glass with ginger ale and ice. Stir.

MARTINEZ COCKTAIL

1 dash Orange Bitters
1 oz. Dry Vermouth
¼ tsp. Triple Sec
1 oz. Gin

Stir with ice and strain into chilled cocktail glass. Garnish with a maraschino cherry.

MARTINI (TRADITIONAL 2-TO-1)

1 ½ oz. Gin
¾ oz. Dry Vermouth

Stir with ice and strain into chilled cocktail glass. Garnish with a twist of lemon peel or olive.

MARTINI (DRY) (5-TO-1)

1 ⅔ oz. Gin
⅓ oz. Dry Vermouth

Follow directions for Martini (Traditional 2-to-1) preparation.

MARTINI (EXTRA DRY) (8-TO-1)

2 oz. Gin
¼ oz. Dry Vermouth

Follow directions for Martini (Traditional 2-to-1) preparation.

MARTINI (MEDIUM)

1 ½ oz. Gin
½ oz. Dry Vermouth
½ oz. Sweet Vermouth

Follow directions for Martini (Traditional 2-to-1) preparation.

MARTINI (SWEET)

1 oz. Gin
1 oz. Sweet Vermouth

Follow directions for Martini (Traditional 2-to-1) preparation.

MAURICE COCKTAIL

1 ounce Orange Juice
½ oz. Sweet Vermouth
½ oz. Dry Vermouth
1 oz. Gin
1 dash Bitters

Shake with ice and strain into chilled cocktail glass.

MAXIM

1½ oz. Gin
1 oz. Dry Vermouth
1 dash Crème de Cacao
    (White)

Shake with ice and strain into chilled cocktail glass. Garnish with a maraschino cherry.

MELON COCKTAIL

2 oz. Gin
¼ tsp. Lemon Juice
¼ tsp. Maraschino Liqueur

Shake with ice and strain into chilled cocktail glass. Garnish with a maraschino cherry.

MERRY WIDOW COCKTAIL NO. 1

1¼ oz. Gin
1¼ oz. Dry Vermouth
½ tsp. Benedictine
½ tsp. Anisette
1 dash Orange Bitters

Stir with ice and strain into chilled cocktail glass. Garnish with a twist of lemon peel.

MR. MANHATTAN COCKTAIL

1 cube Sugar
4 sprigs Mint
¼ tsp. Lemon Juice
1 tsp. Orange Juice
1½ oz. Gin

Muddle ingredients. Shake with ice and strain into chilled cocktail glass.

MONKEY GLAND

2 oz. Gin
1 oz. Orange Juice
¼ oz. Grenadine
1 dash Pernod (or Absinthe
    Substitute)

Shake with ice and strain into chilled cocktail glass. Garnish with an orange twist.

MONTE CARLO IMPERIAL HIGHBALL

2 oz. Gin
½ oz. Crème de Menthe
    (White)
½ oz. Lemon Juice
Champagne, Chilled

Shake first three ingredients with ice and strain into ice-filled highball glass. Fill glass with Champagne and stir.

MONTMARTRE COCKTAIL

1¼ oz. Dry Gin
½ oz. Sweet Vermouth
½ oz. Triple Sec

Stir with ice and strain into chilled cocktail glass. Garnish with a maraschino cherry.

MONTREAL CLUB BOUNCER

1 1/2 oz. Gin
1/2 oz. Anisette

Pour into ice-filled old-fashioned glass and stir.

MORRO

1 oz. Gin
1/2 oz. Dark Rum
1 tbsp. Pineapple Juice
1 tbsp. Lime Juice
1/2 tsp. Superfine Sugar (or
    Simple Syrup)

Shake with ice and strain into sugar-rimmed, ice-filled old fashioned glass.

NEGRONI

3/4 oz. Gin
3/4 oz. Campari
3/4 oz. Sweet or
    Dry Vermouth
1 splash Club Soda (optional)

Stir with ice and strain into chilled cocktail glass, or into ice-filled old-fashioned glass. Add club soda, if desired. Garnish with a twist of lemon peel.

NIGHTMARE

1 1/2 oz. Gin
1/2 oz. Madeira
1/2 oz. Cherry-flavored
    Brandy
1 tsp. Orange Juice

Shake with ice and strain into chilled cocktail glass.

NINETEENTH HOLE

1 1/2 oz. Gin
1 oz. Dry Vermouth
1 tsp. Sweet Vermouth
1 dash Bitters

Stir with ice and strain into chilled cocktail glass. Garnish with an olive.

OBITUARY COCKTAIL

2 oz. Gin
1/4 oz. Dry Vermouth
1/4 oz. Pastis (Pernod or
    Other Absinthe Substi-
    tute)

Stir with ice and strain into chilled cocktail glass.

OPAL COCKTAIL

1 oz. Gin
1/2 oz. Triple Sec
1 tbsp. Orange Juice
1/4 tbsp. Superfine Sugar
    (or Simple Syrup)

Shake with ice and strain into chilled cocktail glass.

OPERA

2 oz. Gin
1/2 oz. Dubonnet
1/4 oz. Maraschino Liqueur
1 dash Orange Bitters

Stir with ice and strain into chilled cocktail glass. Garnish with a lemon twist.

ORANGE BLOSSOM

1 oz. Gin
1 oz. Orange Juice
1/4 tsp. Superfine Sugar (or
    Simple Syrup)

Shake with ice and strain into
chilled cocktail glass.

ORANGE BUCK

1 1/2 oz. Gin
1 oz. Orange Juice
1 tbsp. Lime Juice
Ginger Ale

Shake first three ingredients
with ice and strain into ice-
filled highball glass. Fill with
ginger ale and stir.

ORANGE OASIS

1 1/2 oz. Gin
1/2 oz. Cherry-flavored
    Brandy
4 oz. Orange Juice
Ginger Ale

Shake first three ingredients
with ice and strain into ice-
filled highball glass. Fill with
ginger ale and stir.

THE OUTSIDER

2 oz. Gin
1 oz. Lemon Juice
3/4 oz. Superfine Sugar (or
    Simple Syrup)
1 oz. Fresh Apple Cider
1 splash Ginger Ale

Shake first four ingredients
with ice and strain into ice-
filled collins glass. Top with
splash of ginger ale. Garnish
with a slice of red apple.

PAISLEY MARTINI

2 oz. Gin
1/2 oz. Dry Vermouth
1 tsp. Scotch

Stir in ice-filled old-fashioned
glass. Garnish with a twist of
lemon peel.

PALL MALL

1 1/2 oz. Gin
1/2 oz. Sweet Vermouth
1/2 oz. Dry Vermouth
1/2 oz. Crème de Menthe
    (White)

Stir in ice-filled old-fashioned
glass.

PALM BEACH COCKTAIL

1 1/2 oz. Gin
1 1/2 tsps. Sweet Vermouth
1 1/2 tsps. Grapefruit Juice

Shake with ice and strain into
chilled cocktail glass.

PAPAYA SLING

1 1/2 oz. Gin
1 dash Bitters
1 oz. Lime Juice
1 tbsp. Papaya Syrup
Club Soda

Shake first four ingredients
with ice and strain into ice-
filled collins glass. Fill with
club soda and stir. Garnish
with skewered pineapple
chunks.

PARISIAN

1 oz. Gin
1 oz. Dry Vermouth
1/4 oz. Crème de Cassis

Shake with ice and strain into
chilled cocktail glass.

PARK AVENUE

1 1/2 oz. Gin
1/4 oz. Sweet Vermouth
1 tbsp. Pineapple Juice

Stir with ice and strain into
chilled cocktail glass.

PEGU

2 oz. Gin
1 oz. Orange Curaçao
1 tsp. Lime Juice
1 dash Angostura Bitters
1 dash Orange Bitters

Stir with ice and strain into
chilled cocktail glass.

PEGU CLUB

2 oz. Gin
1/2 oz. Lemon Juice
1/2 oz. Triple Sec
4 dashes Angostura Bitters

Shake with ice and strain into
chilled cocktail glass.

PERFECT COCKTAIL

1 1/2 tsps. Dry Vermouth
1 1/2 tsps. Sweet Vermouth
1 1/2 oz. Gin
1 dash Bitters

Stir with ice and strain into
chilled cocktail glass.

PERFECT 10

1 oz. Gin
1/2 oz. Triple Sec
1/2 oz. Campari
1/4 oz. Lemon Juice
1/4 oz. Superfine Sugar (or
Simple Syrup)

Shake with ice and strain into
chilled cocktail glass. Run a
lemon twist along lip of glass,
and then drop lemon twist in
cocktail.

PETER PAN COCKTAIL

2 dashes Bitters
3/4 oz. Orange Juice
3/4 oz. Dry Vermouth
3/4 oz. Gin

Shake with ice and strain into
chilled cocktail glass.

PICCADILLY COCKTAIL

3/4 oz. Dry Vermouth
1 1/2 oz. Gin
1/4 tsp. Anisette
1/4 tsp. Grenadine

Stir with ice and strain into
chilled cocktail glass.

PINK GIN

1 1/2 oz. Gin
3 or 4 dashes Angostura
Bitters

Stir with ice and strain into
chilled cocktail glass.

PINK LADY

1½ oz. Gin
½ oz. Applejack
¾ oz. Lemon Juice
¼ oz. Grenadine
1 Egg White

Shake with ice and strain into
chilled wine glass.

PLAZA COCKTAIL

¾ oz. Sweet Vermouth
¾ oz. Dry Vermouth
¾ oz. Gin

Shake with ice and strain into
chilled cocktail glass. Garnish
with a wedge of pineapple.

POET'S DREAM

¾ oz. Gin
¾ oz. Dry Vermouth
¾ oz. Benedictine

Stir with ice and strain into
chilled cocktail glass. Garnish
with a twist of lemon peel.

POLLYANNA

3 slices Orange
3 slices Pineapple
2 oz. Gin
½ oz. Sweet Vermouth
½ tsp. Grenadine

Muddle ingredients. Shake
with ice and strain into
chilled cocktail glass.

POLO COCKTAIL

1 tbsp. Lemon Juice
1 tbsp. Orange Juice
1 oz. Gin

Shake with ice and strain into
chilled cocktail glass.

POMPANO

1 oz. Gin
½ oz. Dry Vermouth
1 oz. Grapefruit Juice

Shake with ice and strain into
chilled cocktail glass.

POPPY COCKTAIL

¾ oz. Crème de Cacao
(White)
1½ oz. Gin

Shake with ice and strain into
chilled cocktail glass.

PRINCE'S SMILE

½ oz. Apricot-flavored
Brandy
½ oz. Apple Brandy
1 oz. Gin
¼ tsp. Lemon Juice

Shake with ice and strain into
chilled cocktail glass.

PRINCETON COCKTAIL

1 oz. Gin
1 oz. Dry Vermouth
½ oz. Lime Juice

Stir with ice and strain into
chilled cocktail glass.

QUEEN ELIZABETH

1½ oz. Gin
½ oz. Dry Vermouth
1½ tsps. Benedictine

Stir with ice and strain into
chilled cocktail glass.

GIN

RAMOS GIN FIZZ

1½ oz. Gin
½ oz. Lemon Juice
½ oz. Lime Juice
2 tbsp. Cream
1 Egg White
1 tbsp. Superfine Sugar (or
    Simple Syrup)
3–4 dashes Orange Flower
    Water
¼ oz. Club Soda

Shake first seven ingredients
with ice for at least one
minute (or blend on low in a
blender) until foamy. Strain
into chilled wine glass, top
with club soda, and stir.

RED CLOUD

1½ oz. Gin
½ oz. Apricot-flavored
    Brandy
1 tbsp. Lemon Juice
1 tsp. Grenadine

Shake with ice and strain into
chilled cocktail glass.

RED SNAPPER

2 oz. Gin
4 oz. Tomato Juice
½ oz. Lemon Juice
1 pinch Salt
1 pinch Pepper
2–3 dashes Worcestershire
    Sauce
2–3 drops Tabasco Sauce
Celery stalk

Stir with ice in a chilled highball or delmonico glass. Garnish with a celery stalk and a
lemon wedge.

REMSEN COOLER

½ tsp. Superfine Sugar (or
    Simple Syrup)
2 oz. Club Soda or Ginger
    Ale
2 oz. Gin

Combine sugar/syrup and
club soda in collins glass.
Stir. Add ice and gin. Fill
with club soda or ginger ale
and stir again. Garnish with a
spiral of orange or lemon
peel (or both) and dangle
end over rim of glass.

RENAISSANCE COCKTAIL

1½ oz. Gin
½ oz. Dry Sherry
1 tbsp. Light Cream

Shake with ice and strain into
chilled cocktail glass. Garnish
with fresh-grated nutmeg on
top.

RESOLUTE COCKTAIL

½ oz. Lemon Juice
½ oz. Apricot-flavored
  Brandy
1 oz. Gin

Shake with ice and strain into chilled cocktail glass.

ROBERT E. LEE COOLER

½ oz. Lime Juice
½ tsp. Superfine Sugar (or
  Simple Syrup)
2 oz. Club Soda
¼ tsp. Anisette
2 oz. Gin
Ginger Ale

Stir first three ingredients in collins glass. Add ice, anisette, and gin. Fill with ginger ale and stir again. Add a spiral of orange or lemon peel (or both) and dangle end over rim of glass.

ROLLS-ROYCE

½ oz. Dry Vermouth
½ oz. Sweet Vermouth
1½ oz. Gin
¼ tsp. Benedictine

Stir with ice and strain into chilled cocktail glass.

ROSE COCKTAIL (ENGLISH)

½ oz. Apricot-flavored
  Brandy
½ oz. Dry Vermouth
1 oz. Gin
½ tsp. Lemon Juice
1 tsp. Grenadine

Shake with ice and strain into chilled, sugar-rimmed cocktail glass.

ROSE COCKTAIL (FRENCH)

½ oz. Cherry-flavored
  Brandy
½ oz. Dry Vermouth
1½ oz. Gin

Stir with ice and strain into chilled cocktail glass.

ROSELYN COCKTAIL

¾ oz. Dry Vermouth
1½ oz. Gin
½ tsp. Grenadine

Stir with ice and strain into chilled cocktail glass. Garnish with a twist of lemon peel.

RUM RUNNER

1½ oz. Gin
1 oz. Lime Juice
1 oz. Pineapple Juice
1 tsp. Superfine Sugar (or
  Simple Syrup)
1 dash Bitters

Shake with ice and strain into ice-filled, salt-rimmed old-fashioned glass.

SALTY DOG

1½ oz. Gin
5 oz. Grapefruit Juice
¼ tsp. Salt

Pour into ice-filled highball glass. Stir well. (Vodka may be substituted for the gin.)

SAND-MARTIN COCKTAIL

1 tsp. Chartreuse (Green)
1½ oz. Sweet Vermouth
1½ oz. Gin

Stir with ice and strain into chilled cocktail glass.

GIN

SAN SEBASTIAN

1 oz. Gin
1½ tsps. Light Rum
1 tbsp. Grapefruit Juice
1½ tsps. Triple Sec
1 tbsp. Lemon Juice

Shake with ice and strain into
chilled cocktail glass.

SATAN'S WHISKERS

¾ oz. Gin
¾ oz. Dry Vermouth
¾ oz. Sweet Vermouth
½ oz. Orange Juice
½ oz. Grand Marnier
1 dash Orange Bitters

Shake with ice and strain into
chilled cocktail glass.

SENSATION COCKTAIL

½ oz. Lemon Juice
1½ oz. Gin
1 tsp. Maraschino Liqueur

Shake with ice and strain into
chilled cocktail glass. Garnish
with two sprigs of fresh mint.

SEVENTH HEAVEN COCKTAIL

2 tsps. Grapefruit Juice
1 tbsp. Maraschino Liqueur
1½ oz. Gin

Shake with ice and strain into
chilled cocktail glass. Garnish
with a sprig of fresh mint.

SHADY GROVE

1½ oz. Gin
1 oz. Lemon Juice
1 tsp. Superfine Sugar (or
Simple Syrup)
Ginger Beer

Shake gin, lemon juice, and
sugar/syrup with ice and
strain into ice-filled highball
glass. Fill with ginger beer.

SILVER BULLET

1 oz. Gin
1 oz. Kümmel
1 tbsp. Lemon Juice

Shake with ice and strain into
chilled cocktail glass.

SILVER COCKTAIL

1 oz. Dry Vermouth
1 oz. Gin
2 dashes Orange Bitters
¼ tsp. Superfine Sugar (or
Simple Syrup)
½ tsp. Maraschino Liqueur

Stir with ice and strain into
chilled cocktail glass. Garnish
with a twist of lemon peel.

SILVER STREAK

1½ oz. Gin
1 oz. Kümmel

Shake with ice and strain into
chilled cocktail glass.

SMILE COCKTAIL

1 oz. Grenadine
1 oz. Gin
½ tsp. Lemon Juice

Shake with ice and strain into chilled cocktail glass.

SMILER COCKTAIL

½ oz. Sweet Vermouth
½ oz. Dry Vermouth
1 oz. Gin
1 dash Bitters
¼ tsp. Orange Juice

Shake with ice and strain into chilled cocktail glass.

SNOWBALL

1½ oz. Gin
½ oz. Anisette
1 tbsp. Light Cream

Shake with ice and strain into chilled cocktail glass.

SNYDER

1½ oz. Gin
½ oz. Dry Vermouth
½ oz. Triple Sec

Shake with ice and strain into chilled cocktail glass. Garnish with a twist of lemon peel.

SOCIETY COCKTAIL

1½ oz. Gin
¾ oz. Dry Vermouth
¼ tsp. Grenadine

Stir with ice and strain into chilled cocktail glass.

SOUTHERN BRIDE

1½ oz. Gin
1 oz. Grapefruit Juice
1 dash Maraschino Liqueur

Shake with ice and strain into chilled cocktail glass.

SOUTHERN GIN COCKTAIL

2 oz. Gin
2 dashes Orange Bitters
½ tsp. Triple Sec

Stir with ice and strain into chilled cocktail glass. Garnish with a twist of lemon peel.

SOUTH-SIDE COCKTAIL

1 oz. Lemon Juice
1 tsp. Superfine Sugar (or Simple Syrup)
1½ oz. Gin

Shake with ice and strain into chilled cocktail glass. Garnish with two sprigs of fresh mint.

SOUTH-SIDE FIZZ

1 oz. Lemon Juice
1 tsp. Superfine Sugar (or Simple Syrup)
2 oz. Gin
Club Soda

Shake lemon juice, sugar/syrup, and gin with ice and strain into ice-filled highball glass. Fill with club soda and stir. Garnish with fresh mint leaves.

SPENCER COCKTAIL

¾ oz. Apricot-flavored
   Brandy
1½ oz. Gin
1 dash Bitters
¼ tsp. Orange Juice

Shake with ice and strain into
chilled cocktail glass. Garnish
with a maraschino cherry and
a twist of orange peel.

SPHINX COCKTAIL

1½ oz. Gin
1½ tsps. Sweet Vermouth
1½ tsps. Dry Vermouth

Stir with ice and strain into
chilled cocktail glass. Garnish
with a slice of lemon.

SPRING FEELING COCKTAIL

1 tbsp. Lemon Juice
½ oz. Chartreuse (Green)
1 oz. Gin

Shake with ice and strain into
chilled cocktail glass.

STANLEY COCKTAIL

½ oz. Lemon Juice
1 tsp. Grenadine
¾ oz. Gin
¼ oz. Light Rum

Shake with ice and strain into
chilled cocktail glass.

STAR DAISY

1 oz. Lemon Juice
½ tsp. Superfine Sugar (or
   Simple Syrup)
1 tsp. Grenadine
1 oz. Gin
1 oz. Apple Brandy

Shake with ice and strain into
chilled stein or metal cup.
Add an ice cube and garnish
with seasonal fruit.

STRAIGHT LAW COCKTAIL

¾ oz. Gin
1½ oz. Dry Sherry

Stir with ice and strain into
chilled cocktail glass.

STRAITS SLING

2 oz. Gin
½ oz. Cherry Brandy (Dry)
½ oz. Benedictine
1 oz. Lemon Juice
2 dashes Orange Bitters
2 dashes Angostura Bitters
Club Soda

Shake all ingredients except club
soda with ice. Strain into an ice-
filled tumbler or collins glass.
Fill with club soda and stir.

SUNSHINE COCKTAIL

¾ oz. Sweet Vermouth
1½ oz. Gin
1 dash Bitters

Stir with ice and strain into
chilled cocktail glass. Garnish
with a twist of orange peel.

T & T

2 oz. Tanqueray Gin
Tonic Water

Pour gin into ice-filled high-ball glass and fill with tonic water. Stir. Garnish with a lime wedge.

TAILSPIN

¾ oz. Gin
¾ oz. Sweet Vermouth
¾ oz. Chartreuse (Green)
1 dash Campari

Stir with ice and strain into chilled cocktail glass. Garnish with a lemon twist and a maraschino cherry.

TANGO COCKTAIL

1 tbsp. Orange Juice
½ oz. Dry Vermouth
½ oz. Sweet Vermouth
1 oz. Gin
½ tsp. Triple Sec

Shake with ice and strain into chilled cocktail glass.

THE TART GIN COOLER

2 oz. Gin
2 oz. Pink Grapefruit Juice
2 oz. Tonic Water
Peychaud's Bitters to taste

Build, in order given, in ice-filled collins glass.

THIRD-DEGREE COCKTAIL

1½ oz. Gin
¾ oz. Dry Vermouth
1 tsp. Anisette

Stir with ice and strain into chilled cocktail glass.

THREE STRIPES COCKTAIL

1 oz. Gin
½ oz. Dry Vermouth
1 tbsp. Orange Juice

Shake with ice and strain into chilled cocktail glass.

THUNDERCLAP

¾ oz. Gin
¾ oz. Blended Whiskey
¾ oz. Brandy

Shake with ice and strain into chilled cocktail glass.

TILLICUM

2¼ oz. Gin
¾ oz. Dry Vermouth
2 dashes Peychaud's Bitters

Stir with ice and strain into chilled cocktail glass. Garnish with a slice of smoked salmon skewered flat on a pick.

GIN

TOM COLLINS

1 oz. Lemon Juice
1 tsp. Superfine Sugar (or Simple Syrup)
2 oz. Gin
Club Soda

Shake lemon juice, sugar/syrup, and gin with ice and strain into collins glass. Add several ice cubes, fill with club soda, and stir. Garnish with slices of lemon and orange, and a maraschino cherry. Serve with a straw.

TROPICAL SPECIAL

1½ oz. Gin
1 oz. Orange Juice
1 oz. Lime Juice
2 oz. Grapefruit Juice
½ oz. Triple Sec

Shake with ice and strain into ice-filled highball glass. Garnish with fruit slices and a maraschino cherry.

TURF COCKTAIL

¼ tsp. Anisette
2 dashes Bitters
1 oz. Dry Vermouth
1 oz. Gin

Stir with ice and strain into chilled cocktail glass. Add a twist of orange peel.

TUXEDO COCKTAIL

1½ oz. Gin
1½ oz. Dry Vermouth
¼ tsp. Maraschino Liqueur
¼ tsp. Anisette
2 dashes Orange Bitters

Stir with ice and strain into chilled cocktail glass. Garnish with a maraschino cherry.

TWENTIETH-CENTURY COCKTAIL

1½ oz. Gin
¾ oz. Lillet Blonde
¾ oz. Lemon Juice
½ oz. Crème de Cacao (White)

Shake with ice and strain into chilled cocktail glass.

TYPHOON

1 oz. Gin
½ oz. Anisette
1 oz. Lime Juice
Champagne, Chilled

Shake first three ingredients with ice and strain into ice-filled collins glass. Top with Champagne.

UNION JACK COCKTAIL

¾ oz. Sloe Gin
1½ oz. Gin
½ tsp. Grenadine

Shake with ice and strain into chilled cocktail glass.

THE VALENTINO

2 oz. Gin
1/2 oz. Campari
1/2 oz. Sweet Vermouth

Stir over ice and strain into chilled cocktail glass. Garnish with a twist of orange peel.

VESPER

3 oz. Gin
1 oz. Vodka
1/2 oz. Lillet Blonde

Stir with ice and strain into chilled cocktail glass. Garnish with a twist of orange peel.

As mentioned in *James Bond: Casino Royale*

VICTOR

1 1/2 oz. Gin
1/2 oz. Brandy
1/2 oz. Sweet Vermouth

Shake with ice and strain into chilled cocktail glass.

WAIKIKI BEACHCOMBER

3/4 oz. Gin
3/4 oz. Triple Sec
1 tbsp. Fresh Pineapple Juice

Shake with ice and strain into chilled cocktail glass.

WALLICK COCKTAIL

1 1/2 oz. Dry Vermouth
1 1/2 oz. Gin
1 tsp. Triple Sec

Stir with ice and strain into chilled cocktail glass.

WALLIS BLUE COCKTAIL

1 oz. Triple Sec
1 oz. Gin
1 oz. Lime Juice

Moisten rim of old-fashioned glass with lime juice and dip into superfine sugar (or simple syrup). Shake ingredients with ice and strain into sugar-rimmed, ice-filled old-fashioned glass.

WEBSTER COCKTAIL

1/2 oz. Lime Juice
1 1/2 tsps. Apricot-flavored Brandy
1/2 oz. Dry Vermouth
1 oz. Gin

Shake with ice and strain into chilled cocktail glass.

WEMBLY COCKTAIL

3/4 oz. Dry Vermouth
1 1/2 oz. Gin
1/4 tsp. Apricot-flavored Brandy
1/2 tsp. Apple Brandy

Stir with ice and strain into chilled cocktail glass.

WESTERN ROSE

1/2 oz. Apricot-flavored Brandy
1 oz. Gin
1/2 oz. Dry Vermouth
1/4 tsp. Lemon Juice

Shake with ice and strain into chilled cocktail glass.

WHAT THE HELL

1 oz. Gin
1 oz. Dry Vermouth
1 oz. Apricot-flavored
  Brandy
1 dash Lemon Juice

Stir into ice-filled old-fashioned glass.

WHITE LADY

2 oz. Gin
1 oz. Triple Sec
1/2 oz. Lemon Juice

Shake with ice and strain into chilled cocktail glass.

WHITE SPIDER

1 oz. Gin
1 oz. Lemon Juice
1/2 oz. Triple Sec
1 tsp. Superfine Sugar (or
  Simple Syrup)

Shake with ice and strain into chilled cocktail glass.

WHITE WAY COCKTAIL

3/4 oz. Crème de Menthe
  (White)
1 1/2 oz. Gin

Shake with ice and strain into chilled cocktail glass.

WHY NOT?

1 oz. Gin
1 oz. Apricot-flavored
  Brandy
1/2 oz. Dry Vermouth
1 dash Lemon Juice

Shake with ice and strain into chilled cocktail glass.

WILL ROGERS

1 1/2 oz. Gin
1 tbsp. Orange Juice
1/2 oz. Dry Vermouth
1 dash Triple Sec

Shake with ice and strain into chilled cocktail glass.

WOODSTOCK

1 1/2 oz. Gin
1 oz. Lemon Juice
1 1/2 tsps. Maple Syrup
1 dash Orange Bitters

Shake with ice and strain into chilled cocktail glass.

XANTHIA COCKTAIL

3/4 oz. Cherry-flavored
  Brandy
3/4 oz. Chartreuse (Yellow)
3/4 oz. Gin

Stir with ice and strain into chilled cocktail glass.

YALE COCKTAIL

1 1/2 oz. Gin
1/2 oz. Dry Vermouth
1 dash Bitters
1 tsp. Blue Curaçao

Stir with ice and strain into chilled cocktail glass.

YELLOW RATTLER

1 oz. Gin
1 tbsp. Orange Juice
1/2 oz. Dry Vermouth
1/2 oz. Sweet Vermouth

Shake with ice and strain into chilled cocktail glass. Garnish with a cocktail onion.

YOLANDA

½ oz. Brandy
½ oz. Gin
½ oz. Anisette
1 oz. Sweet Vermouth
1 dash Grenadine

Shake with ice and strain into chilled cocktail glass. Garnish with a twist of orange peel.

RUM

Rum was first produced in Brazil, Barbados, and Jamaica after Columbus introduced sugarcane to the West Indies in the late 15th century, and within two centuries it was the favorite spirit of New England. Its popularity endures today as the base of many tropical cocktails, including the Daiquiri, Zombie, Mai Tai, and Piña Colada. Rum is made from molasses, sugarcane juice, or syrup made by reducing the free-run juice of sugarcane.

Rums can be divided into three stylistic types: **Light** rums, sometimes called *white* or *silver*, are traditionally produced in southern Caribbean islands (like Puerto Rico, Trinidad, and Barbados) and aged up to a year in barrels, rendering them very subtle. **Medium** rums, sometimes called *gold* or *amber*, are smoother as a result of either congeners (organic compounds produced during fermentation), the addition of caramel, or occasionally through aging in wood barrels. **Dark** rums, which take their color from being aged anywhere from 3 to 12 years (and in some cases from the addition of caramel), are produced in the tropics: Jamaica, Haiti, or Martinique. While supplying the punch in Planter's Punch and the rich molasses flavor in a variety of tropical and hot drinks, the best dark rums can also be savored like fine brandy.

Subcategories of rum include **spiced** or **flavored** rums, a relatively recent phenomenon, which are infused with spices or aromatics while being distilled. There are also **151-proof** rums, also called *high-proof* rums, which are often added to complete a mixed drink or in desserts or dessert-cocktails that call for flaming—literally igniting the spirit. (Obviously, one should be very careful when playing with fire and high-proof rum!)

RUM

A DAY AT THE BEACH

1 oz. Coconut-flavored Rum
1/2 oz. Amaretto
4 oz. Orange Juice
1/2 oz. Grenadine

Shake rum, amaretto, and orange juice with ice and pour into ice-filled highball glass. Top with grenadine and garnish with a pineapple wedge and a strawberry.

APPLE PIE NO. 1

3/4 oz. Light Rum
3/4 oz. Sweet Vermouth
1 tsp. Apple Brandy
1/2 tsp. Grenadine
1 tsp. Lemon Juice

Shake with ice and strain into chilled cocktail glass.

BAHAMA MAMA

1/2 oz. Dark Rum
1/2 oz. Coconut Liqueur
1/4 oz. 151-proof Rum
1/4 oz. Coffee Liqueur
1/2 oz. Lemon Juice
4 oz. Pineapple Juice

Combine all ingredients and pour into ice-filled highball glass. Garnish with a strawberry or a maraschino cherry.

BAJITO (BAHITO)

4 Fresh Mint Leaves
4 Fresh Basil Leaves
5 slices Fresh Lime
1 tbsp. Superfine Sugar (or Simple Syrup)
3 oz. Dark Rum

In shaker glass muddle mint and basil with lime slices and sugar/syrup. Top with ice and then rum. Shake well and strain into ice-filled rocks glass.

BANANA COW

1 oz. Light Rum
1 oz. Crème de Banana
1 1/2 oz. Cream
1 dash Grenadine

Shake ingredients with crushed ice and strain into chilled cocktail glass. Garnish with a banana slice and fresh grated nutmeg on top.

BEACHCOMBER

1 1/2 oz. Light Rum
1/2 oz. Triple Sec
1/2 oz. Grenadine
1/2 oz. Superfine Sugar (or Simple Syrup)
1/2 oz. Lemon Juice

Shake with ice and strain into chilled, sugar-rimmed cocktail glass. Garnish with a lime wheel.

BERMUDA RUM SWIZZLE

2 oz. Dark Rum
1 oz. Lime Juice
1 oz. Pineapple Juice
1 oz. Orange Juice
1/4 oz. Falernum

Shake with ice and strain into ice-filled highball glass. Garnish with a slice of orange and a maraschino cherry.

BERMUDA TRIANGLE

1 oz. Peach Schnapps
1/2 oz. Spiced Rum
3 oz. Orange Juice

Pour ingredients into ice-filled old-fashioned glass.

BLACK DEVIL

2 oz. Light Rum
1/2 oz. Dry Vermouth

Stir with ice and strain into chilled cocktail glass. Add a black olive.

BLACK MARIA

2 oz. Coffee-flavored Brandy
2 oz. Light Rum
4 oz. Strong Black Coffee
2 tsps. Superfine Sugar (or Simple Syrup)

Stir in brandy snifter and add ice.

BLUE HAWAIIAN

1 oz. Light Rum
1 oz. Blue Curaçao
2 oz. Pineapple Juice
1 oz. Cream of Coconut

Combine all ingredients with 1 cup crushed ice in blender on high speed. Pour into chilled highball glass. Garnish with a slice of pineapple and a maraschino cherry.

BOLERO

1 1/2 oz. Light Rum
1/4 oz. Apple Brandy
1/4 tsp. Sweet Vermouth

Stir with ice and strain into chilled cocktail glass.

BORINQUEN

1 1/2 oz. Light Rum
1 tbsp. Passion Fruit Syrup
1 oz. Lime Juice
1 oz. Orange Juice
1 tsp. 151-proof Rum

Combine all ingredients with half a cup of ice in blender on low speed. Pour into chilled old-fashioned glass.

BOSTON COOLER

1 oz. Lemon Juice
1 tsp. Superfine Sugar (or
    Simple Syrup)
2 oz. Club Soda
2 oz. Light Rum
Club Soda or Ginger Ale

Into collins glass pour lemon juice, sugar/syrup, and club soda. Stir. Fill glass with ice and add rum. Fill with club soda or ginger ale and stir again. Add spiral of orange or lemon peel and dangle end over rim of glass.

BOSTON SIDECAR

³/₄ oz. Brandy
³/₄ oz. Light Rum
³/₄ oz. Triple Sec
¹/₂ oz. Lime Juice

Shake with ice and strain into chilled cocktail glass.

BUCK JONES

1¹/₂ oz. Light Rum
1 oz. Sweet Sherry
¹/₂ oz. Lime Juice
Ginger Ale

Pour first three ingredients into ice-filled highball glass and stir. Fill with ginger ale.

BURGUNDY BISHOP

¹/₂ oz. Lemon Juice
1 tsp. Superfine Sugar (or
    Simple Syrup)
1 oz. Light Rum
Red Wine

Shake lemon juice, sugar/syrup, and rum with ice and strain into ice-filled highball glass. Fill with red wine and stir. Garnish with fruits.

CABLE CAR

2 oz. Spiced Rum
1 oz. Triple Sec
¹/₃ oz. Lemon Juice

Shake with ice and strain into chilled, cinnamon-sugar-rimmed cocktail glass. Garnish with a twist of lemon peel and a dust of cinnamon.

CAIPIRINHA

2 oz. Cachaça (Brazilian
    White Rum)
1 tsp. Sugar
1 whole Lime

Wash the lime and cut it into quarters. Muddle sugar and limes in a tumbler. Add cachaça and stir. Fill with ice and stir again.

CANADO SALUDO

1 1/2 oz. Light Rum
1 oz. Orange Juice
1 oz. Pineapple Juice
1/2 oz. Lemon Juice
1/2 oz. Grenadine
5 dashes Bitters

Combine all ingredients in ice-filled highball glass. Garnish with pineapple slices, an orange slice, and a maraschino cherry.

CAPTAIN'S BLOOD

1 1/2 oz. Dark Rum
1/4 oz. Lime Juice
1/4 oz. Superfine Sugar (or Simple Syrup)
2 dashes Angostura Bitters

Shake with ice and strain into chilled cocktail glass. Garnish with a spiral of lemon peel.

CARIBBEAN CHAMPAGNE

1/2 oz. Light Rum
1/2 oz. Crème de Banana
Champagne, Chilled

Pour rum and banana liqueur into Champagne flute. Fill with Champagne and stir gently. Add a slice of banana.

CARIBBEAN ROMANCE

1 1/2 oz. Light Rum
1 oz. Amaretto
1 1/2 oz. Orange Juice
1 1/2 oz. Pineapple Juice
1 splash Grenadine

Shake rum, amaretto, and juices with ice and strain into ice-filled highball glass. Float grenadine on top and garnish with an orange, lemon, or lime slice.

CASA BLANCA

2 oz. Light Rum
1 1/2 tsps. Lime Juice
1 1/2 tsps. Triple Sec
1 1/2 tsps. Maraschino Liqueur

Shake with ice and strain into chilled cocktail glass.

CHANTILLY COCKTAIL

1 1/2 oz. Rum
3/4 oz. Apricot-flavored Brandy
2 dashes Peach Bitters
1 oz. Lemon Juice
1 oz. Superfine Sugar (or Simple Syrup)

Shake with ice and strain into chilled, cinnamon-sugar-rimmed cocktail glass. Garnish with an orange peel spiral wrapped around a cinnamon stick.

CHERIE

1 oz. Lime Juice
1/2 oz. Triple Sec
1 oz. Light Rum
1/2 oz. Cherry-flavored Brandy

Shake with ice and strain into chilled cocktail glass. Add a maraschino cherry.

RUM

CHERRY RUM

1¼ oz. Light Rum
1½ tsps. Cherry-flavored
Brandy
1 tbsp. Light Cream

Shake with ice and strain into
chilled cocktail glass.

CHINESE COCKTAIL

1 tbsp. Grenadine
1½ oz. Jamaica Rum
1 dash Bitters
1 tsp. Maraschino Liqueur
1 tsp. Triple Sec

Shake with ice and strain into
chilled cocktail glass.

CHOCOLATE RUM

1 oz. Light Rum
½ oz. Crème de Cacao
(Brown)
½ oz. Crème de Menthe
(White)
1 tbsp. Light Cream
1 tsp. 151-proof Rum

Shake with ice and strain into
ice-filled old-fashioned glass.

COCOMACOQUE

1 oz. Lemon Juice
2 oz. Pineapple Juice
2 oz. Orange Juice
1½ oz. Light Rum
2 oz. Red Wine

Shake all ingredients except
wine. Pour into ice-filled
collins glass and top with
wine. Add a pineapple stick.

CONTINENTAL

1¾ oz. Light Rum
1 tbsp. Lime Juice
1½ tsps. Crème de Menthe
(Green)
½ tsp. Superfine Sugar (or
Simple Syrup)

Shake with ice and strain into
chilled cocktail glass. Add a
twist of lemon peel.

COOL CARLOS

1½ oz. Dark Rum
2 oz. Cranberry Juice
2 oz. Pineapple Juice
1 splash Superfine Sugar
(or Simple Syrup)
1 splash Lemon Juice
1 oz. Orange Curaçao

Shake first four ingredients
with ice. Strain into ice-filled
collins glass and float curaçao
on top. Garnish with
pineapple and orange slices
and a maraschino cherry.

CORKSCREW

1½ oz. Light Rum
½ oz. Dry Vermouth
½ oz. Peach-flavored
Brandy

Shake with ice and strain into
chilled cocktail glass. Garnish
with a lime slice.

CREAM PUFF

2 oz. Light Rum
1 oz. Light Cream
1/2 tsp. Superfine Sugar (or Simple Syrup)
Club Soda

Shake first three ingredients with ice and strain into chilled highball glass over two ice cubes. Fill with club soda and stir.

CREOLE

1 1/2 oz. Light Rum
1 dash Tabasco Sauce
1 tsp. Lemon Juice
1 1/2 oz. Beef Bouillon
Salt and Pepper to taste

Shake with ice and strain into ice-filled old-fashioned glass.

CUBA LIBRE

1/2 oz. Lime Juice
2 oz. Light Rum
Cola

Put lime juice and twist of lime into highball glass and add rum. Top with ice and fill with cola.

CUBAN COCKTAIL NO. 1

1/2 oz. Lime Juice
1/2 tsp. Superfine Sugar (or Simple Syrup)
2 oz. Light Rum

Shake with ice and strain into chilled cocktail glass.

CUBAN SPECIAL

1 tbsp. Pineapple Juice
1/2 oz. Lime Juice
1 oz. Light Rum
1/2 tsp. Triple Sec

Shake with ice and strain into chilled cocktail glass. Garnish with a slice of pineapple and a maraschino cherry.

DAIQUIRI

1 oz. Lime Juice
1 tsp. Superfine Sugar (or Simple Syrup)
1 1/2 oz. Light Rum

Shake with ice and strain into chilled cocktail glass.

DARK 'N' STORMY

2 oz. Dark Rum
4 oz. Ginger Beer

Mix in an old-fashioned glass over ice.

(Dark 'n' Stormy is a registered trademark of Gosling Brothers Limited, Hamilton, Bermuda.)

DERBY DAIQUIRI

1 1/2 oz. Light Rum
1 oz. Orange Juice
1 tbsp. Lime Juice
1 tsp. Sugar

Combine all ingredients with 1/2 cup of shaved ice in blender on low speed. Pour into Champagne flute.

RUM

DIABOLO

2 oz. Rum
1/2 oz. Triple Sec
1/2 oz. Dry Vermouth
2 dashes Angostura Bitters

Stir with ice and strain into
chilled cocktail glass. Garnish
with a twist of orange peel.

DINGO

1/2 oz. Light Rum
1/2 oz. Amaretto
1/2 oz. Whiskey (Tennessee
    Sour Mash)
1 oz. Superfine Sugar (or
    Simple Syrup)
1 oz. Lemon Juice
2 oz. Orange Juice
1 splash Grenadine

Shake with ice and pour into
ice-filled highball glass. Garnish with an orange slice.

EL PRESIDENTE COCKTAIL NO. 1

1 oz. Lime Juice
1 tsp. Pineapple Juice
1 tsp. Grenadine
1 1/2 oz. Light Rum

Shake with ice and strain into
chilled cocktail glass.

EL PRESIDENTE COCKTAIL NO. 2

3/4 oz. Dry Vermouth
1 1/2 oz. Light Rum
1 dash Bitters

Stir with ice and strain into
chilled cocktail glass.

FAIR-AND-WARMER COCKTAIL

3/4 oz. Sweet Vermouth
1 1/2 oz. Light Rum
1/2 tsp. Triple Sec

Stir with ice and strain into
chilled cocktail glass.

FIREMAN'S SOUR

2 oz. Lime Juice
1/2 tsp. Superfine Sugar (or
    Simple Syrup)
1/2 tbsp. Grenadine
2 oz. Light Rum
Club Soda (optional)

Shake sugar/syrup, grena
dine, lime juice, and rum
with ice and strain into
chilled sour glass. Fill with
club soda, if desired. Garnish
with a half-slice of lemon and
a maraschino cherry.

FLORIDITA

1 1/2 oz. Rum
1/2 oz. Lime Juice
1/2 oz. Sweet Vermouth
1/8 oz. Crème de Cacao
    (White)
1/8 oz. Grenadine

Shake with ice and strain into
chilled cocktail glass. Garnish
with a lime twist.

FOG CUTTER

1 1/2 oz. Light Rum
1/2 oz. Brandy
1/2 oz. Gin
1 oz. Orange Juice
1 1/2 oz. Lemon Juice
1 1/2 tsps. Orgeat Syrup
   (Almond Syrup)
1 tsp. Sweet Sherry

Shake all ingredients except
sherry and strain into ice-
filled collins glass. Top with
sherry.

FORT LAUDERDALE

1 1/2 oz. Light Rum
1/2 oz. Sweet Vermouth
1 oz. Orange Juice
1/4 oz. Lime Juice

Shake with ice and strain into
ice-filled old-fashioned glass.
Add a slice of orange.

GAUGUIN

2 oz. Light Rum
1 tbsp. Passion Fruit Syrup
1 tbsp. Lemon Juice
1 tbsp. Lime Juice

Combine all ingredients with
a cup of crushed ice in
blender on low speed. Serve
in chilled old-fashioned glass.
Garnish with a maraschino
cherry.

GOLDEN FRIENDSHIP

Equal parts:
Amaretto
Sweet Vermouth
Light Rum
Ginger Ale

Mix first three ingredients in
collins glass with ice, then fill
with ginger ale. Garnish with
an orange spiral and a
maraschino cherry.

GORILLA MILK

1 oz. Light Rum
1/2 oz. Coffee Liqueur
1/2 oz. Irish Cream Liqueur
1/2 oz. Crème de Banana
1 oz. Light Cream

Shake with ice and pour into
ice-filled hurricane or parfait
glass. Garnish with a banana
slice.

HARVEST NECTAR

1 1/2 oz. Rum
1 oz. Pineapple Juice
1 oz. Cranberry Juice
1 oz. Orange Juice
1 oz. Lemon-lime Soda

Shake with ice and strain into
ice-filled pint glass.

HAVANA COCKTAIL

1 1/2 oz. Pineapple Juice
1/2 tsp. Lemon Juice
3/4 oz. Light Rum

Shake with ice and strain into
chilled cocktail glass.

HOP TOAD

½ oz. Lime Juice
¾ oz. Apricot-flavored
  Brandy
¾ oz. Light Rum

Stir with ice and strain into
chilled cocktail glass.

HURRICANE

1 oz. Dark Rum
1 oz. Light Rum
1 tbsp. Passion Fruit Syrup
2 tsps. Lime Juice

Shake with ice and strain into
chilled cocktail glass.

HURRICANE LEAH

¼ oz. Light Rum
¼ oz. Gin
¼ oz. Vodka
¼ oz. Tequila
¼ oz. Blue Curaçao
1 dash Cherry Brandy
1½ oz. Superfine Sugar (or
  Simple Syrup)
1½ oz. Lemon Juice
3 oz. Orange Juice

Pour into ice-filled hurricane
or parfait glass and stir. Garnish with an orange wheel.

JACQUELINE

1 oz. Triple Sec
2 oz. Dark Rum
1 oz. Lime Juice
1 pinch Superfine Sugar (or
  Simple Syrup)

Shake with ice and strain into
chilled cocktail glass.

JADE

1½ oz. Light Rum
½ tsp. Crème de Menthe
  (Green)
½ tsp. Triple Sec
1 tbsp. Lime Juice
1 tsp. Superfine Sugar (or
  Simple Syrup)

Shake with ice and strain into
chilled cocktail glass. Add a
lime slice.

JAMAICAN CRAWLER

1 oz. Light Rum
1 oz. Melon Liqueur
3 oz. Pineapple Juice
1 splash Grenadine

Combine first three ingredients with ice and stir well.
Pour into collins glass, and
float grenadine on top.

KNICKERBOCKER SPECIAL COCKTAIL

1 tsp. Raspberry Syrup
1 tsp. Lemon Juice
1 tsp. Orange Juice
2 oz. Light Rum
½ tsp. Triple Sec

Shake with ice and strain into
chilled cocktail glass. Garnish
with a small slice of
pineapple.

LEMON-COCONUT COLADA

1½ oz. Citrus-flavored Rum
1½ oz. Coconut-flavored Rum
2 oz. Coco Lopez
1 oz. Heavy Cream
4 oz. Pineapple Juice
½ oz.–1 oz. Lemon Juice

Shake all ingredients with ice and strain into ice-filled hurricane glass. Garnish with lemon zest.

LITTLE DEVIL COCKTAIL

½ oz. Lemon Juice
1½ tsps. Triple Sec
¾ oz. Light Rum
¾ oz. Gin

Shake with ice and strain into chilled cocktail glass.

LITTLE PRINCESS COCKTAIL

1½ oz. Sweet Vermouth
1½ oz. Light Rum

Shake with ice and strain into chilled cocktail glass.

LOOK OUT BELOW

1½ oz. 151-proof Rum
¼ oz. Lime Juice
1 tsp. Grenadine

Shake with ice and strain into ice-filled old-fashioned glass.

LOUNGE LIZARD

1 oz. Dark Rum
½ oz. Amaretto
Cola

Pour rum and amaretto into ice-filled collins glass. Fill with cola. Garnish with a slice of lime.

MAI-TAI

1 oz. Light Rum
1 oz. Gold Rum
½ oz. Orange Curaçao
½ oz. Orgeat Syrup (Almond Syrup)
½ oz. Lime Juice
1 oz. Dark Rum

Shake all but the dark rum with ice. Strain into chilled old-fashioned glass. Top with the dark rum. Garnish with a maraschino cherry.

Created by Victor "Trader Vic" Bergeron

MAI-TAI (ORIGINAL TRADER VIC FORMULA)

2 oz. Jamaican Rum
½ oz. French Garnier Orgeat
½ oz. Orange Curaçao
¼ oz. Rock Candy Syrup
1 oz. Lime Juice

Hand-shake and garnish with half of the lime shell inside the drink and float a sprig of fresh mint at the edge of the glass.

MALMAISON

1 oz. Lemon Juice
1 oz. Light Rum
1/2 oz. Cream Sherry

Shake with ice and strain into chilled, Anisette-rimmed cocktail glass.

MANDEVILLE

1 1/2 oz. Light Rum
1 oz. Dark Rum
1 tsp. Anisette
1 tbsp. Lemon Juice
1 tbsp. Cola
1/4 tsp. Grenadine

Shake with ice and strain into ice-filled old-fashioned glass.

MARIPOSA

1 oz. Light Rum
1/2 oz. Brandy
1 tbsp. Lemon Juice
1 tbsp. Orange Juice
1 dash Grenadine

Shake with ice and strain into chilled cocktail glass.

MARY PICKFORD COCKTAIL

1 oz. Light Rum
1 oz. Pineapple Juice
1/4 tsp. Grenadine
1/4 tsp. Maraschino Liqueur

Shake with ice and strain into chilled cocktail glass.

MIAMI

1 1/2 oz. Light Rum
1/2 oz. Crème de Menthe (White)
1 dash Lemon Juice

Shake with ice and strain into chilled cocktail glass.

MIDNIGHT EXPRESS

1 1/2 oz. Dark Rum
1/2 oz. Triple Sec
3/4 oz. Lime Juice
1 splash Superfine Sugar (or Simple Syrup)
1 splash Lemon Juice

Shake with ice and pour into ice-filled old-fashioned glass.

MISSISSIPPI PLANTER'S PUNCH

1 tbsp. Superfine Sugar (or Simple Syrup)
1 oz. Lemon Juice
1/2 oz. Light Rum
1/2 oz. Bourbon
1 oz. Brandy
Club Soda

Shake all but club soda with ice and strain into ice-filled collins glass. Fill with club soda and stir.

MOJITO

2 tsp. Sugar
4 sprigs Fresh Mint
1 Lime, halved
2 oz. Light Rum
Club Soda

Muddle sugar and mint with soda water in pint glass. Squeeze both halves of lime into the glass, leaving one hull in the mixture. Add rum, stir, and fill with ice. Top with club soda. Garnish with a mint sprig.

MONKEY WRENCH

1½ oz. Light Rum
Grapefruit Juice

Pour rum into ice-filled collins glass. Fill with grapefruit juice and stir.

MOON QUAKE SHAKE

1½ oz. Dark Rum
1 oz. Coffee-flavored Brandy
1 tbsp. Lemon Juice

Shake with ice and strain into chilled cocktail glass.

NEVADA COCKTAIL

1½ oz. Light Rum
1 oz. Grapefruit Juice
1 oz. Lime Juice
1 dash Bitters
3 tsps. Superfine Sugar (or Simple Syrup)

Shake with ice and strain into chilled cocktail glass.

NEW ORLEANS BUCK

1½ oz. Light Rum
1 oz. Orange Juice
½ oz. Lemon Juice
Ginger Ale

Shake all ingredients except ginger ale with ice and strain into ice-filled collins glass. Fill with ginger ale and stir.

NIGHT CAP

2 oz. Light Rum
1 tsp. Superfine Sugar (or Simple Syrup)
Warm Milk

Pour rum and sugar/syrup in Irish coffee glass, fill with warm milk, and stir. Garnish with fresh-grated nutmeg on top.

THE OLD CUBAN

¾ oz. Lime Juice
1 oz. Superfine Sugar (or Simple Syrup)
6 Mint Leaves
1½ oz. Rum (aged)
2 dashes Angostura Bitters
2 oz. Champagne

In a mixing glass, muddle lime juice, sugar/syrup, and mint. Add rum and bitters, top with ice, and shake well. Strain into a chilled cocktail glass and top with Champagne. Garnish with a sugar-dried vanilla bean and mint flecks.

RUM

PALMETTO COCKTAIL

1 1/2 oz. Light Rum
1 1/2 oz. Dry Vermouth
2 dashes Bitters

Stir with ice and strain into chilled cocktail glass.

PASSION DAIQUIRI

1 1/2 oz. Light Rum
1 oz. Lime
1 tsp. Superfine Sugar (or Simple Syrup)
1 tbsp. Passion Fruit Juice

Shake with ice and strain into chilled cocktail glass.

PIÑA COLADA

3 oz. Light Rum
3 tbsps. Coconut Milk
3 tbsps. Crushed Pineapple

Combine all ingredients with 2 cups of crushed ice in blender on high speed. Strain into chilled collins glass and serve with a straw.

PINEAPPLE COCKTAIL

3/4 oz. Pineapple Juice
1 1/2 oz. Light Rum
1/2 tsp. Lemon Juice

Shake with ice and strain into chilled cocktail glass.

PINEAPPLE FIZZ

1 oz. Pineapple Juice
1/2 tsp. Superfine Sugar (or Simple Syrup)
2 oz. Light Rum
Club Soda

Shake juice, sugar/syrup, and rum with ice and strain into chilled highball glass over two ice cubes. Fill with club soda and stir.

PINK CREOLE

1 1/2 oz. Light Rum
1 tbsp. Lime Juice
1 tsp. Grenadine
1 tsp. Light Cream

Shake with ice and strain into chilled cocktail glass. Add a black cherry soaked in rum.

PINK PARADISE

1 1/2 oz. Coconut-flavored Rum
1 oz. Amaretto
3 oz. Cranberry Juice
1 1/2 oz. Pineapple Juice

Combine all ingredients in ice-filled hurricane or parfait glass. Garnish with a pineapple wedge and a maraschino cherry.

PLANTER'S COCKTAIL

1/2 oz. Lemon Juice
1/2 tsp. Superfine Sugar (or Simple Syrup)
1 1/2 oz. Jamaica Rum

Shake with ice and strain into chilled cocktail glass.

PLANTER'S PUNCH NO. 1

2 oz. Lime Juice
2 tsps. Superfine Sugar (or Simple Syrup)
2 oz. Club Soda
2 dashes Bitters
2½ oz. Light Rum
1 dash Grenadine

Mix first three ingredients in ice-filled collins glass, and stir until glass is frosted. Add bitters and rum. Stir and top with grenadine. Garnish with slices of lemon, orange, and pineapple, and a maraschino cherry. Serve with a straw.

PLANTER'S PUNCH NO. 2

1 oz. Lime Juice
¼ oz. Lemon Juice
2 oz. Orange Juice
1 tsp. Pineapple Juice
2 oz. Light Rum
1 oz. Jamaica Rum
2 dashes Triple Sec
1 dash Grenadine

Pour first five ingredients into ice-filled collins glass. Stir until glass is frosted. Add Jamaica Rum, stir, and top with triple sec and grenadine. Garnish with slices of orange, lemon, and pineapple, a maraschino cherry, and a sprig of mint dipped in sugar. Serve with a straw.

POKER COCKTAIL

1½ oz. Sweet Vermouth
1½ oz. Light Rum

Stir with ice and strain into chilled cocktail glass.

QUAKER'S COCKTAIL

¾ oz. Light Rum
¾ oz. Brandy
½ oz. Lemon Juice
2 tsps. Raspberry Syrup

Shake with ice and strain into chilled cocktail glass.

QUARTER DECK COCKTAIL

½ oz. Cream Sherry
1½ oz. Light Rum
½ oz. Lime Juice

Stir with ice and strain into chilled cocktail glass.

RAIN MAN

1¼ oz. 151-proof Rum
¾ oz. Melon Liqueur
4 oz. Orange Juice

Shake and pour into ice-filled hurricane or parfait glass.

RED STRING BIKINI

1 oz. Beachcomber Apple Rum
2 oz. Cranberry Juice

Pour into ice-filled highball glass and stir.

ROBSON COCKTAIL

2 tsps. Lemon Juice
1 tbsp. Orange Juice
1½ tsps. Grenadine
1 oz. Jamaica Rum

Shake with ice and strain into chilled cocktail glass.

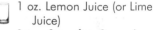

RUM COBBLER

1 tsp. Superfine Sugar (or Simple Syrup)
2 oz. Club Soda
2 oz. Light Rum

In goblet, dissolve sugar in club soda. Fill goblet with shaved ice and add rum. Stir and garnish with fruits in season. Serve with a straw.

RUM COLLINS

1 oz. Lime Juice
1 tsp. Superfine Sugar (or Simple Syrup)
2 oz. Light Rum
Club Soda

Shake juce, sugar/syrup, and rum with ice and strain into chilled collins glass. Add several ice cubes, fill with club soda, and stir. Garnish with a slice of lemon and a maraschino cherry. Serve with a straw.

RUM COOLER

½ tsp. Superfine Sugar (or Simple Syrup)
2 oz. Club Soda
2 oz. Light Rum
Club Soda or Ginger Ale

In collins glass, dissolve sugar in club soda. Stir. Fill glass with ice and add rum. Fill with club soda or ginger ale and stir again. Insert a spiral of orange or lemon peel (or both) and dangle end over rim of glass.

RUM DAISY

½ oz. Lemon Juice
½ tsp. Superfine Sugar (or Simple Syrup)
1 tsp. Grenadine
2 oz. Light Rum

Shake with ice and strain into chilled stein or metal cup. Add one large ice cube and garnish with fruit.

RUM FIX

1 oz. Lemon Juice (or Lime Juice)
1 tsp. Superfine Sugar (or Simple Syrup)
1 tsp. Water
2½ oz. Light Rum

Stir together in highball glass and fill glass with ice. Add rum. Stir and add a slice of lemon. Serve with a straw.

RUM HIGHBALL

2 oz. Light or Dark Rum
Ginger Ale or Club Soda

Pour rum into highball glass over ice cubes and fill with ginger ale or club soda. Add a twist of lemon peel and stir.

RUM MARTINI

4–5 parts Light Rum
1 dash Dry Vermouth

Serve over ice in cocktail glass with a twist of lemon.

RUM OLD-FASHIONED

½ tsp. Superfine Sugar (or
   Simple Syrup)
1 dash Bitters
1 tsp. Water
1½ oz. Light Rum
1 tsp. 151-proof Rum

Stir sugar, bitters, and water
in old-fashioned glass. When
sugar is dissolved, add ice
cubes and light rum. Add a
twist of lime peel and float
the 151-proof rum on top.

RUM RELAXER

1½ oz. Light Rum
1 oz. Pineapple Juice
½ oz. Grenadine
Lemon-lime Soda

Shake first three ingredients
with ice and pour into hurricane or parfait glass. Fill glass
with lemon-lime soda. Garnish with an orange slice and
a maraschino cherry.

RUM RICKEY

½ oz. Lime Juice
1½ oz. Light Rum
Club Soda

Pour lime juice and rum into
ice-filled highball glass and
fill with club soda. Stir. Add a
wedge of lime.

RUM SCREWDRIVER

1½ oz. Light Rum
5 oz. Orange Juice

Combine all ingredients in
ice-filled highball glass.

RUM SOUR

1 oz. Lemon Juice
½ tsp. Superfine Sugar (or
   Simple Syrup)
2 oz. Light Rum

Shake with ice and strain into
chilled sour glass. Garnish
with a half-slice of lemon and
a maraschino cherry.

RUM SWIZZLE

1 oz. Lime Juice
1 tsp. Superfine Sugar (or
   Simple Syrup)
2 oz. Club Soda
2 dashes Bitters
2 oz. Light or Dark Rum

Put lime juice, sugar/syrup,
and club soda into collins
glass. Fill glass with ice and
stir. Add bitters and rum. Fill
with club soda and serve
with a swizzle stick.

RUM TODDY

½ tsp. Superfine Sugar (or
   Simple Syrup)
2 tsps. Water
2 oz. Light or Dark Rum

In old-fashioned glass, dissolve sugar/syrup in water.
Stir and add rum and a large
cube of ice. Stir again and
add a twist of lemon peel.

SANTIAGO COCKTAIL

½ tsp. Superfine Sugar (or
    Simple Syrup)
¼ tsp. Grenadine
1 oz. Lime Juice
1½ oz. Light Rum

Shake with ice and strain into
chilled cocktail glass.

SAXON COCKTAIL

½ oz. Lime Juice
½ tsp. Grenadine
1¾ oz. Light Rum

Shake with ice and strain into
chilled cocktail glass. Serve
with a twist of orange peel.

SEWER WATER

1 splash Grenadine
1 oz. 151-proof Rum
½ oz. Gin
¾ oz. Melon Liqueur
Pineapple Juice
Lime Juice

In hurricane or parfait glass,
splash grenadine. Add ice,
then rum, gin, and melon
liqueur. Fill with pineapple
juice and float lime juice on
top.

SHANGHAI COCKTAIL

½ oz. Lemon Juice
1 tsp. Anisette
1 oz. Jamaica Light Rum
½ tsp. Grenadine

Shake with ice and strain into
chilled cocktail glass.

SIR WALTER COCKTAIL

¾ oz. Light Rum
¾ oz. Brandy
1 tsp. Grenadine
1 tsp. Triple Sec
1 tsp. Lemon Juice

Shake with ice and strain into
chilled cocktail glass.

SLOPPY JOE'S COCKTAIL NO. 1

1 oz. Lime Juice
¼ tsp. Triple Sec
¼ tsp. Grenadine
¾ oz. Light Rum
¾ oz. Dry Vermouth

Shake with ice and strain into
chilled cocktail glass.

SPANISH TOWN COCKTAIL

2 oz. Light Rum
1 tsp. Triple Sec

Stir with ice and strain into
chilled cocktail glass.

STONE COCKTAIL

½ oz. Light Rum
½ oz. Sweet Vermouth
1 oz. Dry Sherry

Stir with ice and strain into
chilled cocktail glass.

RUM

STONE WALL

¼ oz. Fresh Skinned
   Ginger
¾ oz. Demerara Syrup
   (Cane Syrup)
1½ oz. Fresh Apple Cider
1½ oz. Rum
1½ oz. Jamaican Ginger
   Beer

Muddle ginger and syrup in
mixing glass. Add cider and
rum and shake with ice.
Strain into ice-filled rocks
glass and top with ginger
beer. Garnish with a lime
squeeze and a green apple
slice.

STRAWBERRY DAIQUIRI

1 oz. Light Rum
½ oz. Strawberry Schnapps
1 oz. Lime Juice
1 tsp. Superfine Sugar (or
   Simple Syrup)
1 oz. Fresh or Frozen
   Strawberries

Shake with ice and strain into
chilled cocktail glass.

SUSIE TAYLOR

½ oz. Lime Juice
2 oz. Light Rum
Ginger Ale

Pour lime juice and rum into
ice-filled collins glass and fill
with ginger ale. Stir.

TAHITI CLUB

2 oz. Light Rum
1 tbsp. Lemon Juice
1 tbsp. Lime Juice
1 tbsp. Pineapple Juice
½ tsp. Maraschino Liqueur

Shake with ice and strain into
ice-filled old-fashioned glass.
Add a slice of lemon.

THIRD-RAIL COCKTAIL

¾ oz. Light Rum
¾ oz. Apple Brandy
¾ oz. Brandy
¼ tsp. Anisette

Shake with ice and strain into
chilled cocktail glass.

THE THOMAS TRIBUTE

3 Eggs (whites and yolks
   separated)
2 oz. Rum
1 tsp. Cinnamon
½ tsp. Cloves
1 lb. Sugar
½ tsp. Allspice
½ tsp. Cream of Tartar
2 oz. Brandy

Beat egg whites to stiff peaks
and yolks until they are as thin
as water. Mix yolks and whites
together, and then add the rum,
spices, and cream of tartar.
Thicken with sugar until consis-
tency of a light batter. Serve in a
coffee mug, combining 1 table-
spoonful of the above mixture
and 2 oz. of brandy, and then
fill the glass with boiling water.
Garnish with fresh-grated
nutmeg on top.

RUM

THREE MILLER COCKTAIL

1 1/2 oz. Light Rum
3/4 oz. Brandy
1 tsp. Grenadine
1/4 tsp. Lemon Juice

Shake with ice and strain into chilled cocktail glass.

TORRIDORA COCKTAIL

1 1/2 oz. Light Rum
1/2 oz. Coffee-flavored Brandy
1 1/2 tsps. Light Cream
1 tsp. 151-proof Rum

Shake all but 151-proof rum with ice and strain into chilled cocktail glass. Float 151-proof rum on top.

TROPICA COCKTAIL

1 1/4 oz. Light Rum
5 oz. Pineapple Juice
2 oz. Grapefruit Juice
1 dash Grenadine

Mix ingredients in ice-filled collins glass. Garnish with a pineapple wedge.

THE VACATION COCKTAIL

1 tsp. Ginger, Chopped
3/4 oz. Lime Juice
1 tsp. Superfine Sugar (or Simple Syrup)
1 oz. Mango Puree
1/2 oz. Cranberry Juice
1/2 oz. Orange Juice
1/2 oz. Light Rum
1/2 oz. Spiced Rum
1/2 oz. Dark Rum

Muddle ginger, lime juice, and sugar/syrup in mixing glass. Add all but spiced rum, cover with ice, and shake. Strain into chilled cocktail glass and float spiced rum on top. Garnish with a mango slice.

VAN VLEET

3 oz. Light Rum
1 oz. Maple Syrup
1 oz. Lemon Juice

Shake with ice and strain into ice-filled old fashioned glass.

WHITE LILY COCKTAIL

3/4 oz. Triple Sec
3/4 oz. Light Rum
3/4 oz. Gin
1/4 tsp. Anisette

Shake with ice and strain into chilled cocktail glass.

WHITE LION COCKTAIL

1 oz. Lemon Juice
1 tsp. Superfine Sugar (or Simple Syrup)
2 dashes Bitters
½ tsp. Grenadine
1½ oz. Light Rum

Shake with ice and strain into chilled cocktail glass.

WIKI WAKI WOO

½ oz. Vodka
½ oz. Rum
½ oz. 151-proof Rum
½ oz. Tequila
½ oz. Triple Sec
1 oz. Amaretto
1 oz. Orange Juice
1 oz. Pineapple Juice
1 oz. Cranberry Juice

Combine all ingredients with ice, and pour into hurricane or parfait glass. Garnish with an orange slice and a maraschino cherry.

X.Y.Z. COCKTAIL

1 tbsp. Lemon Juice
½ oz. Triple Sec
1 oz. Light Rum

Shake with ice and strain into chilled cocktail glass.

ZOMBIE

1 tsp. Brown Sugar
1 oz. Lemon Juice
1 oz. Lime Juice
1 oz. Pineapple Juice
1 oz. Passion Fruit Syrup
1 dash Angostura Bitters
1 oz. Gold Rum
1 oz. 151-proof Rum
1 oz. White Rum

Dissolve brown sugar in juices. Shake all ingredients with ice and pour into chilled collins glass. Garnish with a mint sprig.

TEQUILA

equila is made with the fermented sap of the mature blue agave plant and produced only in and around the town of Tequila, in Mexico's Jalisco province. Mexican law decrees that, in order to be classified tequila, the spirit must be produced from blue agave plants grown within a delineated region in the five Mexican states of Jalisco, Nayarit, Mihoacan, Guanajuato, and Taumaulipas. If a spirit is produced outside of the delineated area, or with another variety of agave plant, it is called Mezcal, and not the "real deal."

Tequila falls into two main categories: **Mixto,** made from no less than 51-percent blue agave, with sugars from cane or other sources added during fermentation; and **100% Blue Agave,** distilled from the fermented sugars of blue agave plants only, and aged and bottled in Mexico.

According to Mexican law, there are four types of Tequila: *blanco, joven abocado, reposado,* and *añejo. Blanco,* also known as *white, silver,* or *plata,* can be mixto or 100% blue agave that is aged less the 60 days in wood and is usually stored in stainless steel tanks during its resting period. *Joven abocado,* also called *gold,* is something of a noncategory; it is almost always mixto tequila that typically gets its color and flavor from the addition of caramel. *Reposado* can also have color and flavor added but must be aged at least 60 days and up to a year in wood. *Añejo* is aged in wood for at least a year, but more often longer, rendering it smooth, complex, and elegant, akin to fine brandy.

Tequila is quite mixable, combining easily with citrus and other fruit juices—à la the Margarita—as well as with plain old tonic with ice. Its inherent vegetal character works particularly well in savory drinks, like the traditional Tequila con Sangrita (a spicy and refreshing nonalcoholic chaser made with fresh orange juice, grenadine, and ground chile peppers), or when standing in for a Bloody Mary's vodka in a Bloody Maria.

TEQUILA

ALAMO SPLASH

1 1/2 oz. Tequila
1 oz. Orange Juice
1/2 oz. Pineapple Juice
1 splash Lemon-lime Soda

Mix with ice and strain into chilled collins glass.

BIG RED HOOTER

1 oz. Tequila
3/4 oz. Amaretto
Pineapple Juice
1 oz. Grenadine

Pour tequila and amaretto into ice-filled collins glass. Fill with pineapple juice and top with grenadine. Garnish with a maraschino cherry and serve with a straw.

BLOODY MARIA

1 oz. Tequila
2 oz. Tomato Juice
1 dash Lemon Juice
1 dash Tabasco Sauce
1 dash Celery Salt

Shake all ingredients with ice. Strain into ice-filled old-fashioned glass. Add a slice of lemon.

BLUE MARGARITA

1 1/2 oz. Tequila
1/2 oz. Blue Curaçao
1 oz. Lime Juice

Shake ingredients with ice and strain into chilled salt-rimmed cocktail glass.

BRAVE BULL

1 1/2 oz. Tequila
1 oz. Coffee Liqueur

Pour into ice-filled old-fashioned glass and stir. Add a twist of lemon.

CACTUS BERRY

1 1/4 oz. Tequila
1 1/4 oz. Red Wine
1 oz. Triple Sec
3 1/4 oz. Superfine Sugar (or Simple Syrup)
3 1/4 oz. Lemon Juice
1 splash Lemon-lime Soda
1 dash Lime Juice

Shake with ice and pour into large, chilled, salt-rimmed cocktail or margarita glass.

CATALINA MARGARITA

1 1/2 oz. Tequila
1 oz. Peach Schnapps
1 oz. Blue Curaçao
2 oz. Superfine Sugar (or Simple Syrup)
2 oz. Lemon Juice

Shake with ice and strain into chilled cocktail or margarita glass.

CHAPALA

1 1/2 oz. Tequila
1 tbsp. Orange Juice
1 tbsp. Lemon Juice
1 dash Triple Sec
2 tsps. Grenadine

Shake with ice and strain into ice-filled old-fashioned glass. Add a slice of orange.

DIABLO

1 1/2 oz. Tequila
3/4 oz. Crème de Cassis
1/2 oz. Lime Juice
Ginger Ale

Shake first three ingredients
with ice. Strain into a chilled
collins glass. Top with ginger
ale. Garnish with a lime
wheel.

FROSTBITE

1 oz. Tequila
3/4 oz. Crème de Cacao
(White)
3/4 oz. Cream

Shake with ice and strain into
chilled cocktail glass. Garnish
with fresh-grated nutmeg on
top.

GUADALAJARA

2 oz. Tequila
1 oz. Dry Vermouth
1/2 oz. Benedictine

Stir with ice and strain into
chilled cocktail glass. Garnish
with a lemon twist.

HAIRY SUNRISE

3/4 oz. Tequila
3/4 oz. Vodka
1/2 oz. Triple Sec
3 oz. Orange Juice
2–3 dashes Grenadine

Shake all ingredients with ice
except grenadine. Strain into
chilled collins glass. Float
grenadine on top and garnish
with a lime slice.

HOT PANTS

1 1/2 oz. Tequila
1/2 oz. Peppermint
Schnapps
1 tbsp. Grapefruit Juice
1 tsp. Powdered Sugar

Shake with ice and pour into
salt-rimmed old-fashioned
glass.

LA BOMBA

1 1/4 oz. Gold Tequila
3/4 oz. Triple Sec
1 1/2 oz. Pineapple Juice
1 1/2 oz. Orange Juice
2 dashes Grenadine

Combine all ingredients
except grenadine with ice
and shake just three times.
Pour into sugar-rimmed cocktail glass. Add grenadine and
garnish with a lime wheel.

MARGARITA

1 1/2 oz. Tequila
1/2 oz. Triple Sec
1 oz. Lemon Juice or Lime
Juice

Shake ingredients with ice
and strain into chilled, salt-
rimmed cocktail glass.

MEXICANA

1 1/2 oz. Tequila
1 oz. Lemon Juice
1 tbsp. Pineapple Juice
1 tsp. Grenadine

Shake with ice and strain into
chilled cocktail glass.

MEXICAN MADRAS

3 oz. Cranberry Juice
1/2 oz. Orange Juice
1 oz. Gold Tequila
1 dash Lime Juice

Shake with ice and strain into old-fashioned glass. Garnish with an orange slice.

MEXICOLA

2 oz. Tequila
1/2 oz. Lime Juice
Cola

Pour tequila and lime juice into ice-filled collins glass. Fill with cola and stir.

PACIFIC SUNSHINE

1 1/2 oz. Tequila
1 1/2 oz. Blue Curaçao
3/4 oz. Superfine Sugar (or Simple Syrup)
3/4 oz. Lemon Juice
1 dash Bitters

Mix with ice and pour, with ice, into chilled, salt-rimmed parfait or hurricane glass. Garnish with a lemon wheel.

PURPLE GECKO

1 1/2 oz. Tequila
1/2 oz. Blue Curaçao
1/2 oz. Red Curaçao
1 oz. Cranberry Juice
1/2 oz. Superfine Sugar (or Simple Syrup)
1/2 oz. Lemon Juice
1/2 oz. Lime Juice

Shake with ice and pour into chilled, salt-rimmed cocktail or margarita glass. Garnish with a lime wedge.

PURPLE PANCHO

1 oz. Tequila
1/2 oz. Blue Curaçao
1/2 oz. Sloe Gin
2 oz. Lime Juice
1 oz. Superfine Sugar (or Simple Syrup)
1 oz. Lemon Juice

Shake with ice and pour into chilled, salt-rimmed cocktail or margarita glass. Garnish with a lime wheel.

ROSITA

1 1/2 oz. Tequila
1/2 oz. Sweet Vermouth
1/2 oz. Dry Vermouth
1/2 oz. Campari
1 dash Bitters

Stir with ice and strain into ice-filled old-fashioned glass. Garnish with lemon twist.

SHADY LADY

1 oz. Tequila
1 oz. Melon Liqueur
4 oz. Grapefruit Juice

Combine all ingredients in ice-filled highball glass and stir. Garnish with a lime and a maraschino cherry.

SILK STOCKINGS

1 1/2 oz. Tequila
1 oz. Crème de Cacao
1 1/2 oz. Cream
1 dash Grenadine

Shake ingredients with ice and strain into chilled cocktail glass. Sprinkle cinnamon on top.

SLOE TEQUILA

1 oz. Tequila
½ oz. Sloe Gin
1 tbsp. Lime Juice

Combine all ingredients with a half-cup of crushed ice in blender on low speed. Pour into old-fashioned glass. Add ice cubes and a twist of cucumber peel.

SOUTH OF THE BORDER

1 oz. Tequila
¾ oz. Coffee-flavored Brandy
½ oz. Lime Juice

Shake with ice and strain into chilled sour glass. Add a lime slice.

STRAWBERRY MARGARITA

1 oz. Tequila
½ oz. Triple Sec
½ oz. Strawberry Schnapps
1 oz. Lemon Juice or Lime Juice
1 oz. Fresh or Frozen Strawberries

Shake with ice and strain into chilled glass (salt-rimmed, if desired).

TEQUILA CANYON

1½ oz. Tequila
⅛ oz. Triple Sec
4 oz. Cranberry Juice
¼ oz. Pineapple Juice
¼ oz. Orange Juice

Pour first three ingredients into ice-filled collins glass and stir gently. Top with pineapple and orange juices. Garnish with a lime wheel. Serve with a straw.

TEQUILA COLLINS

½ oz. Lemon Juice
1 tsp. Superfine Sugar (or Simple Syrup)
2 oz. Tequila
Club Soda

Shake first three ingredients with ice and strain into chilled collins glass. Add several ice cubes, fill with club soda, and stir. Garnish with slices of lemon and orange, and a maraschino cherry. Serve with a straw.

TEQUILA MANHATTAN

2 oz. Tequila
1 oz. Sweet Vermouth
1 dash Lime Juice

Shake with ice and strain into ice-filled old-fashioned glass. Add a maraschino cherry and an orange slice.

TEQUILA MATADOR

1½ oz. Tequila
3 oz. Pineapple Juice
½ oz. Lime Juice

Shake with crushed ice and strain into chilled Champagne flute.

TEQUILA MOCKINGBIRD

1½ oz. Tequila
¾ oz. Crème de Menthe (Green)
1 oz. Lime Juice

Shake with ice and strain into chilled cocktail glass. Garnish with a lime slice.

TEQUILA OLD-FASHIONED

1/2 tsp. Superfine Sugar (or
    Simple Syrup)
1 dash Bitters
1 tsp. Water
1 1/2 oz. Tequila
1 splash Club Soda

Mix sugar/syrup, bitters, and
water in old-fashioned glass.
Add tequila, ice, and club
soda. Garnish with a
pineapple stick.

TEQUILA PINK

1 1/2 oz. Tequila
1 oz. Dry Vermouth
1 dash Grenadine

Shake with ice and strain into
chilled cocktail glass.

TEQUILA SOUR

1 oz. Lemon Juice
1 tsp. Superfine Sugar (or
    Simple Syrup)
2 oz. Tequila

Shake with ice and strain into
chilled sour glass. Garnish
with a half-slice of lemon and
a maraschino cherry.

TEQUILA STRAIGHT

1 pinch Salt
1 1/2 oz. Tequila
1/2 oz. Lemon Juice

Put salt between thumb and
index finger on back of left
hand. Hold jigger of tequila
in same hand and lemon
wedge in right hand. Taste
salt, drink the tequila, and
then suck the lemon.

TEQUILA SUNRISE

2 oz. Tequila
4 oz. Orange Juice
3/4 oz. Grenadine

Stir tequila and orange juice
with ice and strain into ice-
filled highball glass. Pour in
grenadine slowly and allow to
settle. Before drinking, stir to
complete your sunrise.

TEQUINI

1 1/2 oz. Tequila
1/2 oz. Dry Vermouth
1 dash Bitters (if desired)

Stir with ice and strain into
chilled cocktail glass. Serve
with a twist of lemon peel
and an olive.

TEQUONIC

2 oz. Tequila
1 oz. Lemon Juice (or 1/2
    oz. Lime Juice)
Tonic Water

Pour tequila into ice-filled
old-fashioned glass. Add fruit
juice, fill with tonic water,
and stir.

TIJUANA TAXI

2 oz. Gold Tequila
1 oz. Blue Curaçao
1 oz. Tropical Fruit Schnapps
Lemon-lime Soda

Pour tequila, curaçao, and
schnapps into ice-filled large
highball glass. Fill with
lemon-lime soda and garnish
with an orange slice and a
maraschino cherry.

T.N.T. NO. 2

1 oz. Tequila
Tonic Water

Mix with ice in old-fashioned glass.

TOREADOR

1½ oz. Tequila
½ oz. Crème de Cacao
1 tbsp. Light Cream

Shake with ice and strain into chilled cocktail glass. Top with a little whipped cream and sprinkle lightly with cocoa.

TRAFFIC LIGHT COOLER

¾ oz. Melon Liqueur
1 oz. Gold Tequila
1 splash Superfine Sugar (or Simple Syrup)
1 splash Lemon Juice
2 oz. Orange Juice
½ oz. Sloe Gin

Into ice-filled pilsner glass first pour the melon liqueur and then the tequila to create a green layer. Add the sugar/syrup and lemon juice. Slowly pour the orange juice against side of glass to create the yellow layer. Add a few more ice cubes, if needed. Carefully float the sloe gin on top for the red layer. Garnish with a maraschino cherry and lemon and lime wheels. Stir just before drinking.

VIVA VILLA

1 oz. Lime Juice
1 tsp. Superfine Sugar (or Simple Syrup)
1½ oz. Tequila

Shake with ice and strain into salt-rimmed, ice-filled old-fashioned glass.

WILD THING

1½ oz. Tequila
1 oz. Cranberry Juice
1 oz. Club Soda
½ oz. Lime Juice

Pour into ice-filled old-fashioned glass. Garnish with a lime wheel.

VODKA

According to U.S. law, vodkas produced in the United States must be pure spirits with no additives except water; nonaged; and basically colorless, tasteless, and odorless. That description sounds awfully lackluster for one of the most popular spirits in America today, but it's exactly why it is: Because of its purity, vodka graciously assumes the characteristics of whatever it's mixed with.

Vodka is generally made from grain (corn, rye, or wheat) or potatoes, with grain accounting for nearly all of the vodka available on the international market. Vodka is a rectified spirit, meaning it's distilled at least three times, and then filtered—the most important step—typically through charcoal, although some distillers claim to employ diamond dust and even quartz crystals.

The stylistic differences between one vodka and another—even at the very high end—are subtle, given that discernable flavor isn't a factor. More often vodka is described by its texture on the tongue or mouth-feel, ranging from clean and crisp to viscous and silky. Subtle sensations in the finish—after it's swallowed—can range from slightly sweet to medicinal. The finish could also reveal if a vodka is hot, rough, and raw or, conversely, smooth, round, and rich. Though higher-than-normal proof (above 80-proof) could account for that burning heat, it's more often the mark of an inexpensive bulk vodka, as opposed to one made by a master distiller that's smooth and supple.

That said, the very best vodkas, the so-called super-premium brands (priced higher than $20 per bottle) are perfect when unadorned, say in a Martini, or for a chilled straight shot to accompany caviar, for example. In the end, mixing vodka with just about any of the following recipes will only enhance whatever it touches.

ALFIE COCKTAIL

1½ oz. Lemon-flavored
    Vodka
1 tbsp. Pineapple Juice
1 dash Triple Sec

Shake with ice and strain into
chilled cocktail glass.

AQUEDUCT

1½ oz. Vodka
1½ tsps. Curaçao (White)
1½ tsps. Apricot-flavored
    Brandy
1 tbsp. Lime Juice

Shake with ice and strain into
chilled cocktail glass. Add a
twist of orange peel.

BANANA PUNCH

2 oz. Vodka
1½ tsps. Apricot-flavored
    Brandy
½ oz. Lime Juice
Club Soda

Pour vodka, brandy, and lime
juice into collins glass filled
with crushed ice. Add club
soda and top with slices of
banana and sprigs of mint.

BEER BUSTER

1½ oz. 100-proof Vodka
Chilled Beer or Ale
2 dashes Tabasco Sauce

Pour vodka into highball
glass and fill with beer or ale.
Add Tabasco sauce and stir
lightly.

BIANCA

1½ oz. Citrus-flavored
    Vodka
1 splash Superfine Sugar
    (or Simple Syrup)
1 splash Lemon Juice
¼ oz. Lime Juice
2 oz. Pomegranate Juice

Shake with ice and strain into
chilled, sugar-rimmed cocktail glass. Garnish with twist
of lemon and fresh pome-
granate seeds.

THE BIG CRUSH

2½ oz. Raspberry-flavored
    Vodka
1 oz. Triple Sec
½ oz. Raspberry-flavored
    Liqueur
1 splash Lime Juice
Champagne

Shake first four ingredients
with ice. Strain into chilled
cocktail glass and top with
Champagne. Garnish with
fresh blackberries and raspberries.

BIKINI

2 oz. Vodka
1 oz. Light Rum
½ oz. Milk
1 tsp. Sugar
1 oz. Lemon Juice

Shake with ice and strain into
chilled cocktail glass. Garnish
with a twist of lemon peel.

BLACK CHERRY CHOCOLATE

1½ oz. Effen Black Cherry
  Vodka
1½ oz. White Chocolate
  Liqueur
Splash Cherry-flavored
  Soda or Cherry Juice

Shake with ice and strain into
chilled cocktail glass.

BLACK MAGIC

1½ oz. Vodka
¾ oz. Coffee Liqueur
1 dash Lemon Juice

Stir and serve in ice-filled
old-fashioned glass. Add a
twist of lemon peel.

BLACK RUSSIAN

1½ oz. Vodka
¾ oz. Coffee Liqueur

Pour over ice cubes into old-
fashioned glass.

THE BLOOD ORANGE

2 oz. Orange-flavored
  Vodka
1 oz. Campari

Stir with ice and strain into
chilled cocktail glass. Garnish
with a half wheel of blood
orange.

BLOODY BULL

1 oz. Vodka
2 oz. Tomato Juice
2 oz. Beef Bouillon

Pour into ice-filled highball
glass. Stir, and add a squeeze
of lemon and a slice of lime.

BLOODY MARY

1½ oz. Vodka
3 oz. Tomato Juice
1 dash Lemon Juice
½ tsp. Worcestershire
  Sauce
2–3 drops Tabasco Sauce
Salt and Pepper to taste

Shake with ice and strain into
ice-filled old-fashioned glass.
Garnish with a lime wedge or
a celery stalk.

BLUE LAGOON

1 oz. Vodka
1 oz. Blue Curaçao
Lemonade

Pour first two ingredients
into ice-filled highball glass.
Fill with lemonade. Garnish
with a maraschino cherry.

BLUE LEMONADE

1½ oz. Effen Vodka
4 oz. Lemonade
¾ oz. Blue Curaçao

Pour into ice-filled highball
glass and stir.

BLUE MONDAY COCKTAIL

1½ oz. Vodka
¾ oz. Triple Sec
1 dash Blue Food Coloring

Stir with ice and strain into
chilled cocktail glass.

VODKA

BOLSHOI PUNCH

1 oz. Vodka
2½ oz. Lemon Juice
1 tsp. Powdered Sugar
¼ oz. Rum
¼ oz. Crème de Cassis

Shake and pour into ice-filled old-fashioned glass.

BORDEAUX COCKTAIL

1½ oz. Citrus-flavored Vodka
½ oz. Lillet Blonde

Stir with ice and strain into chilled cocktail glass. Garnish with a twist of lemon peel.

BOSTON GOLD

1 oz. Vodka
½ oz. Crème de Banana
Orange Juice

Pour vodka and banana liqueur into ice-filled highball glass. Fill with orange juice and stir.

BULL FROG

1½ oz. Vodka
5 oz. Lemonade

Pour into ice-filled collins glass and garnish with a slice of lime.

BULL SHOT

1½ oz. Vodka
3 oz. Chilled Beef Bouillon
1 dash Worcestershire Sauce
1 dash Salt
1 dash Pepper

Shake with ice and strain into chilled old-fashioned glass.

CAESAR

Celery Salt
1 oz. Vodka
4 oz. Tomato-Clam Juice
1 pinch Salt
1 pinch Pepper
1 dash Worcestershire Sauce
2–3 dashes Horseradish

Coat rim of a highball or delmonico glass with celery salt, and then fill with ice. Shake ingredients with ice and strain mixture into glass. Garnish with a celery stalk and a lemon wedge.

CAPE CODDER

1½ oz. Vodka
5 oz. Cranberry Juice

Pour into ice-filled highball glass. Stir well. Garnish with a wedge of lime.

CAPPUCCINO COCKTAIL

¾ oz. Coffee-flavored Brandy
¾ oz. Vodka
¾ oz. Light Cream

Shake with ice and strain into chilled cocktail glass.

CARIBBEAN CRUISE

1 oz. Vodka
1/4 oz. Light Rum
1/4 oz. Coconut-flavored Rum
1 splash Grenadine
4 oz. Pineapple Juice

Shake first four ingredients with ice and pour into ice-filled collins glass. Fill with pineapple juice. Garnish with a pineapple wedge and a maraschino cherry.

CASCO BAY LEMONADE

1 1/2 oz. Citrus-flavored Vodka
2 oz. Superfine Sugar (or Simple Syrup)
2 oz. Lemon Juice
1 splash Cranberry Juice
1 splash Lemon-lime Soda

Shake first four ingredients with ice. Pour into ice-filled collins glass. Add lemon-lime soda. Float a lemon slice on top.

CHAMPAGNE FLAMINGO

3/4 oz. Vodka
3/4 oz. Campari
5 oz. Champagne, Chilled

Shake vodka and Campari with ice. Strain into a chilled Champagne flute and top with Champagne. Garnish with a zest of orange.

CHERRY BOMB

1 oz. Effen Black Cherry Vodka
1 tumbler 3/4 full of Energy Drink

Mix in a rocks glass with ice and garnish with a maraschino cherry.

CITRONELLA COOLER

1 oz. Citrus-flavored Vodka
1 dash Lime Juice
2 oz. Lemonade
1 oz. Cranberry Juice

Pour into ice-filled collins glass. Top with a squeeze of fresh lime.

COSMOPOLITAN COCKTAIL

1 1/4 oz. Vodka
1/4 oz. Lime Juice
1/4 oz. Triple Sec
1/4 oz. Cranberry Juice

Shake well with ice and strain into chilled cocktail glass. Garnish with a lime wedge.

CROCODILE COOLER

1 1/2 oz. Citrus-flavored Vodka
1 oz. Melon Liqueur
3/4 oz. Triple Sec
1 oz. Superfine Sugar (or Simple Syrup)
1 oz. Lemon Juice
Lemon-lime Soda

Place first five ingredients into ice-filled parfait or hurricane glass. Fill with soda and stir well. Garnish with a pineapple wedge and a maraschino cherry or lime wheel. Serve with a straw.

VODKA

CUBELTINI

3 Cucumber Slices
5–7 Mint Leaves
1½ oz. Superfine Sugar (or Simple Syrup)
2 oz. Vodka
1 oz. Lime Juice

Muddle the cucumber, mint, and sugar/syrup. Add vodka and lime juice. Shake and strain into chilled martini glass. Garnish with fresh mint.

DESERT SUNRISE

1¼ oz. Vodka
1½ oz. Orange Juice
1½ oz. Pineapple Juice
1 dash Grenadine

Pour first three ingredients over crushed ice in collins glass. Top with grenadine.

ELECTRIC JAM

1¼ oz. Vodka
½ oz. Blue Curaçao
1 oz. Superfine Sugar (or Simple Syrup)
1 oz. Lemon Juice
Lemon-lime Soda

Pour into ice-filled collins glass and stir.

FRENCH MARTINI

1½ oz. Vodka
1 oz. Black Raspberry Liqueur

Stir with ice and strain into chilled cocktail glass.

FRISKY WITCH

1 oz. Vodka
1 oz. Sambuca

Pour into ice-filled old-fashioned glass and stir. Garnish with a black licorice stick.

GABLES COLLINS

1½ oz. Vodka
1 oz. Crème de Noyaux
1 tbsp. Lemon Juice
1 tbsp. Pineapple Juice
Club Soda

Shake first four ingredients with ice and strain into ice-filled collins glass. Fill with club soda. Garnish with a slice of lemon and a pineapple chunk.

GENTLE BEN

1 oz. Vodka
1 oz. Gin
1 oz. Tequila
Orange Juice

Shake first three ingredients with ice and pour into ice-filled collins glass. Fill with orange juice and stir. Garnish with an orange slice and a maraschino cherry.

GEORGIA PEACH

1½ oz. Vodka
½ oz. Peach Schnapps
1 dash Grenadine
Lemonade

Pour first three ingredients into ice-filled collins glass. Fill with lemonade.

GLASS TOWER

1 oz. Vodka
1 oz. Peach Schnapps
1 oz. Rum
1 oz. Triple Sec
1/2 oz. Sambuca
Lemon-lime Soda

Pour first five ingredients into ice-filled collins glass. Fill with lemon-lime soda and garnish with an orange slice and a maraschino cherry.

GODCHILD

1 oz. Amaretto
1 oz. Vodka
1 oz. Heavy Cream

Shake well with ice and strain into chilled Champagne flute.

GODMOTHER

1 1/2 oz. Vodka
3/4 oz. Amaretto

Combine in ice-filled old-fashioned glass.

GRAPE NEHI (AKA PURPLE HOOTER)

1 oz. Vodka
1 oz. Raspberry-flavored Liqueur
1 oz. Lemon Juice

Shake with ice and strain into chilled cocktail glass.

GRAPEFRUIT GIMLET ROYALE

2 oz. Vodka
2 oz. Grapefruit Juice
1 splash Fresh Lime Juice
1 splash Superfine Sugar (or Simple Syrup)
Champagne, Chilled

Shake with ice and strain into chilled cocktail glass. Top off with Champagne.

HANDBALL COOLER

1 1/2 oz. Vodka
Club Soda
1 splash Orange Juice

Pour vodka into ice-filled highball glass. Fill almost to top with club soda. Top with orange juice. Garnish with a lime wedge.

HARRINGTON

1 1/2 oz. Vodka
1/4 oz. Triple Sec
1/8 oz. Chartreuse

Stir with ice and strain into chilled cocktail glass. Twist an orange zest over the drink and then float zest in drink.

HARVEY WALLBANGER

1 oz. Vodka
4 oz. Orange Juice
1/2 oz. Galliano

Pour vodka and orange juice into ice-filled collins glass. Stir. Float Galliano on top.

HEADLESS HORSEMAN

2 oz. Vodka
3 dashes Bitters
Ginger Ale

Pour vodka and bitters into ice-filled collins glass. Fill with ginger ale and stir. Garnish with a slice of orange.

HUNTSMAN COCKTAIL

1½ oz. Vodka
½ oz. Jamaica Rum
½ oz. Lime Juice
½ tsp. Superfine Sugar (or Simple Syrup)

Shake with ice and strain into chilled cocktail glass.

IBIZA

1 oz. Orange-flavored Vodka
½ oz. Campari
1 dash Peach Schnapps
1 dash Apple Schnapps
1 dash Pomegranates au Merlot Syrup
1 oz. Grapefruit Juice

Shake with ice and strain into chilled cocktail glass. Garnish with a grapefruit twist.

ITALIAN SCREWDRIVER

1½ oz. Citrus-flavored Vodka
3 oz. Orange Juice
2 oz. Grapefruit Juice
1 splash Ginger Ale

Mix and pour into ice-filled, sugar-rimmed hurricane or parfait glass. Garnish with a lime wheel.

JACKIE-O

½ oz. Citrus-flavored Vodka
½ oz. Orange-flavored Vodka
½ oz. Crème de Cassis
1 oz. Apricot Nectar
3 tsp. Lemon Juice
2 tsps. Cranberry Juice
Champagne, Chilled

Shake first six ingredients with ice and strain into chilled, pink-sugar-rimmed 10-oz. cocktail glass. Top with Champagne and garnish with an orange slice and a lime wheel.

THE JAMAICAN TEN SPEED

1 oz. Vodka
¾ oz. Melon Liqueur
¼ oz. Crème de Banana
¼ oz. Coconut-flavored Rum
½ oz. Half-and-Half

Shake with ice and strain into chilled cocktail glass.

JERICHO'S BREEZE

1 oz. Vodka
3/4 oz. Blue Curaçao
1 1/4 oz. Superfine Sugar (or
   Simple Syrup)
1 1/4 oz. Lemon Juice
1 splash Lemon-lime Soda
1 splash Orange Juice

Shake with ice until frothy.
Strain into chilled stemmed
goblet. Garnish with a
pineapple spear and a
maraschino cherry.

JUNGLE JUICE

1 oz. Vodka
1 oz. Rum
1/2 oz. Triple Sec
1 splash Superfine Sugar
   (or Simple Syrup)
1 splash Lemon Juice
1 oz. Cranberry Juice
1 oz. Orange Juice
1 oz. Pineapple Juice

Pour into ice-filled collins
glass. Garnish with an orange
slice and a maraschino
cherry.

KANGAROO COCKTAIL

1 1/2 oz. Vodka
3/4 oz. Dry Vermouth

Shake with ice and strain into
chilled cocktail glass. Garnish
with a twist of lemon peel.

KRETCHMA COCKTAIL

1 oz. Vodka
1 oz. Crème de Cacao
   (White)
1 tbsp. Lemon Juice
1 dash Grenadine

Shake with ice and strain into
chilled cocktail glass.

L.A. SUNRISE

1 oz. Vodka
1/2 oz. Crème de Banana
2 oz. Orange Juice
2 oz. Pineapple Juice
1/4 oz. Rum

Pour first four ingredients into
ice-filled hurricane or parfait
glass. Float rum on top. Garnish with a lime wheel and a
maraschino cherry.

LE PARADINI

1 1/2 oz. Vodka
1/2 oz. Raspberry-flavored
   Liqueur
1 1/2 oz. Grand Marnier
1 1/2 oz. Champagne,
   Chilled

Shake first three ingredients
with ice and strain into
chilled cocktail glass. Top
with Champagne.

LEMON CRUSH

2 oz. Citrus-flavored Vodka
1 oz. Limoncello Crema
1 oz. Triple Sec
2 oz. Lemon Juice

Shake with ice and strain into
chilled, sugar-rimmed cocktail glass.

LONG ISLAND ICED TEA

¾ oz. Vodka
¾ oz. Tequila
¾ oz. Gin
¾ oz. Light Rum
¾ oz. Triple Sec
½ oz. Superfine Sugar (or Simple Syrup)
½ oz. Lemon Juice
Cola

Combine first seven ingredients and pour into ice-filled highball glass. Add cola for color. Garnish with a wedge of lime.

MADRAS

1½ oz. Vodka
4 oz. Cranberry Juice
1 oz. Orange Juice

Pour into highball glass over ice. Garnish with a wedge of lime.

MOCHA EXPRESS

2 oz. Vodka
¾ oz. Irish Cream Liqueur
¾ oz. Kahlua
1 oz. Espresso Coffee

Shake with ice and strain into chilled cocktail glass.

MOSCOW MULE

1½ oz. Vodka
½ oz. Lime Juice
Ginger Beer

Pour vodka and lime juice into coffee mug. Add ice cubes and fill with ginger beer. Drop lime wedge in mug for garnish.

NAKED PRETZEL

¾ oz. Vodka
1 oz. Melon Liqueur
½ oz. Crème de Cassis
2 oz. Pineapple Juice

Stir and pour into ice-filled old-fashioned glass.

NIJINSKI BLINI

1 oz. Vodka
2 oz. Pureed Peaches
½ oz. Lemon Juice
1 splash Peach Schnapps
1 splash Champagne, Chilled

Pour into chilled Champagne flute and stir gently.

NINOTCHKA COCKTAIL

1½ oz. Vodka
½ oz. Crème de Cacao (White)
1 tbsp. Lemon Juice

Shake with ice and strain into chilled cocktail glass.

ORANG-A-TANG

1 oz. Vodka
½ oz. Triple Sec
1 splash Grenadine
6 oz. Orange Juice
1 splash Superfine Sugar (or Simple Syrup)
1 splash Lemon Juice
1 oz. 151-proof Rum

Lightly blend all ingredients except rum. Strain into large snifter half-filled with ice. Float rum on top. Garnish with tropical fruits.

PAVLOVA SUPREME

2 oz. Chilled Vodka
1/2 oz. Crème de Cassis

Mix in red-wine glass filled with crushed ice.

PETIT ZINC

1 oz. Vodka
1/2 oz. Triple Sec
1/2 oz. Sweet Vermouth
1/2 oz. Orange Juice (preferably Seville; otherwise, add 1/4 oz. Lemon Juice)

Shake with ice and strain into chilled cocktail glass. Garnish with a wedge of orange.

PINK LEMONADE

1 1/2 oz. Citrus-flavored Vodka
1 splash Triple Sec
1 splash Lime Juice
1 splash Superfine Sugar (or Simple Syrup)
1 splash Lemon Juice
2 oz. Cranberry Juice

Shake and pour into ice-filled collins glass. Garnish with a lemon wheel.

PINK PUSSY CAT

1 1/2 oz. Vodka
Pineapple or Grapefruit Juice
1 dash Grenadine

Pour vodka into ice-filled highball glass. Fill with juice. Add grenadine for color and stir.

POLYNESIAN COCKTAIL

1 1/2 oz. Vodka
3/4 oz. Cherry-flavored Brandy
1 oz. Lime Juice

Shake with ice and strain into chilled sugar-rimmed cocktail glass.

PRETTY IN PINK

2 oz. Vodka
3/4 oz. Creme de Noyeaux
3/4 oz. Lemon Juice
Club Soda

Shake first three ingredients and strain into ice-filled collins glass. Top with club soda.

PURPLE MASK

1 oz. Vodka
1 oz. Grape Juice
1/2 oz. Crème de Cacao (White)

Shake with ice and strain into chilled cocktail glass.

PURPLE PASSION

1 1/2 oz. Vodka
3 oz. Grapefruit Juice
3 oz. Grape Juice
Sugar

Chill, stir, add sugar to taste, and serve in collins glass.

VODKA

PURPLE PASSION TEA

¼ oz. Vodka
¼ oz. Rum
¼ oz. Gin
½ oz. Black Raspberry
  Liqueur
2 oz. Superfine Sugar (or
  Simple Syrup)
2 oz. Lemon Juice
3 oz. Lemon-lime Soda

Pour into ice-filled highball
glass, and stir. Garnish with a
twist of lemon peel.

RED APPLE

1 oz. 100-proof Vodka
1 oz. Apple Juice
1 tbsp. Lemon Juice
1 tsp. Grenadine

Shake with ice and strain into
chilled cocktail glass.

RED HEAD MARTINI

4 whole Strawberries
¾ oz. Lemon Juice
¾ oz. Superfine Sugar (or
  Simple Syrup)
1½ oz. Citrus-flavored
  Vodka
1 splash Moscato d'Asti (or
  Sweet Sparkling Wine)

Muddle strawberries in
mixing glass with lemon juice
and sugar/syrup. Cover with
ice, add vodka, and shake
well. Strain into chilled cocktail glass. Splash with
sparkling wine. Garnish with
a strawberry.

ROBIN'S NEST

1 oz. Vodka
1 oz. Cranberry Juice
½ oz. Crème de Cacao
  (White)

Shake with ice and strain into
chilled cocktail glass.

RUBY RED

2 oz. Grapefruit-flavored
  Vodka
1½ oz. Triple Sec
1 splash Orange Juice
1½ oz. Grapefruit Juice

Shake with ice and strain into
chilled cocktail glass. Garnish
with a tangerine wedge.

RUSSIAN BEAR COCKTAIL

1 oz. Vodka
½ oz. Crème de Cacao
  (White)
1 tbsp. Light Cream

Stir with ice and strain into
chilled cocktail glass.

RUSSIAN COCKTAIL

¾ oz. Crème de Cacao
  (White)
¾ oz. Gin
¾ oz. Vodka

Shake with ice and strain into
chilled cocktail glass.

SAM-TINI

1¼ oz. Vodka
1 splash Sambuca
1 dash Blue Curaçao

Stir with ice and strain into
chilled cocktail glass. Garnish
with a twist of orange.

SCREWDRIVER

1½ oz. Vodka
5 oz. Orange Juice

Pour into ice-filled highball glass. Stir well.

SEABREEZE

1½ oz. Vodka
4 oz. Cranberry Juice
1 oz. Grapefruit Juice

Pour into ice-filled highball glass. Garnish with a wedge of lime.

SHALOM

1½ oz. 100-proof Vodka
1 oz. Madeira
1 tbsp. Orange Juice

Shake with ice and strain into ice-filled old-fashioned glass. Add an orange slice.

SIBERIAN SLEIGHRIDE

1¼ oz. Vodka
¾ oz. Crème de Cacao (White)
½ oz. Crème de Menthe (White)
3 oz. Light Cream

Shake with ice and strain into chilled snifter. Sprinkle with chocolate shavings.

SINO-SOVIET SPLIT

2 oz. Vodka
1 oz. Amaretto
Milk or Light Cream

Combine first two ingredients in ice-filled old-fashioned glass. Fill with milk or cream.

SONIC BLASTER

½ oz. Vodka
½ oz. Light Rum
½ oz. Banana Liqueur
1 oz. Pineapple Juice
1 oz. Orange Juice
1 oz. Cranberry Juice

Shake and pour into ice-filled collins glass. Garnish with orange and lime slices.

SOVIET

1½ oz. Vodka
½ oz. Amontillado Sherry
½ oz. Dry Vermouth

Shake with ice and strain into ice-filled old-fashioned glass. Add a twist of lemon peel.

SPUTNIK

1¼ oz. Vodka
1¼ oz. Peach Schnapps
3 oz. Orange Juice
3 oz. Light Cream

Shake with ice until frothy, and pour into stemmed goblet. Garnish with a slice of fresh peach.

STOCKHOLM 75

¾ oz. Citrus-flavored Vodka
¾ oz. Superfine Sugar (or Simple Syrup)
¾ oz. Lemon Juice
5 oz. Champagne, Chilled

Shake vodka, sugar/syrup, and juice with ice. Strain into chilled, oversized, sugar-rimmed cocktail glass. Fill with Champagne.

VODKA

STUPID CUPID

2 oz. Citrus-flavored Vodka
1/2 oz. Sloe Gin
1 splash Superfine Sugar
   (or Simple Syrup)
1 splash Lemon Juice

Stir with ice and strain into chilled cocktail glass. Garnish with a maraschino cherry.

SURF RIDER

3 oz. Vodka
1 oz. Sweet Vermouth
1/2 cup Orange Juice
1 oz. Lemon Juice
1/2 tsp. Grenadine

Shake with ice and strain into chilled cocktail glass. Garnish with an orange slice and a maraschino cherry.

SWEET MARIA

1 tbsp. Light Cream
1/2 oz. Amaretto
1 oz. Vodka

Shake with ice and strain into chilled cocktail glass.

SWISS MARTINI

3 oz. Vodka
3/4 oz. Cherry-flavored
   Brandy

Stir with ice in mixing glass and strain into chilled cocktail glass. Garnish with a twist of lemon peel or an olive.

THE TITIAN

1 oz. Orange-flavored
   Vodka
1/2 oz. Grand Marnier
1 oz. Passion Fruit Juice
1/2 oz. Lime Juice
1/2 oz. Pomegranate Syrup

Shake with ice and strain into chilled cocktail glass. Garnish with a fresh raspberry.

TOP BANANA

1 oz. Vodka
1 oz. Crème de Banana
2 oz. Orange Juice

Shake with ice and strain into ice-filled old-fashioned glass.

TROPICAL ICED TEA

1/2 oz. Vodka
1/2 oz. Rum
1/2 oz. Gin
1/2 oz. Triple Sec
1/2 oz. Superfine Sugar (or
   Simple Syrup)
1/2 oz. Lemon Juice
1 oz. Pineapple Juice
1 oz. Cranberry Juice
1/2 oz. Grenadine

Combine in mixing glass and strain into ice-filled collins glass. Garnish with seasonal fruits.

TWISTER

2 oz. Vodka
1/3 oz. Lime Juice
Lemon Soda

Pour vodka and lime into collins glass. Add several ice cubes and drop a lime twist into glass. Fill with lemon soda and stir.

VELVET HAMMER

1½ oz. Vodka
1 tbsp. Crème de Cacao
1 tbsp. Light Cream

Shake with ice and strain into chilled cocktail glass.

VELVET PEACH HAMMER

1¾ oz. Vodka
¾ oz. Peach Schnapps
1 splash Superfine Sugar (or Simple Syrup)
1 splash Lemon Juice

Pour vodka and schnapps into ice-filled old-fashioned glass. Stir and top with sugar/syrup and lemon juice. Garnish with a slice of fresh peach.

VICTORY COLLINS

1½ oz. Vodka
3 oz. Unsweetened Grape Juice
3 oz. Lemon Juice
1 tsp. Superfine Sugar (or Simple Syrup)

Shake with ice and strain into ice-filled collins glass. Add a slice of orange.

VODKA AND APPLE JUICE

2 oz. Vodka
Apple Juice

Pour vodka into ice-filled highball glass. Fill with apple juice and stir.

VODKA COLLINS

1 oz. Lemon Juice
1 tsp. Superfine Sugar (or Simple Syrup)
2 oz. Vodka
Club Soda

Shake lemon juice, sugar/syrup, and vodka with ice and strain into chilled collins glass. Add several ice cubes, fill with club soda, and stir. Garnish with slices of lemon and orange and a maraschino cherry. Serve with a straw.

VODKA COOLER

½ tsp. Superfine Sugar (or Simple Syrup)
2 oz. Club Soda
2 oz. Vodka
Club Soda or Ginger Ale

In collins glass stir sugar/syrup with club soda. Fill glass with ice and add vodka. Fill with club soda or ginger ale and stir again. Insert a spiral of orange or lemon peel and dangle end over rim of glass.

VODKA DAISY

1 oz. Lemon Juice
½ tsp. Superfine Sugar (or Simple Syrup)
1 tsp. Grenadine
2 oz. Vodka

Shake with ice and strain into chilled stein or metal cup. Add ice cubes and garnish with fruits.

VODKA

VODKA GIMLET

1 oz. Lime Juice
1 tsp. Superfine Sugar (or Simple Syrup)
1½ oz. Vodka

Shake with ice and strain into chilled cocktail glass.

VODKA GRASSHOPPER

¾ oz. Vodka
¾ oz. Crème de Menthe (Green)
¾ oz. Crème de Cacao (White)

Shake with ice and strain into chilled cocktail glass.

VODKA ON THE ROCKS

2 oz. Vodka

Put two or three ice cubes in old-fashioned glass and add vodka. Serve with a twist of lemon peel.

VODKA SALTY DOG

1½ oz. Vodka
5 oz. Grapefruit Juice
¼ tsp. Salt

Pour into ice-filled highball glass. Stir well.

VODKA "7"

2 oz. Vodka
½ oz. Lime Juice
Lemon-lime Soda

Pour vodka and lime juice into ice-filled collins glass. Drop a twist of lime in glass, fill with lemon-lime soda, and stir.

VODKA SLING

1 tsp. Superfine Sugar (or Simple Syrup)
1 tsp. Water
1 oz. Lemon Juice
2 oz. Vodka

Dissolve sugar/syrup in water and lemon juice. Add vodka. Pour into ice-filled old-fashioned glass and stir. Add a twist of orange peel.

VODKA SOUR

1 oz. Lemon Juice
½ tsp. Superfine Sugar (or Simple Syrup)
2 oz. Vodka

Shake with ice and strain into chilled sour glass. Garnish with a half-slice of lemon and a maraschino cherry.

VODKA STINGER

1 oz. Vodka
1 oz. Crème de Menthe (White)

Shake with ice and strain into chilled cocktail glass.

VODKA AND TONIC

2 oz. Vodka
Tonic Water

Pour vodka into highball glass over ice. Add tonic and stir. Garnish with a lemon wedge.

WARSAW COCKTAIL

1 1/2 oz. Vodka
1/2 oz. Blackberry-flavored
   Brandy
1/2 oz. Dry Vermouth
1 tsp. Lemon Juice

Shake with ice and strain into chilled cocktail glass.

WHITE RUSSIAN

1 oz. Coffee Liqueur
2 oz. Vodka
Milk or Cream

Pour coffee liqueur and vodka in ice-filled old-fashioned glass and fill with milk or cream.

WHISKEY

Whiskey is an umbrella term for four distinctly different spirits—Irish, Scotch, Bourbon, and Rye—all based on a common foundation. There is often confusion about how to spell it (though very little confusion about what to *do* with it). In Ireland and the United States, it's spelled with an "e," while in Scotland and Canada it's spelled without one. Regardless of where it comes from or how it's spelled, at its core Whiskey is distilled from a fermented mash of grain (usually corn, rye, barley, or wheat) and then aged in oak barrels, which, depending on the type of wood used, impact the spirits color, flavor, and aroma.

Irish whiskey has a subtle sweetness from corn-based grain whiskey and a honey, toasty flavor imparted by barley and barley malt. In **Scotch** whisky production, part of the grain-drying process takes place over a peat-fueled fire, with the peat smoke coming in direct contact with the drying malt, ultimately flavoring the final product. On this side of the Atlantic, American whiskey falls into two categories: *straight* or *blended*. Straight whiskey must be made from at least 51 percent of a grain, must not exceed 160-proof, must be aged in oak barrels for two years, and may only be diluted by water to no less than 80-proof. Blended whiskey is a combination of at least two 100-proof straight whiskeys blended with either neutral spirits, grain spirits, or light whiskeys. But it gets more complicated.

Straight whiskey is made in three styles: Bourbon, Tennessee, and Rye. **Bourbon** can be made with one of two types of mash: **sweet mash,** which employs fresh yeast to start fermentation or **sour mash,** which combines a new batch of sweet mash with residual mash from the previous fermentation. Within the Bourbon category are two styles: **wheat** and **rye.** Although Bourbon is made primarily with corn (up to, but no more than, 80 percent; higher than that and it must be labeled "corn whiskey"), the remaining grain in the mash is either rye or wheat and, if it's a sour mash, a small amount of barley malt to get the fermentation going.

Tennessee whiskey is similar to Bourbon in almost every way, except that before the whiskey goes into charred barrels to mature, it is painstakingly filtered through 10 feet of sugar maple charcoal. This can take up to two weeks per batch to drip through.

Rye, once the leading brown spirit before Prohibition, is similar in taste to Bourbon, but it is decidedly spicier and slightly more bitter in flavor. Though wheat and barley are commonly used to make rye whiskey, by U.S. law it must be made with a minimum of 51 percent rye, whereas in Canada anything goes.

In the following recipes, we list a specific whiskey if it's traditional or integral to the drink. Where simply "whiskey" is listed, feel free to experiment.

AFFINITY COCKTAIL

1 oz. Dry Vermouth
1 oz. Sweet Vermouth
1 oz. Whisky (Scotch)
3 dashes Orange Bitters

Stir with ice and strain into chilled cocktail glass.

ALGONQUIN

1½ oz. Whiskey (Rye)
1 oz. Dry Vermouth
1 oz. Pineapple Juice

Shake with ice and strain into chilled cocktail glass.

ALLEGHENY

1 oz. Whiskey (Bourbon)
1 oz. Dry Vermouth
1½ tsps. Blackberry-
    flavored Brandy
1½ tsps. Lemon Juice

Shake with ice and strain into chilled cocktail glass. Add a twist of lemon peel on top.

AMERICANA

¼ oz. Whiskey (Tennessee)
½ tsp. Superfine Sugar (or
    Simple Syrup)
1–2 dashes Bitters
Champagne, Chilled

Combine first three ingredients in ice-filled collins glass, stirring until sugar is dissolved. Fill with Champagne and add a slice of peach.

AQUARIUS

1½ oz. Whisky (Scotch)
½ oz. Cherry-flavored
    Brandy
1 oz. Cranberry Juice

Shake with ice and strain into old-fashioned glass over ice.

BASIN STREET

2 oz. Whiskey (Bourbon)
1 oz. Triple Sec
1 oz. Lemon Juice

Shake well with ice and strain into chilled cocktail glass.

BEADLESTONE COCKTAIL

1½ oz. Dry Vermouth
1½ oz. Whisky (Scotch)

Stir with ice and strain into chilled cocktail glass.

BEALS COCKTAIL

1½ oz. Whisky (Scotch)
½ oz. Dry Vermouth
½ oz. Sweet Vermouth

Stir with ice and strain into chilled cocktail glass.

BLACK HAWK

1¼ oz. Whiskey (Bourbon)
1¼ oz. Sloe Gin

Stir with ice and strain into chilled cocktail glass. Garnish with a maraschino cherry.

BLARNEY STONE COCKTAIL

2 oz. Whiskey (Irish)
1/2 tsp. Anisette
1/2 tsp. Triple Sec
1/4 tsp. Maraschino Liqueur
1 dash Bitters

Shake with ice and strain into chilled cocktail glass. Garnish with a twist of orange peel and an olive.

BLOOD-AND-SAND COCKTAIL

1 tbsp. Orange Juice
1/2 oz. Whisky (Scotch)
1/2 oz. Cherry-flavored Brandy
1/2 oz. Sweet Vermouth

Shake with ice and strain into chilled cocktail glass.

BOBBY BURNS COCKTAIL

1 1/2 oz. Sweet Vermouth
1 1/2 oz. Whisky (Scotch)
1 1/4 tsps. Benedictine

Stir with ice and strain into chilled cocktail glass. Garnish with a twist of lemon peel.

BOURBON A LA CRÈME

2 oz. Whiskey (Bourbon)
1 oz. Crème de Cacao (Brown)
1–2 Vanilla Beans

Combine with ice in mixing glass and refrigerate for at least 1 hour. Shake well and serve straight up in an old-fashioned glass.

BOURBON AND WATER

2 oz. Whiskey (Bourbon)
4 oz. Water

Pour bourbon and water into old-fashioned glass. Add ice and stir. Garnish with a twist of lemon peel.

BOURBON COBBLER

2 1/2 oz. Whiskey (Bourbon)
1 tbsp. Lemon Juice
2 tsps. Grapefruit Juice
1 1/2 tsps. Almond Extract

Combine all ingredients in mixing glass, and then pour into ice-filled old-fashioned glass. Garnish with a peach slice.

BOURBON CRUSTA

2 oz. Whiskey (Bourbon)
1/2 oz. Triple Sec
1/2 oz. Maraschino Liqueur
1/2 oz. Lemon Juice
2 dashes Orange Bitters

Shake with ice and strain into chilled cocktail glass. Garnish with an orange peel.

BOURBON HIGHBALL

2 oz. Whiskey (Bourbon)
Ginger Ale or Club Soda

Combine in ice-filled highball glass and stir. Garnish with a twist of lemon peel.

BOURBON ON THE ROCKS

2 oz. Whiskey (Bourbon)

Pour bourbon into old-fashioned glass half-filled with ice.

WHISKEY

BRIGHTON PUNCH

¾ oz. Whiskey (Bourbon)
¾ oz. Brandy
¾ oz. Benedictine
2 oz. Orange Juice
1 oz. Lemon Juice
Club Soda

Shake first five ingredients with ice and pour into ice-filled collins glass. Fill with club soda and stir gently. Garnish with orange and lemon slices and serve with a straw.

BROOKLYN

1½ oz. Whiskey (Rye or Bourbon)
½ oz. Sweet Vermouth
1 dash Amer Picon
1 dash Maraschino Liqueur

Stir with ice and strain into chilled cocktail glass.

BUDDY'S FAVORITE

1½ oz. Whiskey (Bourbon)
6 oz. Cold Water

Pour ingredients into highball glass. Stir and serve without ice.

BULL AND BEAR

1½ oz. Whiskey (Bourbon)
¾ oz. Orange Curaçao
1 tbsp. Grenadine
1 oz. Lemon Juice

Shake with ice and strain into chilled cocktail glass. Garnish with a maraschino cherry and an orange slice.

CABLEGRAM

1 oz. Lemon Juice
1 tsp. Superfine Sugar (or Simple Syrup)
2 oz. Whiskey
Ginger Ale

Stir first three ingredients with ice cubes in highball glass and fill with ginger ale.

CALIFORNIA LEMONADE

2 oz. Lemon Juice
1 oz. Lime Juice
1 tbsp. Superfine Sugar (or Simple Syrup)
2 oz. Whiskey
¼ tsp. Grenadine
Club Soda

Shake first five ingredients with ice and strain into chilled collins glass over shaved ice. Fill with club soda and garnish with slices of orange and lemon, and a maraschino cherry. Serve with straws.

CAMERON'S KICK COCKTAIL

¾ oz. Whisky (Scotch)
¾ oz. Irish Whiskey
½ oz. Lemon Juice
2 dashes Orange Bitters

Shake with ice and strain into chilled cocktail glass.

CANADIAN BREEZE

1½ oz. Whisky (Canadian)
1 tsp. Pineapple Juice
1 tbsp. Lemon Juice
½ tsp. Maraschino Liqueur

Shake with ice and strain into ice-filled old-fashioned glass. Garnish with a pineapple wedge or spear and a maraschino cherry.

CANADIAN CHERRY

1½ oz. Whisky (Canadian)
½ oz. Maraschino Liqueur
1½ tsps. Lemon Juice
1½ tsps. Orange Juice

Shake all ingredients and strain into ice-filled old-fashioned glass. Moisten glass rim with maraschino liquer.

CANADIAN COCKTAIL

1½ oz. Whisky (Canadian)
1 dash Bitters
1½ tsps. Triple Sec
1 tsp. Superfine Sugar (or Simple Syrup)

Shake with ice and strain into chilled cocktail glass.

CANADIAN PINEAPPLE

1½ oz. Whisky (Canadian)
1 tsp. Pineapple Juice
1 tbsp. Lemon Juice
½ tsp. Maraschino Liqueur

Shake with ice and strain into ice-filled old-fashioned glass. Add a stick of pineapple.

CANAL STREET DAISY

¾ oz. Lemon Juice
1 oz. Orange Juice
1 oz. Whisky (Scotch)
Club Soda

Pour juices and scotch into ice-filled collins glass. Add club soda and an orange slice.

CHAPEL HILL

1½ oz. Whiskey (Bourbon)
½ oz. Triple Sec
1 tbsp. Lemon Juice

Shake with ice and strain into chilled cocktail glass. Add a twist of orange peel.

CHAPLIN

¾ oz. Whiskey (Bourbon)
¾ oz. Dry Sherry
¾ oz. Rammazotti Amaro
⅛ oz. Triple Sec
2 dashes Orange Bitters

Stir with ice and strain into chilled cocktail glass. Garnish with a twist of lemon peel.

CHAS

1¼ oz. Whiskey (Bourbon)
⅛ oz. Amaretto
⅛ oz. Benedictine
⅛ oz. Triple Sec
⅛ oz. Orange Curaçao

Stir with ice and strain into chilled cocktail glass. Garnish with an orange twist.

COFFEE OLD-FASHIONED

1½ tsp. Instant Coffee
½ cup Water
2 tsps. Superfine Sugar (or Simple Syrup)
2 dashes Bitters
1 oz. Whiskey (Bourbon)
2 oz. Club Soda

Dissolve coffee in water; stir in sugar/syrup, bitters, and bourbon. Add club soda and pour into ice-filled old-fashioned glass. Garnish with an orange slice and a maraschino cherry.

COMMODORE COCKTAIL

2 oz. 1792 Ridgemont Reserve Bourbon Whiskey
¾ oz. Crème de Cacao (White)
½ oz. Lemon Juice
1 dash Grenadine

Shake with ice and strain into chilled Champagne flute.

COWBOY COCKTAIL

1½ oz. Whiskey (Bourbon)
1 tbsp. Light Cream

Shake with ice and strain into chilled cocktail glass.

CREOLE LADY

1½ oz. Whiskey (Bourbon)
1½ oz. Madeira
1 tsp. Grenadine

Stir with ice and strain into chilled cocktail glass. Serve with one green and one red maraschino cherry.

DAISY DUELLER

1½ oz. Whiskey (Tennessee)
1½ tsps. Lemon Juice
1½ tsps. Superfine Sugar (or Simple Syrup)
Several drops Triple Sec
Club Soda

Shake first four ingredients with ice. Strain into chilled highball glass. Add ice and fill with soda. Garnish with fruit slices.

DE LA LOUISIANE

¾ oz. Whiskey (Rye)
¾ oz. Sweet Vermouth
¾ oz. Benedictine
3 dashes Pastis (Pernod or Other Absinthe Substitute)
3 dashes Peychaud's Bitters

Stir with ice and strain into chilled cocktail glass. Garnish with a maraschino cherry.

THE DEBONAIR

2½ oz. Whisky (Single Malt Scotch)
1 oz. Original Canton Delicate Ginger Liqueur

Stir and strain into a chilled cocktail glass. Garnish with a lemon twist.

THE DELMARVA COCKTAIL

2 oz. Whiskey (Rye)
½ oz. Dry Vermouth
½ oz. Crème de Menthe (White)
½ oz. Lemon Juice

Shake and strain into a chilled cocktail glass. Garnish with a mint leaf.

DERBY

2 oz. Whiskey (Bourbon)
¼ oz. Benedictine
1 dash Angostura Bitters

Stir with ice and strain into chilled cocktail glass. Garnish with a lemon peel.

DINAH COCKTAIL

¾ oz. Lemon Juice
½ tsp. Superfine Sugar (or Simple Syrup)
1½ oz. Whiskey (Bourbon)

Shake well with ice and strain into chilled cocktail glass. Garnish with a mint leaf.

DIXIE JULEP

1 tsp. Superfine Sugar (or Simple Syrup)
2½ oz. Whiskey (Bourbon)

Combine sugar/syrup and bourbon in collins glass. Fill with crushed ice and stir gently until glass is frosted. Garnish with sprigs of mint. Serve with straws.

DIXIE WHISKEY COCKTAIL

½ tsp. Superfine Sugar (or Simple Syrup)
1 dash Bitters
¼ tsp. Triple Sec
½ tsp. Crème de Menthe (White)
2 oz. Whiskey (Bourbon)

Shake with ice and strain into chilled cocktail glass.

DOUBLE STANDARD SOUR

1 oz. Lemon Juice (or ½ oz. Lime Juice)
½ tsp. Superfine Sugar (or Simple Syrup)
¾ oz. Whiskey
¾ oz. Gin
½ tsp. Grenadine

Shake with ice and strain into chilled sour glass. Garnish with a half-slice of lemon and a maraschino cherry.

WHISKEY

EASTERN SOUR

2 oz. Whiskey (Bourbon)
1 1/2 oz. Orange Juice
1 oz. Lime Juice
1/4 oz. Orgeat Syrup
(Almond Syrup)
1/4 oz. Superfine Sugar (or
Simple Syrup)

Shake with ice and strain into
ice-filled tumbler. Garnish
with spent shell of lime.

EVERYBODY'S IRISH COCKTAIL

1 tsp. Crème de Menthe
(Green)
1 tsp. Chartreuse (Green)
2 oz. Whiskey (Irish)

Stir with ice and strain into
chilled cocktail glass. Garnish
with a green olive.

FANCY-FREE COCKTAIL

2 oz. Whiskey (Bourbon)
1/2 oz. Maraschino Liqueur
1 dash Angostura Bitters
1 dash Orange Bitters

Stir with ice and strain into
chilled cocktail glass.

FANCY WHISKEY

2 oz. Whiskey (Bourbon or
Rye)
1 dash Bitters
1/4 tsp. Triple Sec
1/4 tsp. Superfine Sugar (or
Simple Syrup)

Shake with ice and strain into
chilled cocktail glass. Add a
twist of lemon peel.

FLYING SCOTCHMAN

1 oz. Sweet Vermouth
1 oz. Whisky (Scotch)
1 dash Bitters
1/4 tsp. Superfine Sugar (or
Simple Syrup)

Stir with ice and strain into
chilled cocktail glass.

FOX RIVER COCKTAIL

1 tbsp. Crème de Cacao
(Brown)
2 oz. Whiskey (Bourbon or
Rye)
4 dashes Bitters

Stir with ice and strain into
chilled cocktail glass.

FRISCO SOUR

3/4 oz. Lemon Juice
1/2 oz. Lime Juice
1/2 oz. Benedictine
2 oz. Whiskey (Bourbon or
Rye)

Shake with ice and strain into
chilled sour glass. Garnish
with slices of lemon and
lime.

GENTLEMAN'S COCKTAIL

1 1/2 oz. Whiskey (Bourbon)
1/2 oz. Brandy
1/2 oz. Crème de Menthe
Club Soda

Pour bourbon, brandy, and
crème de menthe into ice-
filled highball glass. Add club
soda and garnish with a twist
of lemon peel.

GODFATHER

1½ oz. Whisky (Scotch)
¾ oz. Amaretto

Combine in ice-filled old-fashioned glass.

HEATHER BLUSH

1 oz. Whisky (Scotch)
1 oz. Strawberry Liqueur
3 oz. Chilled Sparkling
   Wine

Pour scotch and liqueur into Champagne flute. Top with sparkling wine. Garnish with a strawberry.

HIGHLAND COOLER

½ tsp. Superfine Sugar (or
   Simple Syrup)
2 oz. Club Soda
2 oz. Whisky (Scotch)
Club Soda (or Ginger Ale)

Combine sugar/syrup and soda in collins glass; stir. Add ice cubes and scotch. Fill with soda and stir again. Insert a spiral of orange or lemon peel (or both) and dangle end over rim of glass.

HIGHLAND FLING COCKTAIL

¾ oz. Sweet Vermouth
1½ oz. Whisky (Scotch)
2 dashes Orange Bitters

Stir with ice and strain into chilled cocktail glass. Garnish with an olive.

HOLE-IN-ONE

1¾ oz. Whisky (Scotch)
¾ oz. Vermouth
¼ tsp. Lemon Juice
1 dash Orange Bitters

Shake with ice and strain into chilled cocktail glass.

HOOT MON COCKTAIL

¾ oz. Sweet Vermouth
1½ oz. Whisky (Scotch)
1 tsp. Benedictine

Stir with ice and strain into chilled cocktail glass. Twist a lemon peel and drop into glass.

HORSE'S NECK (WITH A KICK)

2 oz. Whiskey (Bourbon)
Ginger Ale

Peel rind of whole lemon in spiral fashion and put in collins glass with one end hanging over the rim. Fill glass with ice cubes. Add whiskey. Fill with ginger ale and stir well.

HOT TODDY

12 oz. Boiling Water
2 oz. Whiskey (Bourbon)
½ oz. Honey

Preheat an Irish coffee glass with half the boiling water; then discard. Pour honey and Bourbon into glass and top with remaining water. Garnish with a large, clove-studded lemon twist.

WHISKEY

IMPERIAL FIZZ

1 oz. Lemon Juice
1/2 oz. Light Rum
1 1/2 oz. Whiskey (Bourbon
    or Rye)
1 tsp. Superfine Sugar (or
    Simple Syrup)
Club Soda

Shake first four ingredients
with ice and strain into highball glass. Add two ice cubes.
Fill with club soda and stir.

INCIDER COCKTAIL

1 1/2 oz. Whiskey
Apple Cider

Mix whiskey with a generous
helping of apple cider in an
old-fashioned glass. Top with
ice and stir. Garnish with a
slice of apple.

IRISH RICKEY

1/2 oz. Lime Juice
1 1/2 oz. Whiskey (Irish)
Club Soda

Pour lime juice and whiskey
into ice-filled highball glass.
Fill with club soda and stir.
Garnish with a wedge of
lime.

IRISH SHILLELAGH

1 oz. Lemon Juice
1 tsp. Superfine Sugar (or
    Simple Syrup)
1 1/2 oz. Whiskey (Irish)
1 tbsp. Sloe Gin
1 tbsp. Light Rum

Shake with ice and strain into
chilled punch cup. Garnish
with fresh raspberries, strawberries, a maraschino cherry,
and two peach slices.

WHISKEY (IRISH)

1/2 tsp. Triple Sec
1/2 tsp. Anisette
1/4 tsp. Maraschino Liqueur
1 dash Bitters
2 oz. Whiskey (Irish)

Stir with ice and strain into
chilled cocktail glass. Garnish
with an olive.

WHISKEY (IRISH) HIGHBALL

2 oz. Whiskey (Irish)
Ginger Ale or Club Soda

Pour whiskey into ice-filled
highball glass. Fill with ginger
ale or club soda. Garnish
with a twist of lemon peel, if
desired, and stir.

JOCOSE JULEP

2½ oz. Whiskey (Bourbon)
½ oz. Crème de Menthe
    (Green)
1 oz. Lime Juice
1 tsp. Sugar
5 Chopped Mint Leaves
Club Soda

Combine all ingredients
except club soda in blender
without ice until smooth.
Pour into ice-filled collins
glass. Fill with club soda and
stir. Garnish with a sprig of
mint.

JOHN COLLINS

1 oz. Lemon Juice
1 tsp. Superfine Sugar (or
    Simple Syrup)
2 oz. Whiskey (Bourbon)
Club Soda

Shake first three ingredients
with ice and strain into
collins glass. Add several
cubes of ice, fill with club
soda, and stir. Garnish with
slices of orange and lemon,
and a maraschino cherry.
Serve with straws.

KENTUCKY BLIZZARD

1½ oz. Whiskey (Bourbon)
1½ oz. Cranberry Juice
½ oz. Lime Juice
½ oz. Grenadine
1 tsp. Sugar

Shake all ingredients with ice.
Strain into chilled cocktail
glass or over fresh ice in old-
fashioned glass. Garnish with
a half-slice of orange.

KENTUCKY COCKTAIL

¼ oz. Pineapple Juice
1½ oz. 1792 Ridgemont
    Reserve Bourbon Whiskey

Shake with ice and strain into
chilled cocktail glass.

KENTUCKY COLONEL COCKTAIL

½ oz. Benedictine
1½ oz. Whiskey (Bourbon)

Stir with ice and strain into
chilled cocktail glass. Add a
twist of lemon peel.

THE KENTUCKY LONGSHOT

2 oz. Whiskey (Bourbon)
½ oz. Ginger Liqueur
½ oz. Peach-flavored
    Brandy
1 dash Angostura Bitters
1 dash Peychaud's Bitters
3 pieces Candied Ginger,
    for garnish

Stir and strain into chilled
cocktail glass. Add gar-
nishes—if using long strips
hang over the lip of the glass;
smaller pieces can be
dropped into the drink.

KING COLE COCKTAIL

1 slice Orange
1 slice Pineapple
½ tsp. Superfine Sugar (or
    Simple Syrup)
2 oz. Whiskey
2 Ice Cubes

Muddle first three ingredients
well in old-fashioned glass.
Add whiskey and ice cubes
and stir.

KISS ON THE LIPS

2 oz. Whiskey (Bourbon)
6 oz. Apricot Nectar

Pour into ice-filled collins glass and stir. Serve with a straw.

KLONDIKE COOLER

1/2 tsp. Superfine Sugar (or Simple Syrup)
2 oz. Club Soda
2 oz. Whiskey (Bourbon)
Club Soda or Ginger Ale

Mix sugar/syrup and club soda in collins glass. Fill glass with ice and add whiskey. Fill with club soda or ginger ale and stir again. Insert a spiral of orange or lemon peel (or both) and dangle end over rim of glass.

LADIES' COCKTAIL

1 3/4 oz. Whiskey (Bourbon)
1/2 tsp. Anisette
2 dashes Bitters

Stir with ice and strain into chilled cocktail glass. Serve with a pineapple stick on top.

LAWHILL COCKTAIL

3/4 oz. Dry Vermouth
1 1/2 oz. Whiskey (Rye)
1/4 tsp. Anisette
1/4 tsp. Maraschino Liqueur
1 dash Bitters

Stir with ice and strain into chilled cocktail glass.

LIBERAL

1 1/2 oz. Whiskey (Rye)
1/2 oz. Sweet Vermouth
1/4 oz. Amer Picon
1 dash Orange Bitters

Stir with ice and strain into chilled cocktail glass. Garnish with an orange twist.

LIMESTONE COCKTAIL

1 1/2 oz. Whiskey (Bourbon)
1 oz. Lemon Juice
1 tsp. Superfine Sugar (or Simple Syrup)
Club Soda

Stir first three ingredients in ice-filled highball glass. Fill with club soda; stir again.

LINSTEAD COCKTAIL

1 oz. Whiskey (Bourbon)
1 oz. Pineapple Juice
1/2 tsp. Superfine Sugar (or Simple Syrup)
1/4 tsp. Anisette
1/4 tsp. Lemon Juice

Shake with ice and strain into chilled cocktail glass.

LOCH LOMOND

1 oz. Whisky (Scotch)
1/2 oz. Peach Schnapps
1 oz. Blue Curaçao
3 oz. Grapefruit Juice
1/2 oz. Lemon Juice

Shake all ingredients with ice and strain into ice-filled parfait or hurricane glass. Garnish with a slice of star fruit.

LOUISVILLE COOLER

1½ oz. 1792 Ridgemont
    Reserve Bourbon Whiskey
1 oz. Orange Juice
1 tbsp. Lime Juice
1 tsp. Superfine Sugar (or
    Simple Syrup)

Shake all ingredients with ice.
Strain into old-fashioned
glass over fresh ice. Garnish
with a half-slice of orange.

LOUISVILLE LADY

1 oz. Whiskey (Bourbon)
¾ oz. Crème de Cacao
    (White)
¾ oz. Cream

Shake with ice and strain into
chilled cocktail glass.

MAGNOLIA MAIDEN

1¼ oz. Whiskey (Bourbon)
1¼ oz. Mandarine
    Napoléon
1 splash Superfine Sugar
    (or Simple Syrup)
1 splash Club Soda

Shake bourbon, Mandarine
Napoléon, and sugar/syrup
with ice. Strain into ice-filled
old-fashioned glass. Top with
club soda.

MAMIE GILROY

½ oz. Lime Juice
2 oz. Whisky (Scotch)
Ginger Ale

Combine in ice-filled collins
glass and stir.

MANHASSET

1½ oz. Whiskey (Bourbon)
1½ tsp. Dry Vermouth
1½ tsp. Sweet Vermouth
1 tbsp. Lemon Juice

Shake with ice and strain into
chilled cocktail glass.

MANHATTAN

2 oz. Whiskey (Rye or
    Bourbon)
½ oz. Sweet Vermouth
1 dash Angostura Bitters

Stir with ice and strain into
chilled cocktail glass. Garnish
with a maraschino cherry.

MANHATTAN (DRY)

2 oz. Whiskey (Rye or
    Bourbon)
½ oz. Dry Vermouth
1 dash Angostura Bitters

Stir with ice and strain into
chilled cocktail glass. Garnish
with an olive.

MIAMI BEACH COCKTAIL

¾ oz. Whisky (Scotch)
¾ oz. Dry Vermouth
¾ oz. Grapefruit Juice

Shake with ice and strain into
chilled cocktail glass.

MINT JULEP

4 sprigs Mint
1 tsp. Superfine Sugar (or Simple Syrup)
2 tsps. Water
2½ oz. Whiskey (Bourbon)

In silver julep cup, silver mug, or collins glass, muddle mint leaves, sugar/syrup, and water. Fill glass or mug with shaved or crushed ice and add bourbon. Top with more ice and garnish with a mint sprig and straws.

MINT JULEP (SOUTHERN STYLE)

5–6 sprigs Mint
1 tsp. Superfine Sugar (or Simple Syrup)
2 tsps. Water
2½ oz. Whiskey (Bourbon)

In silver mug or collins glass, dissolve sugar/syrup with water. Fill with finely shaved ice and add Bourbon. Stir until glass is heavily frosted, adding more ice if necessary. (Do not hold glass with hand while stirring.) Garnish with sprigs of fresh mint so that the tops are about 2 inches above rim of glass. Use short straws so that it will be necessary to bury nose in mint, which is intended for scent rather than taste.

MODERN COCKTAIL

1½ oz. Whisky (Scotch)
½ tsp. Lemon Juice
¼ tsp. Anisette
½ tsp. Jamaica Rum
1 dash Orange Bitters

Shake with ice and strain into chilled cocktail glass. Garnish with a maraschino cherry.

MONTANA STUMP PULLER

2 oz. Whisky (Canadian)
1 oz. Crème de Menthe (White)

Stir with ice and strain into shot glass.

MONTE CARLO

2 oz. Whiskey (Rye)
½ oz. Benedictine
2 dashes Angostura Bitters

Stir with ice and strain into chilled cocktail glass.

NARRAGANSETT

1½ oz. Whiskey (Bourbon)
1 oz. Sweet Vermouth
1 dash Anisette

Stir in ice-filled old-fashioned glass. Garnish with a twist of lemon peel.

NEVINS

1½ oz. Whiskey (Bourbon)
1½ tsps. Apricot-flavored Brandy
1 tbsp. Grapefruit Juice
1½ tsps. Lemon Juice
1 dash Bitters

Shake with ice and strain into chilled cocktail glass.

NEW YORK COCKTAIL (AKA NEW YORKER)

1 oz. Lime Juice (or 2 oz. Lemon Juice)
1 tsp. Superfine Sugar (or Simple Syrup)
1 1/2 oz. Whiskey (Rye)
1/2 tsp. Grenadine

Shake with ice and strain into chilled cocktail glass. Garnish with a twist of lemon peel.

NEW YORK SOUR

1 oz. Lemon Juice
1 tsp. Superfine Sugar (or Simple Syrup)
2 oz. Whiskey (Rye or Bourbon)
Red Wine

Shake first three ingredients with ice and strain into chilled sour glass, leaving about 1/2-inch of space. Float red wine on top. Garnish with a half-slice of lemon and a maraschino cherry.

OLD-FASHIONED COCKTAIL

1 cube Sugar
1 dash Bitters
1 tsp. Water
2 oz. Whiskey (Rye or Bourbon)

In old-fashioned glass, muddle sugar cube, bitters, and water. Add whiskey, and stir. Add a twist of lemon peel and ice cubes. Garnish with a slice of orange and a maraschino cherry. Serve with a swizzle stick.

OLD PAL COCKTAIL

1/2 oz. Grenadine
1/2 oz. Sweet Vermouth
1 1/4 oz. Whiskey (Rye)

Stir with ice and strain into chilled cocktail glass.

OPENING COCKTAIL

1/2 oz. Grenadine
1/2 oz. Sweet Vermouth
1 1/2 oz. Whiskey (Rye)

Stir with ice and strain into chilled cocktail glass.

ORIENTAL COCKTAIL

1 oz. Whiskey (Rye)
1/2 oz. Sweet Vermouth
1/2 oz. Triple Sec
1/2 oz. Lime Juice

Shake with ice and strain into chilled cocktail glass.

PADDY COCKTAIL

1 1/2 oz. Whiskey (Irish)
1 1/2 oz. Sweet Vermouth
1 dash Bitters

Stir with ice and strain into chilled cocktail glass.

PALMER COCKTAIL

2 oz. Whiskey (Rye)
1 dash Bitters
1/2 tsp. Lemon Juice

Stir with ice and strain into chilled cocktail glass.

PENDENNIS TODDY

1 cube Sugar
1 tsp. Water
2 oz. Whiskey (Bourbon)

Muddle cube of sugar with
water in sour glass. Fill with
ice, add Bourbon, and stir.
Garnish with two slices of
lemon.

PREAKNESS COCKTAIL

3/4 oz. Sweet Vermouth
1 1/2 oz. Whiskey (Rye)
1 dash Bitters
1/2 tsp. Benedictine

Stir with ice and strain into
chilled cocktail glass. Garnish
with a twist of lemon peel.

QUEBEC

1 1/2 oz. Whisky (Canadian)
1/2 oz. Dry Vermouth
1 1/2 tsps. Amer Picon (or
    Bitters)
1 1/2 tsps. Maraschino
    Liqueur

Shake with ice and strain into
chilled, sugar-rimmed cocktail glass.

RED HOOK

2 oz. Whiskey (Rye)
1/4 oz. Maraschino Liqueur
1/4 oz. Punt e Mes

Stir with ice and strain into
chilled cocktail glass. Garnish
with a maraschino cherry.

RED-HOT PASSION

1/2 oz. Whiskey (Bourbon)
1/2 oz. Amaretto
1/2 oz. Whiskey (Tennessee
    Sour Mash)
1/4 oz. Sloe Gin
1 splash Triple Sec
1 splash Orange Juice
1 splash Pineapple Juice

Pour all ingredients over ice
into parfait or hurricane glass
and stir gently. Garnish with
an orange slice.

RED RAIDER

1 oz. Whiskey (Bourbon)
1/2 oz. Triple Sec
1 oz. Lemon Juice
1 dash Grenadine

Shake with ice and strain into
chilled cocktail glass.

ROB ROY

3/4 oz. Sweet Vermouth
1 1/2 oz. Whisky (Scotch)

Stir with ice and strain into
chilled cocktail glass.

ROBERT BURNS

1 1/2 oz. Whisky (Scotch)
1/2 oz. Sweet Vermouth
1 dash Orange Bitters
1 dash Pernod (or Absinthe
    Substitute)

Stir with ice and strain into
chilled cocktail glass.

RORY O'MORE

¾ oz. Sweet Vermouth
1½ oz. Whiskey (Irish)
1 dash Orange Bitters

Stir with ice and strain into
chilled cocktail glass.

RUSTY NAIL

¾ oz. Whisky (Scotch)
¼ oz. Drambuie

Serve in old-fashioned glass
with ice cubes. Float Drambuie on top.

RYE HIGHBALL

2 oz. Whiskey (Rye)
Ginger Ale or Club Soda

Pour whiskey into ice-filled
highball glass. Fill with ginger
ale or club soda and ice
cubes. Garnish with a twist
of lemon peel and stir.

RYE COCKTAIL

1 dash Bitters
1 tsp. Superfine Sugar (or
    Simple Syrup)
2 oz. Whiskey (Rye)

Shake with ice and strain into
chilled cocktail glass. Garnish
with a maraschino cherry.

SANTIAGO SCOTCH PLAID

1½ oz. Whisky (Scotch)
½ oz. Dry Vermouth
2 dashes Angostura Bitters

Stir with ice and strain into
chilled cocktail glass. Garnish
with a lemon twist.

SAZERAC

½ tsp. Pernod (or Absinthe
    Substitute)
1 dash Peychaud's Bitters
1 cube Sugar (or ½ tsp.
    Simple Syrup)
2 oz. Whiskey (Rye)

Coat chilled old-fashioned
glass with Pernod. Pour most
of it out, then add bitters.
Add sugar cube (or simple
syrup) and muddle. Add
whiskey. Garnish with a twist
of lemon peel.

SCOFFLAW

1 oz. Whisky (Canadian)
1 oz. Dry Vermouth
¼ oz. Lemon Juice
1 dash Grenadine
1 dash Orange Bitters

Stir with ice and strain into
chilled cocktail glass. Garnish
with a lemon wedge.

SCOTCH BISHOP COCKTAIL

1 oz. Whisky (Scotch)
1 tbsp. Orange Juice
½ oz. Dry Vermouth
½ tsp. Triple Sec
¼ tsp. Superfine Sugar (or
    Simple Syrup)

Shake with ice and strain into
chilled cocktail glass. Garnish
with a twist of lemon peel.

SCOTCH BOUNTY

1 oz. Whisky (Scotch)
1 oz. Coconut-flavored
   Rum
1 oz. Crème de Cacao
   (White)
1/2 oz. Grenadine
4 oz. Orange Juice

Shake with ice and pour into
hurricane or parfait glass.
Garnish with a pineapple
wedge and a maraschino
cherry. Serve with a straw.

SCOTCH COBBLER

2 oz. Whisky (Scotch)
4 dashes Curaçao
4 dashes Brandy

Combine in ice-filled old-
fashioned glass. Garnish with
a slice of orange and a mint
sprig.

SCOTCH COOLER

2 oz. Whisky (Scotch)
3 dashes Crème de
   Menthe (White)
Chilled Club Soda

Pour scotch and crème de
menthe into ice-filled highball glass. Fill with club soda
and stir.

SCOTCH HIGHBALL

2 oz. Whisky (Scotch)
Ginger Ale or Club Soda

Pour scotch into ice-filled
highball glass and fill with
ginger ale or club soda. Add
a twist of lemon peel and stir.

SCOTCH HOLIDAY SOUR

1 1/2 oz. Whisky (Scotch)
1 oz. Cherry-flavored
   Brandy
1/2 oz. Sweet Vermouth
1 oz. Lemon Juice

Shake with ice and strain into
ice-filled old-fashioned glass.
Add a slice of lemon.

SCOTCH MIST

2 oz. Whisky (Scotch)

Pack old-fashioned glass with
crushed ice. Pour in scotch
and add a twist of lemon
peel. Serve with a short
straw.

SCOTCH OLD-FASHIONED

1 cube Sugar
1 tsp. Water
1 dash Bitters
2 oz. Whisky (Scotch)

In old-fashioned glass,
muddle sugar cube, water,
and bitters. Add scotch and
stir. Add a twist of lemon
peel and ice cubes. Garnish
with slices of orange and
lemon and a maraschino
cherry.

SCOTCH RICKEY

½ oz. Lime Juice
1½ oz. Whisky (Scotch)
Club Soda

Pour lime juice and scotch
into ice-filled highball glass
and fill with club soda. Add a
twist of lime. Stir.

SCOTCH ON THE ROCKS

2 oz. Whisky (Scotch)

Pour scotch into old-
fashioned glass half-filled
with ice.

SCOTCH ROYALE

1 cube Sugar
1½ oz. Whisky (Scotch)
1 dash Bitters
Champagne, Chilled

Place sugar cube in Cham-
pagne flute. Add scotch and
bitters, and fill with Champagne.

SCOTCH SOUR

1½ oz. Whisky (Scotch)
½ oz. Lime Juice
½ tsp. Superfine Sugar (or
   Simple Syrup)

Shake with ice and strain into
chilled sour glass. Garnish
with a half-slice of lemon and
a maraschino cherry.

SCOTCH STINGER

½ oz. Crème de Menthe
   (White)
1½ oz. Whisky (Scotch)

Shake with ice and strain into
chilled cocktail glass.

SCOTTISH GUARD

1½ oz. Whiskey (Bourbon)
½ oz. Lemon Juice
½ oz. Orange Juice
1 tsp. Grenadine

Shake with ice and strain into
chilled cocktail glass.

SEABOARD

1 oz. Whiskey
1 oz. Gin
1 tbsp. Lemon Juice
1 tsp. Superfine Sugar (or
   Simple Syrup)

Shake with ice and strain into
ice-filled old-fashioned glass.
Garnish with mint leaves.

THE SEELBACH COCKTAIL

¾ oz. Whiskey (Bourbon)
½ oz. Triple Sec
7 dashes Angostura Bitters
7 dashes Peychaud's Bitters
4 oz. Champagne, Chilled

Build in the order given in a
Champagne flute. Garnish
with a twist of orange peel.

SHAMROCK

1½ oz. Whiskey (Irish)
½ oz. Dry Vermouth
1 tsp. Crème de Menthe
   (Green)

Stir with ice and strain into
chilled cocktail glass. Garnish
with an olive.

THE SHOOT

1 oz. Whisky (Scotch)
1 oz. Dry Sherry
1 tsp. Orange Juice
1 tsp. Lemon Juice
1/2 tsp. Superfine Sugar (or
    Simple Syrup)

Shake with ice and strain into
chilled cocktail glass.

SILENT THIRD

1 oz. Triple Sec
2 oz. Whisky (Scotch)
1 oz. Lemon Juice

Shake with ice and strain into
chilled cocktail glass.

SOUTHERN BELLE

1 1/4 oz. Whiskey (Ten-
    nessee)
8 oz. Pineapple Juice
1/4 oz. Triple Sec
2 oz. Orange Juice
1 splash Grenadine

Combine whiskey, triple sec,
and juices in ice-filled collins
glass. Top with grenadine and
stir once.

SOUTHERN LADY

2 oz. Whiskey (Bourbon)
1 oz. Whiskey (Tennessee
    Sour Mash)
1 oz. Crème de Noyaux
3 oz. Pineapple Juice
1 oz. Lime Juice
2 oz. Lemon-lime Soda

Shake first four ingredients
with ice and strain into parfait or hurricane glass half-
filled with ice. Fill with soda
to within 1 inch of top of
glass and top with lime juice.
Garnish with a pineapple
wheel and a maraschino
cherry.

SOUTHERN PEACH

1 1/2 oz. Whiskey (Bourbon)
1/8 oz. Grenadine
2 oz. Orange Juice
1 oz. Superfine Sugar (or
    Simple Syrup)
1 oz. Lemon Juice
1 oz. Peach Schnapps

Fill parfait or hurricane glass
with ice. Pour grenadine over
ice; add bourbon. Shake last
four ingredients with ice and
pour slowly into hurricane
glass. Garnish with a peach
slice.

STILETTO

1 oz. Lemon Juice
1 1/2 tsps. Amaretto
1 1/2 oz. Whiskey (Bourbon)

Pour into ice-filled old-
fashioned glass and stir.

STONE FENCE

2 oz. Whisky (Scotch)
2 dashes Bitters
Club Soda or Cider

Pour scotch and bitters into ice-filled highball glass. Fill with club soda or cider. Stir.

SWISS FAMILY COCKTAIL

½ tsp. Anisette
2 dashes Bitters
¾ oz. Dry Vermouth
1½ oz. Whiskey

Stir with ice and strain into chilled cocktail glass.

T-BIRD

1⅛ oz. Whisky (Canadian)
¾ oz. Amaretto
2 oz. Pineapple Juice
1 oz. Orange Juice
2 dashes Grenadine

Shake with ice and strain into ice-filled highball glass. Garnish with an orange slice and a maraschino cherry. Serve with a straw.

T.N.T.

1½ oz. Whiskey (Rye or
    Bourbon)
1½ oz. Anisette

Shake with ice and strain into chilled cocktail glass.

THISTLE COCKTAIL

1½ oz. Sweet Vermouth
1½ oz. Whisky (Scotch)
2 dashes Bitters

Stir with ice and strain into chilled cocktail glass.

THOROUGHBRED COOLER

1 oz. Whiskey (Bourbon)
½ oz. Superfine Sugar (or
    Simple Syrup)
½ oz. Lemon Juice
1 oz. Orange Juice
1 dash Grenadine
Lemon-lime Soda

Pour all ingredients over ice in highball glass. Fill with lemon-lime soda and stir. Add grenadine. Garnish with an orange wedge.

TIPPERARY COCKTAIL

¾ oz. Whiskey (Irish)
¾ oz. Chartreuse (Green)
¾ oz. Sweet Vermouth

Stir with ice and strain into chilled cocktail glass.

TRILBY COCKTAIL

1½ oz. Whiskey (Bourbon)
¾ oz. Sweet Vermouth
2 dashes Orange Bitters

Stir with ice and strain into chilled cocktail glass.

WHISKEY

TWIN HILLS

1½ oz. Whiskey
2 tsps. Benedictine
1½ tsps. Lemon Juice
1½ tsps. Lime Juice
1 tsp. Sugar

Shake with ice and strain into sour glass. Garnish with a slice of lime and a slice of lemon.

VIEUX CARRE

¾ oz. Whiskey (Rye)
¾ oz. Brandy
¾ oz. Sweet Vermouth
¼ oz. Benedictine
1 dash Peychaud's Bitters
1 dash Angostura Bitters

Build, over ice, in a rocks glass.

WALTERS

1½ oz. Whisky (Scotch)
1 tbsp. Orange Juice
1 tbsp. Lemon Juice

Shake with ice and strain into chilled cocktail glass.

WARD EIGHT

¾ oz. Lemon Juice
1 tsp. Superfine Sugar (or Simple Syrup)
2 tsp. (scant) Grenadine
2 oz. Whiskey (Rye)

Shake with ice and strain into red-wine glass filled with ice. Garnish with slices of orange, lemon, and a maraschino cherry. Serve with straws.

WASHINGTON APPLE

2 oz. Black Velvet Reserve Canadian Whisky
2 oz. Sour Apple Schnapps
2 oz. Cranberry Juice

Pour into ice-filled highball glass and stir.

WHISKEY COBBLER

1 tsp. Superfine Sugar (or Simple Syrup)
2 oz. Club Soda
2 oz. Whiskey

Dissolve sugar/syrup in club soda in red-wine glass. Fill with shaved ice and add whiskey. Stir and garnish with seasonal fruit. Serve with a straw.

WHISKEY COCKTAIL

1 dash Bitters
1 tsp. Superfine Sugar (or Simple Syrup)
2 oz. Whiskey

Stir with ice and strain into chilled cocktail glass. Garnish with a maraschino cherry.

WHISKEY COLLINS

1 oz. Lemon Juice
1 tsp. Superfine Sugar (or Simple Syrup)
2 oz. Whiskey
Club Soda

Shake lemon juice, sugar/syrup, and whiskey with ice and strain into chilled collins glass. Add several ice cubes, fill with club soda, and stir. Garnish with slices of lemon and orange and a maraschino cherry. Serve with a straw.

WHISKEY DAISY

1 oz. Lemon Juice
$1/2$ tsp. Superfine Sugar (or
 Simple Syrup)
1 tsp. Grenadine
2 oz. Whiskey

Shake with ice and strain into
chilled beer mug or metal
cup. Add 1 ice cube and garnish with fruit.

WHISKEY FIX

1 oz. Lemon Juice
1 tsp. Superfine Sugar (or
 Simple Syrup)
$2^1/2$ oz. Whiskey

Shake juice and sugar/syrup
with ice and strain into
chilled highball glass. Fill
glass with ice and whiskey.
Stir. Garnish with a slice of
lemon. Serve with straws.

WHISKEY HIGHBALL

2 oz. Whiskey
Ginger Ale or Club Soda

Pour whiskey into ice-filled
highball glass. Fill with ginger
ale or club soda. Garnish
with a twist of lemon peel
and stir.

WHISKEY ORANGE

2 oz. Orange Juice
1 tsp. Superfine Sugar (or
 Simple Syrup)
$1/2$ tsp. Anisette
$1^1/2$ oz. Whiskey

Shake with ice and strain into
ice-filled highball glass. Garnish with slices of orange and
lemon.

WHISKEY RICKEY

$1/2$ oz. Lime Juice
$1^1/2$ oz. Whiskey
Club Soda

Pour lime juice and whiskey
into highball glass over ice
cubes and fill with club soda.
Stir. Drop lime rind into
glass.

WHISKEY SANGAREE

$1/2$ tsp. Superfine Sugar (or
 Simple Syrup)
1 tsp. Water
2 oz. Whiskey
1 splash Club Soda
1 tbsp. Port

Dissolve sugar/syrup in water
in old-fashioned glass. Add
whiskey, ice cubes, and club
soda. Stir and then float Port
on top. Garnish with fresh-
grated nutmeg.

WHISKEY SLING

1 tsp. Superfine Sugar (or
    Simple Syrup)
1 tsp. Water
1 oz. Lemon Juice
2 oz. Whiskey

In old-fashioned glass dissolve sugar/syrup in water and lemon juice. Add ice cubes and whiskey. Stir. Garnish with a twist of lemon peel.

WHISKEY SMASH

1 cube Sugar
1 oz. Club Soda
4 sprigs Mint
2 oz. Whiskey (Bourbon)

Muddle sugar with club soda and mint in old-fashioned glass. Add whiskey and then ice cubes. Stir. Garnish with a slice of orange, a maraschino cherry, and a twist of lemon peel.

WHISKEY SOUR

1 oz. Lemon Juice
1/2 tsp. Superfine Sugar (or
    Simple Syrup)
2 oz. Whiskey

Shake with ice and strain into chilled sour glass. Garnish with a half-slice of lemon and a maraschino cherry.

WHISKEY SQUIRT

1 1/2 oz. Whiskey
1 tbsp. Superfine Sugar (or
    Simple Syrup)
1 tbsp. Grenadine
Club Soda

Shake with ice and strain into chilled highball glass. Fill with club soda and ice cubes. Garnish with cubes of pineapple and strawberries.

WHISKEY SWIZZLE

1 oz. Lime Juice
1 tsp. Superfine Sugar (or
    Simple Syrup)
2 oz. Club Soda
2 dashes Bitters
2 oz. Whiskey

Put lime juice, sugar/syrup, and club soda into collins glass. Fill glass with ice and stir. Add bitters and whiskey. Fill with club soda and serve with a swizzle stick.

WHISPERS-OF-THE-FROST COCKTAIL

3/4 oz. Whiskey (Bourbon)
3/4 oz. Cream Sherry
3/4 oz. Port
1 tsp. Superfine Sugar (or
    Simple Syrup)

Stir with ice and strain into chilled cocktail glass. Garnish with slices of lemon and orange.

WHITE PLUSH

2 oz. Whiskey
1 cup Milk
1 tsp. Superfine Sugar (or Simple Syrup)

Shake with ice and strain into chilled collins glass.

WOODWARD COCKTAIL

1½ oz. Whisky (Scotch)
½ oz. Dry Vermouth
1 tbsp. Grapefruit Juice

Shake with ice and strain into chilled cocktail glass.

▶ Pacific Sunshine

▶ Shady Lady

► Cosmopolitan and Jungle Juice

▶ Titian

► Commodore
Cocktail

► Godfather and Cowboy

► Manhattan

▶ Mint Julep

▶ Scotch Holiday Sour

CORDIALS

AND

LIQUEURS

C ordials and liqueurs have been around since the Middle Ages, when they were concocted in European monasteries primarily for medicinal purposes. The historical distinction between cordials, which are fruit based, and liqueurs, which are herb based, doesn't really exist anymore today, as the terms are often grouped together—though liqueurs is typically used for both. In Europe, liqueurs and cordials have long been savored as after-dinner drinks, while Americans have tended to enjoy them mixed with other ingredients, putting the fuzz in a Fuzzy Navel, adding the nuttiness to a Pink Squirrel, and turning a Grasshopper green.

Liqueurs by today's definition are flavored spirits with between 2.5 percent and 40 percent sweetener, which can come from just about anything, including fruits, herbs, roots, spices, and nuts. The alcohol base used to make liqueurs can be produced from grain, grapes, or other fruits or vegetables, and must be flavored in one of four ways: distillation, infusion, maceration, or percolation.

Liqueurs, however, should never be confused with fruit brandies, which are distilled from a mash of the fruit itself. Be aware that some producers mislabel their liqueurs as brandies, such as "blackberry brandy" or "apricot brandy," when they are technically cordials (or liqueurs). Artificial colors are permitted in liqueurs, and some lesser brands use artificial flavors.

The very best liqueurs come from all over the globe, and many have closely-guarded secret recipes and processes, as well as their own proprietary brand names. A surely incomplete list of the most popular liqueurs would include: Amaretto (made from apricot pits; almond flavored); Amer Picon (bitter, orange-flavored French cordial made from quinine and spices); Anisette or Anis (flavored with anise seed; licorice flavored); Benedictine (secret herb formula; created by Benedictine monks 400 years ago); Chartreuse (yellow and greed herb liqueur; created by Carthusian monks); Crème de Banana (artificial banana flavoring); Crème de Cacao (cacao and vanilla beans); Crème de Cassis (black currants); Crème de Menthe (mint; comes in white and green varieties); Crème de Noyeaux (apricot and peach pits with almonds); Curaçao (orange flavored, made from dried orange peel; comes in orange and blue varieties); Galliano (herbs, roots, and spices); Kümmel (caraway, anise seed, and other herbs); Maraschino (made from cherries grown in Dalmatia, in former Yugoslavia); Sambuca (licorice-flavored, made from white flowers of elderberry bush); Sloe Gin (sloe berries produced by the blackthorn bush); Southern Comfort (Bourbon and peach liqueur); Strega (herbs, spices, and plants); Triple Sec (orange-flavored form of curaçao).

ABSINTHE SPECIAL COCKTAIL

1 1/2 oz. Anisette
1 oz. Water
1/4 tsp. Superfine Sugar (or Simple Syrup)
1 dash Orange Bitters

Shake with ice and strain into chilled cocktail glass.

AMARETTO AND CREAM

1 1/2 oz. Amaretto
1 1/2 oz. Light Cream

Shake with ice and strain into chilled cocktail glass.

AMARETTO MIST

1 1/2 oz. Amaretto

Serve in old-fashioned glass over crushed ice. Garnish with a twist of lemon or a wedge of lime.

AMARETTO ROSE

1 1/2 oz. Amaretto
1/2 oz. Lemon juice
1 tsp. Superfine Sugar (or Simple Syrup)
Club Soda

Pour amaretto and lime juice into ice-filled collins glass and fill with club soda.

AMARETTO SOUR

1 1/2 oz. Amaretto
3/4 oz. Lemon Juice

Shake with ice and strain into chilled sour glass. Garnish with a slice of orange.

AMARETTO STINGER

1 1/2 oz. Amaretto
3/4 oz. Crème de Menthe (White)

Shake with ice and strain into chilled cocktail glass.

AMBER AMOUR

1 1/2 oz. Amaretto
1/4 oz. Superfine Sugar (or Simple Syrup)
1/4 oz. Lemon Juice
Club Soda

Pour amaretto, sugar/syrup, and lemon juice into ice-filled collins glass. Top with club soda and stir. Garnish with a maraschino cherry.

AMORE-ADE

1 1/4 oz. Amaretto
3/4 oz. Triple Sec
3 oz. Club Soda

Combine all ingredients in oversized red-wine glass. Add ice and garnish with a lemon wedge.

APPLE PIE

3 oz. Apple Schnapps
1 Splash Cinnamon Schnapps

Pour into ice-filled old-fashioned glass and garnish with an apple slice and a sprinkle of cinnamon.

ARISE MY LOVE

1 tsp. Crème de Menthe
(Green)
Champagne, Chilled

Put Crème de Menthe into
Champagne flute. Fill with
Champagne.

BANSHEE

1 oz. Crème de Banana
½ oz. Crème de Cacao
(White)
½ oz. Light Cream

Shake with ice and strain into
chilled cocktail glass.

BLACKJACK

1 oz. Cherry-flavored
Brandy
½ oz. Brandy
1 oz. Coffee

Shake with ice and strain into
ice-filled old-fashioned glass.

BLACKTHORN

1½ oz. Sloe Gin
1 oz. Sweet Vermouth

Stir with ice and strain into
chilled cocktail glass. Garnish
with a twist of lemon peel.

BLANCHE

1 oz. Anisette
1 oz. Triple Sec
½ oz. Curaçao (White)

Shake with ice and strain into
chilled cocktail glass.

BOCCIE BALL

1½ oz. Amaretto
1½ oz. Orange Juice
2 oz. Club Soda

Serve in ice-filled highball
glass.

BOSTON ICED COFFEE

6 oz. Coffee (cooled)
1 oz. Crème de Menthe
(White)
1 oz. Crème de Cacao
(White)
1 oz. Brandy

Pour into ice-filled highball
glass and stir. Garnish with a
twist of lemon peel.

BURNING SUN

1½ oz. Strawberry
Schnapps
4 oz. Pineapple Juice

Pour into ice-filled highball
glass and stir. Garnish with a
fresh strawberry.

BUSHWACKER

½ oz. Coffee Liqueur
½ oz. Amaretto
½ oz. Light Rum
½ oz. Irish Cream Liqueur
2 oz. Light Cream

Blend and pour into ice-filled
old-fashioned glass.

CAFÉ CABANA

1 oz. Coffee Liqueur
3 oz. Club Soda

Pour into ice-filled collins
glass. Stir. Garnish with a
lime wedge.

CHOCOLATE-COVERED STRAWBERRY

1 oz. Strawberry Schnapps
1/4 oz. Crème de Cacao (White)
1/2 oz. Cream

Stir with ice and serve over ice in red-wine glass. Garnish with a fresh strawberry.

CRÈME DE MENTHE FRAPPÉ

2 oz. Crème de Menthe (Green)

Fill cocktail glass up to brim with shaved ice. Add Crème de Menthe. Serve with two short straws.

DEPTH CHARGE

Shot of any flavor of schnapps in a glass of beer.

DIANA COCKTAIL

Crème de Menthe (White)
Brandy

Fill cocktail glass with ice, then fill 3/4 full with Crème de Menthe and float brandy on top.

DUCHESS

1 1/2 oz. Anisette
1/2 oz. Dry Vermouth
1/2 oz. Sweet Vermouth

Shake with ice and strain into chilled cocktail glass.

FERRARI

1 oz. Amaretto
2 oz. Dry Vermouth

Mix in an ice-filled old-fashioned glass. Garnish with a twist of lemon peel.

FRENCH CONNECTION

1 1/2 oz. Cognac
3/4 oz. Amaretto

Serve in ice-filled old-fashioned glass.

FRENCH FANTASY

1 oz. Black Raspberry Liqueur
1 oz. Mandarine Napoléon
2 oz. Cranberry Juice
2 oz. Orange Juice

Pour into ice-filled highball glass and stir. Garnish with an orange slice and a maraschino cherry.

FUZZY NAVEL

3 oz. 48-proof Peach Schnapps
3 oz. Orange Juice

Combine schnapps and orange juice and pour over ice in highball glass. Garnish with an orange slice.

GOLDEN CADILLAC

1 oz. Galliano
2 oz. Crème de Cacao
  (White)
1 oz. Light Cream

Combine with a half-cup of crushed ice in blender on low speed for 10 seconds. Strain into chilled Champagne flute.

GOLDEN DREAM

1 tbsp. Orange Juice
½ oz. Triple Sec
1 oz. Galliano
1 tbsp. Light Cream

Shake with ice and strain into chilled cocktail glass.

GOOBER

1½ oz. Vodka
1½ oz. Black Raspberry
  Liqueur
1½ oz. Melon Liqueur
1 oz. Triple Sec
1 oz. Grenadine
3 oz. Pineapple Juice
4 oz. Orange Juice

Shake with ice and strain into ice-filled collins glass. Garnish with an orange slice and a maraschino cherry. Serve with a straw.

GRASSHOPPER

¼ oz. Crème de Menthe
  (Green)
¼ oz. Crème de Cacao
  (White)
¼ oz. Light Cream

Shake with ice and strain into chilled cocktail glass.

HEAT WAVE

1¼ oz. Coconut-flavored
  Rum
½ oz. Peach Schnapps
3 oz. Pineapple Juice
3 oz. Orange Juice
½ oz. Grenadine

Pour first four ingredients into ice-filled hurricane or parfait glass. Top with grenadine. Garnish with a fresh peach slice.

ITALIAN SOMBRERO

1½ oz. Amaretto
3 oz. Light Cream

Put ingredients in blender or shake well. Serve over ice or straight up in Champagne flute.

ITALIAN SURFER

1 oz. Amaretto
1 oz. Brandy
Pineapple Juice

Fill a collins glass with ice. Add amaretto and brandy. Fill with pineapple juice. Garnish with a pineapple spear and a maraschino cherry.

JOHNNIE COCKTAIL

¾ oz. Triple Sec
1½ oz. Sloe Gin
1 tsp. Anisette

Shake with ice and strain into chilled cocktail glass.

LIMONCELLO SUNRISE

1 oz. Caravella Limoncello
3 oz. Orange Juice
1 dash Grenadine

Stir limoncello and orange juice with ice and strain into chilled rocks glass. Top with a dash of grenadine.

LOVER'S KISS

1/2 oz. Amaretto
1/2 oz. Cherry-flavored Brandy
1/2 oz. Crème de Cacao (Brown)
1 oz. Cream

Shake with ice and strain into parfait glass. Top with whipped cream. Sprinkle with chocolate shavings and top with a maraschino cherry.

MARMALADE

1 1/2 oz. Curaçao
Tonic Water

Pour Curaçao into ice-filled highball glass and fill with tonic water. Garnish with an orange slice.

McCLELLAND COCKTAIL

3/4 oz. Triple Sec
1 1/2 oz. Sloe Gin
1 dash Orange Bitters

Shake with ice and strain into chilled cocktail glass.

MELON COOLER

1 oz. Melon Liqueur
1/2 oz. Peach Schnapps
1/2 oz. Raspberry Schnapps
2 oz. Pineapple Juice

Shake with ice and pour into chilled margarita or cocktail glass. Garnish with a lime wheel and a maraschino cherry.

MINT HIGHBALL

2 oz. Crème de Menthe (Green)
Ginger Ale or Club Soda

Pour crème de menthe into highball glass over ice cubes and fill with ginger ale or club soda. Stir. Garnish with a twist of lemon peel.

MINT ON ROCKS

2 oz. Crème de Menthe (Green)

Pour over ice cubes in old-fashioned glass.

MOULIN ROUGE

1 1/2 oz. Sloe Gin
3/4 oz. Sweet Vermouth
1 dash Bitters

Stir with ice and strain into chilled cocktail glass.

PANAMA COCKTAIL

1 oz. Crème de Cacao (White)
1 oz. Light Cream
1 oz. Brandy

Shake with ice and strain into chilled cocktail glass.

PEACH MELBA

1 oz. Peach Schnapps
1/2 oz. Black Raspberry
   Liqueur
3 oz. Cream

Shake with ice and pour into
old-fashioned glass. Garnish
with a peach slice. Serve with
a short straw.

PEPPERMINT ICEBERG

2 oz. Peppermint Schnapps

Pour into ice-filled old-
fashioned glass. Stir and
serve with a peppermint
candy swizzle stick.

PEPPERMINT STICK

1 oz. Peppermint Schnapps
1 1/2 oz. Crème de Cacao
   (White)
1 oz. Light Cream

Shake with ice and strain into
chilled Champagne flute.

PEPPERMINT TWIST

1 1/2 oz. Peppermint
   Schnapps
1/2 oz. Crème de Cacao
   (White)
3 scoops Vanilla Ice Cream

Blend and pour into large
parfait glass. Garnish with a
mint sprig and a peppermint
candy stick. Serve with a
straw.

PINK SQUIRREL

1 oz. Crème de Noyaux
1 tbsp. Crème de Cacao
   (White)
1 tbsp. Light Cream

Shake with ice and strain into
chilled cocktail glass.

PORT AND STARBOARD

1 tbsp. Grenadine
1/2 oz. Crème de Menthe
   (Green)

Pour carefully into pousse
café glass, so that crème de
menthe floats on grenadine.

POUSSE CAFÉ

Equal parts:
Grenadine
Chartreuse (Yellow)
Crème de Cassis
Crème de Menthe (White)
Chartreuse (Green)
Brandy

Pour carefully, in order given,
into pousse café glass so that
each ingredient floats on preceding one.

QUAALUDE

1 oz. Vodka
1 oz. Hazelnut Liqueur
1 oz. Coffee Liqueur
1 splash Milk

Pour into ice-filled old-
fashioned glass.

RASPBERRY ROMANCE

3/4 oz. Coffee Liqueur
3/4 oz. Black Raspberry
   Liqueur
1 1/4 oz. Irish Cream Liqueur
Club Soda

Pour liqueurs into ice-filled
parfait glass. Fill with club
soda and stir.

RITZ FIZZ

Champagne, Chilled
1 dash Lemon Juice
1 dash Blue Curaçao
1 dash Amaretto

Fill flute with Champagne.
Add remaining ingredients
and stir. Garnish with a twist
of lemon peel.

ROAD RUNNER

1 oz. Vodka
1/2 oz. Amaretto
1/2 oz. Coconut Cream

Combine in blender with
half-scoop of crushed ice for
15 seconds. Rim edge of
chilled Champagne flute with
a slice of orange. Dip rim in a
sugar and nutmeg mixture.
Pour cocktail into the prepared glass. Garnish with
fresh-grated nutmeg on top.

ROCKY MOUNTAIN COOLER

1 1/2 oz. Peach Schnapps
4 oz. Pineapple Juice
2 oz. Lemon-lime Soda

Pour into ice-filled collins
glass and stir.

ST. PATRICK'S DAY

1/4 oz. Crème de Menthe
   (Green)
3/4 oz. Chartreuse (Green)
3/4 oz. Irish Whiskey
1 dash Bitters

Stir with ice and strain into
chilled cocktail glass.

SAMBUCA STRAIGHT

2 oz. Sambuca
3 Coffee Beans

Pour Sambuca into snifter
and float coffee beans on top.

SAN FRANCISCO COCKTAIL

3/4 oz. Sloe Gin
3/4 oz. Sweet Vermouth
3/4 oz. Dry Vermouth
1 dash Bitters
1 dash Orange Bitters

Shake with ice and strain into
chilled cocktail glass. Garnish
with a maraschino cherry.

SANTINI'S POUSSE CAFÉ

1/2 oz. Brandy
1 tbsp. Maraschino Liqueur
1/2 oz. Triple Sec
1/2 oz. Rum

Pour in order given into
pousse café glass.

SHEER ELEGANCE

1 1/2 oz. Amaretto
1 1/2 oz. Black Raspberry
   Liqueur
1/2 oz. Vodka

Shake with ice and strain into
chilled cocktail glass.

SLOEBERRY COCKTAIL

1 dash Bitters
2 oz. Sloe Gin

Stir with ice and strain into chilled cocktail glass.

SLOE DRIVER

1½ oz. Sloe Gin
5 oz. Orange Juice

Pour ingredients into ice-filled highball glass and stir.

SLOE GIN COCKTAIL

2 oz. Sloe Gin
1 dash Orange Bitters
¼ oz. Dry Vermouth

Stir with ice and strain into chilled cocktail glass.

SLOE GIN COLLINS

1 oz. Lemon Juice
2 oz. Sloe Gin
Club Soda

Shake lemon juice and sloe gin with ice and strain into chilled collins glass. Add several ice cubes, fill with club soda, and stir. Garnish with slices of lemon and orange and a maraschino cherry. Serve with straws.

SLOE GIN FIZZ

1 oz. Lemon Juice
1 tsp. Superfine Sugar (or Simple Syrup)
2 oz. Sloe Gin
Club Soda

Shake lemon juice, sugar/syrup, and sloe gin with ice and strain into chilled highball glass with two ice cubes. Fill with club soda and stir. Garnish with a slice of lemon.

SLOE GIN RICKEY

½ oz. Lime Juice
2 oz. Sloe Gin
Club Soda

Pour into highball glass over ice cubes. Stir. Drop a lime rind into glass.

SLOE VERMOUTH

1 oz. Sloe Gin
1 oz. Dry Vermouth
1 tbsp. Lemon Juice

Shake with ice and strain into chilled cocktail glass.

SOMETHING DIFFERENT

1 oz. Peach Schnapps
1 oz. Amaretto
2 oz. Pineapple Juice
2 oz. Cranberry Juice

Shake with ice and pour into ice-filled highball glass.

CORDIALS AND LIQUEURS

STRAWBERRY FIELDS FOREVER

2 oz. Strawberry Schnapps
1/2 oz. Brandy
Club Soda

Pour schnapps and brandy into ice-filled highball glass. Fill with club soda. Garnish with a fresh strawberry.

STRAWBERRY SUNRISE

2 oz. Strawberry Schnapps
1/2 oz. Grenadine
Orange Juice

Pour schnapps and grenadine into ice-filled highball glass. Fill with orange juice. Garnish with a fresh strawberry.

SUN KISS

2 oz. Amaretto
4 oz. Orange Juice

Combine amaretto and orange juice in ice-filled collins glass. Garnish with a lime wedge.

THUNDER CLOUD

1/2 oz. Crème de Noyaux
1/2 oz. Blue Curaçao
1/2 oz. Amaretto
1/4 oz. Vodka
1 oz. Superfine Sugar (or Simple Syrup)
1 oz. Lemon Juice
1 oz. Lemon-lime Soda

Layer ingredients in an ice-filled hurricane or parfait glass in order given. Whirl gently with a large straw.

TIKKI DREAM

3/4 oz. Melon Liqueur
41/4 oz. Cranberry Juice

Pour into ice-filled, sugar-rimmed highball glass. Garnish with a wedge of watermelon.

TOASTED ALMOND

11/2 oz. Coffee Liqueur
1 oz. Amaretto
11/2 oz. Cream or Milk

Add all ingredients in ice-filled old-fashioned glass.

TROPICAL COCKTAIL

3/4 oz. Crème de Cacao (White)
3/4 oz. Maraschino Liqueur
3/4 oz. Dry Vermouth
1 dash Bitters

Stir with ice and strain into chilled cocktail glass.

TWIN PEACH

2 oz. Peach Schnapps
Cranberry Juice

Pour schnapps into ice-filled highball glass, fill with cranberry juice, and stir. Garnish with an orange or peach slice.

WATERMELON

1 oz. Strawberry Liqueur
1 oz. Vodka
½ oz. Superfine Sugar (or Simple Syrup)
½ oz. Lemon Juice
1 oz. Orange Juice

Pour in ice-filled collins glass. Garnish with an orange slice and serve with a straw.

YELLOW PARROT COCKTAIL

¾ oz. Anisette
¾ oz. Chartreuse (Yellow)
¾ oz. Apricot-flavored Brandy

Shake with ice and strain into chilled cocktail glass.

ZERO MIST

2 oz. Crème de Menthe
1 oz. Water

For each serving, chill liqueur and water in freezer compartment of refrigerator for 2 hours or longer (does not have to be frozen solid). Serve in cocktail glasses.

SHOOTERS

When this book debuted 70 years ago, a "shot" was 2 ounces of straight whiskey knocked back in a single gulp—just like the scenes in those dusty old Westerns. Today, shots are called shooters, slammers, even tooters, usually preceded by fanciful names—B-52, Sex on the Beach, Kamikaze—and concocted with virtually any spirit and mixer handy in a well-stocked bar.

The universal appeal of shooters is at least partly attributable to the fact that many are fairly low in alcohol content, appealing to those with lighter tastes. Frequently made with several juices, as well as lower proof liqueurs, the small size of the shooter limits the amount of spirit contained in a single drink. Some, like the Rattlesnake, are skillfully layered works of art, similar to a Pousse Café. Others, like the Bloody Caesar, incorporate surprising ingredients such as clams or oysters.

Of course, the granddaddy of all shooters—a lick of salt, washed down with a shot of straight tequila, followed by a suck on a wedge of lime and the obligatory shudder—is not only still alive and kicking, it has inspired similar drinks like the Lemon Drop and the Cordless Screwdriver.

On the pages that follow, you'll find recipes for all the drinks already mentioned, plus a multitude of others. The common denominator they all share is that they were created with a sense of humor and wit, which is how they should be enjoyed, too. Once you get the hang of making them, you can experiment with bumping up the recipes to make large batches for parties. You might also feel inspired to create your own, which is how every one of these recipes came to fruition. A little imagination and creativity can create a great little drink.

SHOOTERS

AFFAIR

1 oz. Strawberry Schnapps
1 oz. Cranberry Juice
1 oz. Orange Juice

Stir with ice and strain into chilled cordial glass.

ALABAMA SLAMMER

1 oz. Amaretto
1 oz. Whiskey (Tennessee Sour Mash)
1/2 oz. Sloe Gin
1 splash Lemon Juice

Stir with ice and strain into chilled shot glass. Add lemon juice.

ANGEL'S DELIGHT

1 1/2 tsps. Grenadine
1 1/2 tsps. Triple Sec
1 1/2 tsps. Sloe Gin
1 1/2 tsps. Light Cream

Into cordial glass pour carefully, in order given, so that each ingredient floats on preceding one without mixing.

ANGEL'S KISS

1/4 oz. Crème de Cacao (White)
1/4 oz. Sloe Gin
1/4 oz. Brandy
1/4 oz. Light Cream

Into cordial glass pour carefully, in order given, so that each ingredient floats on preceding one without mixing.

ANGEL'S TIP

1/4 oz. Crème de Cacao (White)
1/4 oz. Light Cream

Into cordial glass pour Crème de Cacao and then gently float cream on top. Garnish with a maraschino cherry on a cocktail pick across mouth of glass.

ANGEL'S WING

1/2 oz. Crème de Cacao (White)
1/2 oz. Brandy
1 tbsp. Light Cream

Into cordial glass pour carefully, in order given, so that each ingredient floats on preceding one without mixing.

B-52

1/2 oz. Coffee Liqueur
1/2 oz. Irish Cream Liqueur
1/2 oz. Mandarine Napoléon

Into shot glass pour carefully, in order given, so that each ingredient floats on preceding one without mixing.

BANANA BOMBER

1 oz. 99 Bananas Flavored
    Schnapps
¾ oz. Triple Sec
Splash Grenadine

Shake with ice and strain into
chilled shot glass.

BANANA SLIP

1½ oz. Crème de Banana
1½ oz. Irish Cream Liqueur

Into cordial glass pour Crème
de Banana and then gently
float cream on top.

BETWEEN-THE-SHEETS

1 oz. Lemon Juice
½ oz. Brandy
½ oz. Triple Sec
½ oz. Light Rum

Shake with ice and strain into
chilled shot glass.

BLOODY CAESAR SHOOTER

1 Littleneck Clam
1 oz. Vodka
1½ oz. Tomato Juice
2 drops Worcestershire
    Sauce
2 drops Tabasco Sauce
1 dash Horseradish Sauce
Celery Salt

Put clam in the bottom of a
shot glass. Shake vodka,
Worcestershire, tomato juice,
Tabasco, and horseradish
with ice, and strain into
chilled shot glass. Sprinkle
with celery salt and garnish
with a lime wedge.

BLUE MARLIN

1 oz. Light Rum
½ oz. Blue Curaçao
1 oz. Lime Juice

Stir with ice and strain into
chilled shot glass.

BONZAI PIPELINE

½ oz. Vodka
1 oz. Tropical Fruit
    Schnapps

Stir with ice and strain into
chilled shot glass.

BUZZARD'S BREATH

½ oz. Amaretto
½ oz. Peppermint
    Schnapps
½ oz. Coffee Liqueur

Stir with ice and strain into
chilled shot glass.

C.C. KAZI

1½ oz. Tequila
2 oz. Cranberry Juice
1 tsp. Lime Juice

Shake with ice and strain into
chilled cordial glass.

CAPRI

¾ oz. Crème de Cacao
    (White)
¾ oz. Crème de Banana
¾ oz. Light Cream

Shake with ice and strain into
chilled cordial glass.

CARAMEL APPLE

1 oz. 99 Apples Flavored
    Schnapps
2 oz. Butterscotch Schnapps

Shake with ice and strain into
chilled shot glass.

CHARLIE CHAPLIN

1 oz. Sloe Gin
1 oz. Apricot-flavored
    Brandy
1 oz. Lemon Juice

Shake with ice and strain into
chilled cordial glass.

CORDLESS SCREWDRIVER

1¾ oz. Vodka
Orange Wedge
Sugar

Chill vodka and strain into
shot glass. Dip orange wedge
in sugar. Shoot the vodka
and immediately take a draw
on the orange.

COSMOS

1½ oz. Vodka
½ oz. Lime Juice

Shake with ice and strain into
chilled shot glass.

FIFTH AVENUE

½ oz. Crème de Cacao
    (Brown)
½ oz. Apricot-flavored
    Brandy
1 tbsp. Light Cream

Into cordial glass pour carefully, in order given, so that
each ingredient floats on preceding one without mixing.

FLYING GRASSHOPPER

¾ oz. Crème de Menthe
    (Green)
¾ oz. Crème de Cacao
    (White)
¾ oz. Vodka

Stir with ice and strain into
chilled cordial glass.

4TH OF JULY TOOTER

1 oz. Grenadine
1 oz. Vodka
1 oz. Blue Curaçao

Into cordial or shot glass
pour carefully, in order given,
so that each ingredient floats
on preceding one without
mixing.

FOXY LADY

1 oz. Amaretto
½ oz. Crème de Cacao
    (Brown)
1 oz. Heavy Cream

Shake with ice and strain into
chilled cordial glass.

GALACTIC ALE

¾ oz. Vodka
¾ oz. Blue Curaçao
½ oz. Lime Juice
¼ oz. Black Raspberry
    Liqueur

Shake with ice and strain into
chilled shot glass

GREEN DEMON

½ oz. Vodka
½ oz. Rum
½ oz. Melon Liqueur
½ oz. Lemonade

Shake with ice and strain into chilled shot glass.

INTERNATIONAL INCIDENT

¼ oz. Vodka
¼ oz. Coffee Liqueur
¼ oz. Amaretto
¼ oz. Hazelnut Liqueur
½ oz. Irish Cream Liqueur

Shake with ice and strain into chilled shot glass.

IRISH CHARLIE

1 oz. Irish Cream Liqueur
1 oz. Crème de Menthe
   (White)

Stir with ice and strain into chilled cordial glass.

IRISH FLAG

1 oz. Crème de Menthe
   (Green)
1 oz. Irish Cream Liqueur
1 oz. Mandarine Napoléon

Into cordial glass pour carefully, in order given, so that each ingredient floats on preceding one without mixing.

JOHNNY ON THE BEACH

¾ oz. Vodka
½ oz. Melon Liqueur
½ oz. Black Raspberry
   Liqueur
¼ oz. Pineapple Juice
¼ oz. Orange Juice
¼ oz. Grapefruit Juice
¼ oz. Cranberry Juice

Stir with ice and strain into chilled shot glass.

KAMIKAZE

½ oz. Lime Juice
½ oz. Triple Sec
½ oz. Vodka

Shake with ice and strain into chilled shot glass.

LEMON DROP

1½ oz. Vodka
Lemon wedge
Sugar

Chill vodka and strain into chilled shot glass. Dip lemon wedge in sugar. Shoot the vodka and immediately take a draw on the lemon.

MELON BALL

1 oz. Melon Liqueur
1 oz. Vodka
1 oz. Pineapple Juice

Shake with ice and strain into chilled cordial glass.

MOCHA MINT

Y ¾ oz. Coffee-flavored
Brandy
¾ oz. Crème de Cacao
(White)
¾ oz. Crème de Menthe
(White)

Shake with ice and strain into
chilled cordial glass.

MONKEY SHINE SHOOTER

Y ½ oz. Bourbon Liqueur
½ oz. Crème de Banana
½ oz. Irish Cream Liqueur

Shake with ice and strain into
chilled cordial glass.

NUTTY PROFESSOR

⊔ ½ oz. Mandarine
Napoléon
½ oz. Hazelnut Liqueur
½ oz. Irish Cream Liqueur

Stir and strain into shot glass.

OH MY GOSH

⊔ 1 oz. Amaretto
1 oz. Peach Schnapps

Stir with ice and strain into
chilled shot glass.

PARISIAN BLONDE

Y ¾ oz. Light Rum
¾ oz. Triple Sec
¾ oz. Jamaica Rum

Shake with ice and strain into
chilled cordial glass.

PEACH BUNNY

Y ¾ oz. Peach-flavored
Brandy
¾ oz. Crème de Cacao
(White)
¾ oz. Light Cream

Shake with ice and strain into
chilled cordial glass.

PEACH TART

⊔ 1 oz. Peach Schnapps
½ oz. Lime Juice

Stir with ice and strain into
chilled shot glass.

PEPPERMINT PATTIE

Y 1 oz. Crème de Cacao
(White)
1 oz. Crème de Menthe
(White)

Shake with ice and strain into
chilled cordial glass.

PIGSKIN SHOT

1 oz. Vodka
1 oz. Melon Liqueur
1/4 oz. Superfine Sugar (or
   Simple Syrup)
1/4 oz. Lemon Juice

Shake with ice and strain into
chilled shot glass.

PINEAPPLE UPSIDE-DOWN CAKE

1/2 oz. Irish Cream Liqueur
1/2 oz. Vodka
1/2 oz. Butterscotch
   Schnapps
1/2 oz. Pineapple Juice

Stir and strain into shot glass.

PURPLE HOOTER

1 1/2 oz. Citrus-flavored
   Vodka
1/2 oz. Triple Sec
1/4 oz. Black Raspberry
   Liqueur

Shake with ice and strain into
chilled shot glass.

RATTLESNAKE

1 oz. Coffee Liqueur
1 oz. Crème de Cacao
   (White)
1 oz. Irish Cream Liqueur

Into cordial or shot glass pour
carefully, in order given, so
that each ingredient floats on
preceding one without
mixing.

ROCKY MOUNTAIN

1 oz. Whiskey (Tennessee
   Sour Mash)
1 oz. Amaretto
1/2 oz. Lime Juice

Shake with ice and strain into
chilled shot glass.

SAMBUCA SLIDE

1 oz. Sambuca
1/2 oz. Vodka
1/2 oz. Light Cream

Stir with ice and strain into
chilled shot glass.

SCOOTER

1 oz. Amaretto
1 oz. Brandy
1 oz. Light Cream

Shake with cracked ice. Strain
into chilled cordial glass.

SEX ON THE BEACH

1/2 oz. Black Raspberry
   Liqueur
1/2 oz. Melon Liqueur
1/2 oz. Vodka
1 oz. Pineapple Juice
Cranberry Juice

Stir first four ingredients with
ice and strain into chilled
cordial or shot glass. Top
with cranberry juice.

SHAVETAIL

1 1/2 oz. Peppermint
   Schnapps
1 oz. Pineapple Juice
1 oz. Light Cream

Shake with ice and strain into
chilled cordial glass.

SHOOTERS

SILVER SPIDER

½ oz. Vodka
½ oz. Rum
½ oz. Triple Sec
½ oz. Crème de Menthe (White)

Stir with ice and strain into chilled shot glass.

SOUR APPLE

¼ oz. Vodka
¼ oz. Apple Liqueur
½ oz. Melon Liqueur
½ oz. Lemon-lime Soda

Shake and strain into cordial glass.

STALACTITE

1¼ oz. Sambuca
¼ oz. Irish Cream Liqueur
¼ oz. Black Raspberry Liqueur

Pour Sambuca into cordial glass and then float Irish Cream on top. Then carefully pour raspberry liqueur, drop by drop, as top layer. The raspberry liqueur will pull the Irish cream through the Sambuca and settle on the bottom.

STARS AND STRIPES

⅓ oz. Grenadine
⅓ oz. Heavy Cream
⅓ oz. Blue Curaçao

Into cordial glass, pour carefully, in order given, so that each ingredient floats on preceding one without mixing.

TERMINATOR

½ oz. Coffee Liqueur
½ oz. Irish Cream Liqueur
½ oz. Sambuca
½ oz. Mandarine Napoléon
½ oz. Vodka

Into cordial glass pour carefully, in order given, so that each layer floats on preceding one without mixing.

TO THE MOON

½ oz. Coffee Liqueur
½ oz. Amaretto
½ oz. Irish Cream Liqueur
½ oz. 151-proof Rum

Stir with ice and strain into chilled shot glass.

TRAFFIC LIGHT

½ oz. Crème de Noyaux
½ oz. Galliano
½ oz. Melon Liqueur

Layer liqueurs in order given in cordial glass.

WOO WOO

½ oz. Peach Schnapps
½ oz. Vodka
1 oz. Cranberry Juice

Shake with ice and strain into chilled shot glass.

FROZEN
DRINKS

Frozen drinks are certainly perfect for summertime sipping, but they're also enjoyed year-round—much as ice cream is. In fact, some are creamy concoctions made with ice cream. Others are tropical in nature, combining spirits or liqueurs with fruit juices, and blended with ice. Served in tall, generous glasses and garnished with an assortment of seasonal fruits, they're best sipped slowly—to prevent brain-freeze—through a straw.

Ice cream–based frozen drinks, often mixed with liqueurs such as Crème de Cacao, Amaretto, or Irish cream and topped with whipped cream, also make delicious dessert substitutes. Just imagine sipping a Strawberry Shortcake or a Raspberry Cheesecake after a meal, and you sort of get the picture.

The most important ingredient to consider when planning to mix up frozen drinks is ice—and more than you think you could possibly need. Depending on the size and shape of the ice you use, it will melt differently when mixed with warm mixers and alcohol, and it will blend differently, too. And speaking of blending, having an electric blender to pulverize the ice will allow you to make professional-style smoothies at home.

You'll find plenty of delicious recipes for every season in this section. Next time it's 90 in the shade, you and your blender can quickly dispatch a Tidal Wave or a Maui Breeze to cool down. And when you have a hankering for a creamy treat any time of year, you'll find a recipe that will put you on Cloud Nine.

THE ALL-AMERICAN DAIQUIRI

Blue Layer:
¾ oz. Light Rum or Vodka
¾ oz. Superfine Sugar (or Simple Syrup)
¾ oz. Lemon Juice
½ oz. Blueberry Flavoring

Red Layer:
¾ oz. Light Rum or Vodka
2 oz. Strawberry Daiquiri Mix

White Layer:
Whipped Cream

For red and blue layers, combine ingredients in blender with 1 cup crushed ice and blend until very thick. Layer frozen colors—blue, red, and white—in parfait glass. Top with a maraschino cherry and an American flag frill pick.

APPLE COLADA

2 oz. Apple Schnapps
1 oz. Cream of Coconut
1 oz. Half-and-Half

Combine all ingredients with 1 cup crushed ice in blender until smooth. Pour into highball glass and serve with a straw. Garnish with an apple slice and a maraschino cherry.

APPLE GRANNY CRISP

1 oz. Apple Schnapps
½ oz. Brandy
½ oz. Irish Cream Liqueur
2 scoops Vanilla Ice Cream
Graham Cracker Crumbs

Combine all ingredients in blender until smooth. Serve topped with whipped cream and cinnamon.

APPLE RIVER INNER TUBE

1 oz. Brandy
1 oz. Crème de Cacao (Brown)
1½ scoops Vanilla Ice Cream

Combine all ingredients with 1 cup crushed ice in blender until smooth. Pour into parfait glass. Garnish with half a spiced apple ring.

APRICOT CREAM SPRITZ

¾ cup Milk
½ cup Apricot Nectar

2 tbsps. Apricot-flavored Brandy
2 cups Sparkling Wine

Combine first three ingredients in blender with ¼ cup crushed ice until smooth. Pour equal amounts into 6 large red-wine glasses. Add about ⅓ cup sparkling wine to each glass. Stir gently. (Makes 6 servings.)

BANANA DAIQUIRI

1 ½ oz. Light Rum
1 tbsp. Triple Sec
1 ½ oz. Lime Juice
1 tsp. Sugar
1 Medium Banana, sliced

Combine all ingredients in blender with 1 cup crushed ice and blend until smooth. Pour into Champagne flute. Garnish with a maraschino cherry.

BANANA DI AMORE

1 oz. Amaretto
1 oz. Crème de Banana
2 oz. Orange Juice
½ oz. Superfine Sugar (or Simple Syrup)
½ oz. Lemon Juice

Combine all ingredients with 1 cup crushed ice in blender until smooth. Serve in red-wine glass, garnished with orange and banana slices.

BANANA FOSTER

2 scoops Vanilla Ice Cream
1 ½ oz. Spiced Rum
½ oz. Banana Liqueur
1 Medium Banana, sliced

Combine all ingredients in blender until smooth. Pour into large brandy snifter and sprinkle with cinnamon.

BAY CITY BOMBER

½ oz. Vodka
½ oz. Rum
½ oz. Tequila
½ oz. Gin
½ oz. Triple Sec
1 oz. Orange Juice
1 oz. Pineapple Juice
1 oz. Cranberry Juice
½ oz. Superfine Sugar (or Simple Syrup)
½ oz. Lemon Juice
¼ oz. 151-proof Rum

Combine all ingredients except rum with 1 cup crushed ice in blender until smooth. Pour into parfait glass. Float rum on top. Garnish with a maraschino cherry and an orange slice.

BEACH BUM'S COOLER

1 ¼ oz. Irish Cream
¼ oz. Banana Liqueur
1 ½ oz. Piña Colada Mix
¾ oz. Light Rum
¼ Banana
2 scoops Vanilla Ice Cream
1 splash Cream

Combine all ingredients in blender until smooth. Pour into parfait glass and garnish with a pineapple slice and a paper umbrella.

THE BIG CHILL

1½ oz. Dark Rum
1 oz. Pineapple Juice
1 oz. Orange Juice
1 oz. Cranberry Juice
1 oz. Cream of Coconut

Combine all ingredients in
blender with 1 cup of
crushed ice and blend until
smooth. Pour into 12-oz. pilsner glass and garnish with a
pineapple wedge and a
maraschino cherry.

THE BLIZZARD

1 oz. Brandy
1 oz. Irish Cream Liqueur
1 oz. Coffee Liqueur
1 oz. Light Rum
2 scoops Vanilla Ice Cream
1 splash Light Cream

Combine all ingredients in
blender until smooth. Pour
into a large snifter and garnish with fresh-grated
nutmeg on top.

BLUE CLOUD COCKTAIL

1 oz. Amaretto
½ oz. Blue Curaçao
2 oz. Vanilla Ice Cream

Combine all ingredients in
blender and blend until
smooth. Pour into brandy
snifter. Top with whipped
cream and a maraschino
cherry.

BLUE VELVET

1 oz. Black Raspberry
   Liqueur
1 oz. Melon Liqueur
4 oz. Vanilla Ice Cream
Blue Curaçao

Combine liqueurs and ice
cream with 1 cup crushed ice
in blender until smooth. Pour
into parfait glass and top
with whipped cream and
drizzle with Blue Curaçao.
Garnish with a maraschino
cherry.

BLUSHIN' RUSSIAN

1 oz. Coffee Liqueur
¾ oz. Vodka
1 scoop Vanilla Ice Cream
4 Large Fresh Strawberries

Combine all ingredients in
blender until smooth. Pour
into parfait glass. Garnish
with a chocolate-covered
strawberry.

THE BRASS FIDDLE

2 oz. Peach Schnapps
¾ oz. Tennessee Whiskey
2 oz. Pineapple Juice
1 oz. Orange Juice
1 oz. Grenadine

Combine first four ingredients in blender with 1 cup
ice and blend until smooth.
Pour into parfait glass that
has been swirled with grenadine. Garnish with a
pineapple slice and a
maraschino cherry.

BUNKY PUNCH

1 1/2 oz. Vodka
1 oz. Melon Liqueur
1 oz. Peach Schnapps
1 1/2 oz. Cranberry Juice
2 oz. Orange Juice
1/2 oz. Grape Juice

Combine all ingredients with 1 cup crushed ice in blender until smooth. Pour into parfait glass and garnish with a slice of lime.

CANYON QUAKE

3/4 oz. Irish Cream Liqueur
3/4 oz. Brandy
1 oz. Amaretto
2 oz. Light Cream

Combine all ingredients with 1 cup crushed ice in blender until smooth. Pour into large snifter.

CAVANAUGH'S SPECIAL

1 oz. Coffee Liqueur
1 oz. Crème de Cacao (White)
1 oz. Amaretto
2 scoops Vanilla Ice Cream

In snifter, pour coffee liqueur and set aside. In blender, combine next three ingredients with 1 cup ice until smooth. Pour over coffee and top with whipped cream and chocolate sprinkles.

CHAMPAGNE CORNUCOPIA

1 oz. Cranberry Juice
2 scoops Rainbow Sherbet
1 oz. Vodka
3/4 oz. Peach Schnapps
1 oz. Champagne

Pour cranberry juice into oversized red-wine glass. Combine sherbet, vodka, and schnapps in blender until smooth. Pour over cranberry juice to produce a swirl effect and layer Champagne on top. Garnish with an orange slice.

CHERRY REPAIR KIT

1/2 oz. Half-and-Half
1/2 oz. Crème de Cacao (White)
1/2 oz. Amaretto
6 Maraschino Cherries
1/2 oz. Maraschino Liqueur

Combine all ingredients with 1 cup crushed ice in blender until smooth. Garnish with a maraschino cherry and serve with a straw.

FROZEN DRINKS

CHI-CHI

1 1/2 oz. Vodka
1 oz. Cream of Coconut
4 oz. Pineapple Juice

Combine all ingredients with
1 cup crushed ice in blender
until smooth. Pour into red-
wine glass. Garnish with a
slice of pineapple and a
maraschino cherry.

CHILLY IRISHMAN

3 oz. Cold Espresso
1 oz. Irish Whiskey
1/2 oz. Coffee Liqueur
1/2 oz. Irish Cream Liqueur
1 scoop Vanilla Ice Cream
1 dash Superfine Sugar (or
    Simple Syrup)

Combine all ingredients in
blender with 4 cups of
crushed ice and blend until
smooth. Pour into parfait
glass. Garnish with a 3- or 4-
leaf clover.

CHOCO-BANANA SMASH

1 1/4 oz. Irish Cream Liqueur
1/4 oz. Vanilla Extract
1/2 oz. Light Cream
1/2 scoop Vanilla Ice Cream
1/2 Medium Banana, sliced

Combine all ingredients with
1 cup crushed ice in blender
until smooth. Pour into parfait
glass. Garnish with a
maraschino cherry and 1-inch
banana slice on a cocktail
pick. Top with whipped cream
and chocolate sprinkles.

CHOCOLATE ALMOND CREAM

1 qt. Vanilla Ice Cream
1/2 cup Amaretto
1/2 cup Crème de Cacao
    (White)

Combine all ingredients in
blender until smooth. Pour
into parfait glasses. Garnish
with shaved chocolate.
(Makes 4 to 6 servings.)

CITRUS BANANA FLIP

1 Medium Banana, cut in
    pieces
10 oz. Club Soda
2/3 cup Orange Juice
    Concentrate
2/3 cup Milk
1/2 cup Dark Rum
1/2 cup Lime Juice
3 tbsps. Brown Sugar

Combine all ingredients with
1 cup crushed ice in blender
until smooth. Pour into
collins glasses. (Makes 4 to 6
servings.)

CLOUD 9

8 oz. Vanilla Ice Cream
1 oz. Irish Cream Liqueur
1/2 oz. Black Raspberry
    Liqueur
1 oz. Amaretto

Combine all ingredients in
blender and blend until
smooth. Pour into parfait
glass. Top with whipped
cream and a chocolate–peanut
butter cup, split in half.

COOL OPERATOR

1 oz. Melon Liqueur
1/2 oz. Lime Juice
1/2 oz. Vodka
1/2 oz. Light Rum
4 oz. Grapefruit Juice
2 oz. Orange Juice

Combine all ingredients with 1 cup crushed ice in blender until smooth. Pour into parfait glass. Garnish with a melon wedge and a maraschino cherry.

CRANBERRY COOLER

1 1/2 oz. Bourbon
1 1/2 oz. Cranberry Juice
1/2 oz. Lime Juice
1 tsp. Sugar

Combine all ingredients with 1 cup crushed ice in blender until smooth. Pour into parfait glass.

CREAMY GIN SOUR

1/2 cup Gin
1/2 cup Lime Juice
1/2 cup Lemon Juice
1/2 cup Heavy Cream
1/4 cup Triple Sec
1 tbsp. Sugar
10 oz. Club Soda

Combine all ingredients with 1 cup crushed ice in blender until smooth. Pour into large red-wine glasses. (Makes 4 to 6 servings.)

DEATH BY CHOCOLATE

1 oz. Irish Cream Liqueur
1/2 oz. Crème de Cacao (Brown)
1/2 oz. Vodka
1 scoop Chocolate Ice Cream

Combine all ingredients in blender with 1 cup of crushed ice and blend until smooth. Pour into parfait glass. Garnish with whipped cream and chocolate curls. Serve with a straw.

DEVIL'S TAIL

1 1/2 oz. Light Rum
1 oz. Vodka
1 tbsp. Lime Juice
1 1/2 tsps. Grenadine
1 1/2 tsps. Apricot-flavored Brandy

Combine all ingredients in blender with 1 cup of crushed ice and blend until smooth. Pour into Champagne flute. Add a twist of lime peel.

DI AMORE DREAM

1 1/2 oz. Amaretto di Amore
3/4 oz. Crème de Cacao (White)
2 oz. Orange Juice
2 scoops Vanilla Ice Cream

Combine all ingredients in blender until smooth. Pour into parfait glass. Garnish with an orange slice.

DREAMY MONKEY

1 oz. Vodka
1/2 oz. Crème de Banana
1/2 oz. Crème de Cacao
    (Brown)
1 Banana
2 scoops Vanilla Ice Cream
1 oz. Light Cream

Combine all ingredients in
blender (use half of the
banana) and blend until
smooth. Pour into parfait
glass. Top with whipped
cream and garnish with
remaining banana half.

FROSTY NOGGIN

1 1/2 oz. Rum
3/4 oz. Crème de Menthe
    (White)
3 oz. Prepared Dairy
    Eggnog
3 cups Vanilla Ice Cream

Combine all ingredients in
blender and blend until
smooth. Pour into parfait
glass. Top with whipped
cream. Garnish with a few
drops of green crème de
menthe and a cookie.

FROZEN BERKELEY

1 1/2 oz. Light Rum
1/2 oz. Brandy
1 tbsp. Passion Fruit Syrup
1 tbsp. Lemon Juice

Combine all ingredients in
blender with 1 cup of
crushed ice and blend until
smooth. Pour into Cham-
pagne flute.

FROZEN CAPPUCCINO

1/2 oz. Irish Cream Liqueur
1/2 oz. Coffee Liqueur
1/2 oz. Hazelnut Liqueur
1 scoop Vanilla Ice Cream
1 dash Light Cream

Combine all ingredients in
blender with 1 cup of
crushed ice and blend until
smooth. Pour into cinnamon-
sugar-rimmed parfait glass.
Garnish with a cinnamon
stick and a straw.

FROZEN CITRON NEON

1 1/2 oz. Citrus-flavored
    Vodka
1 oz. Melon Liqueur
1/2 oz. Blue Curaçao
1/2 oz. Lime Juice
1/2 oz. Superfine Sugar (or
    Simple Syrup)
1/2 oz. Lemon Juice

Combine all ingredients in
blender with 1 cup of
crushed ice and blend until
smooth. Pour into parfait
glass. Garnish with a lemon
slice and a maraschino
cherry.

FROZEN DAIQUIRI

1 1/2 oz. Light Rum
1 tbsp. Triple Sec
1 1/2 oz. Lime Juice
1 tsp. Sugar

Combine all ingredients in
blender with 1 cup of
crushed ice and blend until
smooth. Pour into Cham-
pagne flute. Top with a
maraschino cherry.

FROZEN FUZZY

1 oz. Peach Schnapps
$1/2$ oz. Triple Sec
$1/2$ oz. Lime Juice
$1/2$ oz. Grenadine
1 splash Lemon-lime Soda

Combine all ingredients in blender with 1 cup of crushed ice and blend until smooth. Pour into Champagne flute. Garnish with a lime wedge.

FROZEN MARGARITA

$1 1/2$ oz. Tequila
$1/2$ oz. Triple Sec
1 oz. Lemon Juice or
    Lime Juice

Combine all ingredients in blender with 1 cup of crushed ice and blend until smooth. Pour into cocktail glass. Garnish with a slice of lemon or lime.

FROZEN MATADOR

$1 1/2$ oz. Tequila
2 oz. Pineapple Juice
1 tbsp. Lime Juice

Combine all ingredients in blender with 1 cup of crushed ice and blend until smooth. Pour into old-fashioned glass. Add a pineapple stick.

FROZEN MINT DAIQUIRI

2 oz. Light Rum
1 tbsp. Lime Juice
6 Mint Leaves
1 tsp. Sugar

Combine all ingredients in blender with 1 cup of crushed ice and blend until smooth. Pour into old-fashioned glass.

FROZEN PINEAPPLE DAIQUIRI

$1 1/2$ oz. Light Rum
4 Pineapple Chunks
1 tbsp. Lime Juice
$1/2$ tsp. Sugar

Combine all ingredients in blender with 1 cup of crushed ice and blend until smooth. Pour into Champagne flute.

FRUITY SMASH

1 pint Vanilla Ice Cream
$1/3$ cup Cherry-flavored
    Brandy
$1/3$ cup Crème de Banana

Combine all ingredients in blender with 1 cup of crushed ice and blend until smooth. Pour into large cocktail glasses. Garnish with maraschino cherries. (Makes 4 to 6 servings.)

GAELIC COFFEE

¾ oz. Irish Whiskey
¾ oz. Irish Cream Liqueur
1½ oz. Crème de Cacao
   (Brown)
2 oz. Milk
1 tsp. Instant Coffee

Combine all ingredients in blender with 1 cup of crushed ice and blend until smooth. Pour into Irish coffee cup. Top with whipped cream and sprinkle with green crème de menthe for color.

GEORGIO

2 oz. Coffee Liqueur
2 oz. Irish Cream Liqueur
1 Banana, ripe
½ cup Light Cream

Combine all ingredients in blender with 1 cup of crushed ice and blend until smooth. Pour equal amounts into 2 parfait glasses. Top with whipped cream and a light dusting of cocoa. Garnish with a sprig of fresh mint. (Makes 2 servings.)

GULF STREAM

1 oz. Blue Curaçao
3 oz. Champagne
½ oz. Light Rum
½ oz. Brandy
6 oz. Lemonade
1 oz. Lime Juice

Combine all ingredients in blender with 1 cup of crushed ice and blend until smooth. Pour into sugar-rimmed parfait glass. Garnish with a whole strawberry.

HUMMER

1 oz. Coffee Liqueur
1 oz. Light Rum
2 large scoops Vanilla Ice
   Cream

Combine all ingredients in blender until smooth. Serve in highball glass.

ICED COFFEE À L'ORANGE

1 qt. Vanilla Ice Cream
4 tsps. Instant Coffee
1 cup Triple Sec

Combine all ingredients in blender until smooth. Pour into parfait glasses. Garnish with orange slices. (Makes 5 to 6 servings.)

ICY RUMMED CACAO

1 qt. Vanilla Ice Cream
1/2 cup Dark Rum
1/2 cup Crème de Cacao
   (Brown)

Combine all ingredients in
blender until smooth. Pour
into parfait glasses. Garnish
with shaved chocolate.
(Makes 4 to 6 servings.)

IRISH DREAM

1/2 oz. Hazelnut Liqueur
1/2 oz. Irish Cream Liqueur
3/4 oz. Crème de Cacao
   (Brown)
4 oz. Vanilla Ice Cream

Combine all ingredients in
blender with 1 cup of
crushed ice and blend until
smooth. Pour into frosted pilsner glass. Top with whipped
cream and chocolate sprinkles.

ITALIAN DREAM

1 1/2 oz. Irish Cream Liqueur
1/2 oz. Amaretto
2 oz. Light Cream

Combine all ingredients in
blender with 1 cup of
crushed ice and blend until
smooth. Pour into parfait
glass.

JACK'S JAM

1/2 oz. Peach Schnapps
1/2 oz. Apple Schnapps
1/2 oz. Strawberry Liqueur
1/4 oz. Banana Liqueur
2 oz. Lemon Juice
1 oz. Orange Juice
2 tbsps. Powdered Sugar

Combine all ingredients in
blender with 1 cup of
crushed ice and blend until
smooth. Pour into parfait
glass. Garnish with a sprig of
fresh mint and a maraschino
cherry.

JAMAICAN BANANA

1/2 oz. Light Rum
1/2 oz. Crème de Cacao
   (White)
1/2 oz. Crème de Banana
2 scoops Vanilla Ice Cream
1 oz. Half-and-Half
1 Whole Banana

Combine all ingredients in
blender with 1 cup of
crushed ice and blend until
smooth. Pour into large
brandy snifter and garnish
with 2 slices banana, a strawberry, and fresh-grated
nutmeg.

KOKOMO JOE

1 oz. Light Rum
1 oz. Banana Liqueur
5 oz. Orange Juice
3 oz. Piña Colada Mix
½ Banana

Combine all ingredients in blender with 1 cup of crushed ice and blend until smooth. Garnish with a slice of orange.

LEBANESE SNOW

1½ oz. Strawberry Liqueur
1 oz. Crème de Banana
1 oz. Light Cream

Combine all ingredients in blender with 1 cup of crushed ice and blend until smooth. Garnish with a strawberry.

LICORICE MIST

1¼ oz. Sambuca
½ oz. Coconut Liqueur
2 oz. Light Cream

Combine all ingredients in blender with 1 cup of crushed ice and blend until smooth. Pour into parfait glass. Cut off ends of licorice stick and use it as a straw/garnish.

LONELY NIGHT

¾ oz. Coffee Liqueur
1¼ oz. Irish Cream Liqueur
1¼ oz. Hazelnut Liqueur
1 scoop Vanilla Ice Cream

Combine all ingredients in blender with 1 cup of crushed ice and blend until smooth. Pour into parfait glass. Top with whipped cream and shaved chocolate.

MARASCHINO CHERRY

1 oz. Rum
½ oz. Amaretto
½ oz. Peach Schnapps
1 oz. Cranberry Juice
1 oz. Pineapple Juice
1 dash Grenadine

Combine all ingredients in blender with 1 cup of crushed ice and blend until smooth. Garnish with whipped cream and a maraschino cherry.

MAUI BREEZE

½ oz. Amaretto
½ oz. Triple Sec
½ oz. Brandy
½ oz. Superfine Sugar (or Simple Syrup)
½ oz. Lemon Juice
2 oz. Orange Juice
2 oz. Guava Juice

Combine all ingredients in blender with 1 cup of crushed ice and blend until smooth. Pour into parfait glass. Garnish with a pineapple spear, a maraschino cherry, and an orchid.

MISSISSIPPI MUD

1 1/2 oz. Whiskey (Tennessee
   Sour Mash)
1 1/2 oz. Coffee Liqueur
2 scoops Vanilla Ice Cream

Combine all ingredients in
blender until smooth. Spoon
into cocktail glass and top
with shaved chocolate.

MONT BLANC

1 oz. Black Raspberry
   Liqueur
1 oz. Vodka
1 oz. Light Cream
1 scoop Vanilla Ice Cream

Combine all ingredients in
blender until smooth. Pour
into oversized red-wine glass.

NUTTY COLADA

3 oz. Amaretto
3 tbsps. Coconut Milk
3 tbsps. Crushed Pineapple

Combine all ingredients in
blender with 1 cup of
crushed ice and blend until
smooth. Pour into collins
glass and serve with a straw.

ORANGE BLOSSOM SPECIAL

1 oz. Peach Schnapps
2 1/2 oz. Lemon-lime Soda
3 oz. Orange Sherbet
1 1/2 oz. Vanilla Ice Cream
2 1/2 oz. Light Cream

Combine all ingredients in
blender with 1 cup of
crushed ice and blend until
smooth. Pour into parfait
glass and garnish with a
maraschino cherry and an
orange slice.

ORANGE TREE

1 1/2 oz. Amaretto
3/4 oz. Crème de Noyaux
1 1/2 oz. Orange Juice
3/4 oz. Vanilla Ice Cream

Combine all ingredients in
blender until smooth. Pour
into parfait glass. Top with
whipped cream and garnish
with a thin slice of orange.

OVER THE RAINBOW

2 oz. Spiced Rum
1 oz. Orange Curaçao
2 scoops Rainbow Sherbet
4 slices Fresh Peach,
   peeled
2 Strawberries

Combine all ingredients in
blender with 1 cup ice and
blend until smooth. Pour
into parfait glass. Garnish
with a strawberry and a
peach slice.

PEACH MELBA FREEZE

¾ oz. Peach Schnapps
¾ oz. Black Raspberry
   Liqueur
¾ oz. Hazelnut Liqueur
4 oz. Vanilla Ice Cream
¾ oz. Light Cream
1 oz. Melba Sauce (or
   Raspberry Jam)

Combine all ingredients in
blender and blend until
smooth. Pour into parfait
glass. Garnish with a peach
slice.

PEACHY AMARETTO

1 cup Vanilla Ice Cream
1 cup Peaches
1 cup Amaretto

Combine all ingredients in
blender and blend until
smooth. Pour into parfait
glasses. (Makes 3 to 4 servings.)

PEPPERMINT PENGUIN

½ oz. Crème de Menthe
   (Green)
½ oz. Chocolate Mint
   Liqueur
3 Chocolate Sandwich
   Cookies
3 oz. Light Cream

Combine all ingredients in
blender with 1 cup of
crushed ice and blend until
smooth. Pour into hurricane
or parfait glass. Top with
whipped cream. Garnish with
a cookie and a maraschino
cherry.

PINEAPPLE BANANA REFRESHER

2 cups Pineapple Juice
1 cup Pineapple Sherbet
½ cup Crème de Banana
½ cup Dark Rum

Combine all ingredients in
blender until smooth. Pour
into highball glasses. Garnish
with a pineapple wedge and
a banana slice. (Makes 4 to 5
servings.)

PISTACHIO MINT ICE CREAM

1 oz. Hazelnut Liqueur
½ oz. Crème de Menthe
   (Green)
1 oz. Vodka
2 oz. Heavy Cream

Shake all ingredients with ice.
Strain into cocktail glass and
garnish with a mint leaf.

RASPBERRY CHEESECAKE

1 tbsp. Cream Cheese,
   softened
1 oz. Crème de Cacao
   (White)
1 oz. Black Raspberry
   Liqueur
2 scoops Vanilla Ice Cream

Combine all ingredients in
blender with 1 cup of
crushed ice and blend until
smooth. Pour into parfait
glass.

SMOOTH MOVE

1 oz. Rum
2 oz. Pineapple Juice
2 oz. Prune Juice
1 oz. Superfine Sugar (or Simple Syrup)
1 oz. Lemon Juice

Combine all ingredients in blender with 1 cup of crushed ice and blend until smooth. Pour into sugar-rimmed parfait glass. Garnish with a pineapple spear and a maraschino cherry.

SPARKLING STRAWBERRY MIMOSA

2 oz. Frozen Sliced Strawberries in Syrup, Partially Thawed
2 oz. Orange Juice
4 oz. Champagne, Chilled

Combine all ingredients in blender until smooth. Pour into ice-filled parfait glass. Fill with Champagne and garnish with a whole strawberry and an orange slice.

STRAWBERRIES AND CREAM

1 oz. Strawberry Schnapps
1½ tbsps. Sugar
2 oz. Half-and-Half
2 Whole Strawberries

Place first three ingredients in blender with 2 cups crushed ice and blend until smooth. Add strawberries and blend for 10 seconds. Pour into parfait glass and serve with a straw. Garnish with a fresh strawberry.

STRAWBERRY ALEXANDRA

5 oz. Frozen Sliced Strawberries in Syrup, Partially Thawed
1 scoop Vanilla Ice Cream
1 oz. Crème de Cacao (White)
1 oz. Brandy

Combine all ingredients in blender and blend until smooth. Pour into stemmed glass. Top with sweetened whipped cream. Garnish with chocolate curls. Serve with a straw and a spoon.

STRAWBERRY BANANA SPRITZ

1 pint Vanilla Ice Cream
1 cup Strawberries, Fresh or Frozen
1 cup Crème de Banana
10 oz. Club Soda

Combine all ingredients in blender and blend until smooth. Pour into parfait glasses. Garnish with whole strawberries. (Makes 4 to 6 servings.)

STRAWBERRY DAWN

1 oz. Gin
1 oz. Cream of Coconut
4 Fresh Strawberries (or ⅓ cup Frozen Strawberries)

Combine all ingredients in blender with 1 cup of crushed ice and blend until smooth. Pour into cocktail glass. Garnish with a strawberry slice and a mint sprig.

FROZEN DRINKS

STRAWBERRY SHORTCAKE

1 oz. Amaretto
3/4 oz. Crème de Cacao
(White)
3 oz. Strawberries in Syrup
5 oz. Vanilla Ice Cream

Combine all ingredients in
blender until smooth. Pour
into oversized red-wine glass.
Top with whipped cream and
garnish with a fresh strawberry.

SURF'S UP

1/2 oz. Crème de Banana
1/2 oz. Crème de Cacao
(White)
5 oz. Pineapple Juice
1 oz. Light Cream

Shake all ingredients with ice.
Pour into parfait glass. Garnish
with an orange slice and a
maraschino cherry.

SWEET-TART

2 oz. Vodka
3 oz. Cranberry Juice
3 oz. Pineapple Juice
1 dash Lime Juice

Combine all ingredients in
blender with 1 cup of
crushed ice and blend until
smooth. Garnish with a lime
wheel.

TENNESSEE WALTZ

1 1/4 oz. Peach Schnapps
2 oz. Pineapple Juice
1 oz. Passion Fruit Juice
4 oz. Vanilla Ice Cream

Combine all ingredients in
blender until smooth. Pour
into parfait glass. Garnish
with whipped cream and a
strawberry.

TEQUILA FROST

1 1/4 oz. Tequila
1 1/4 oz. Pineapple Juice
1 1/4 oz. Grapefruit Juice
1/2 oz. Honey
1/2 oz. Grenadine
2 oz. Vanilla Ice Milk

Combine all ingredients in
blender until smooth. Pour
into parfait glass. Garnish
with an orange slice and a
maraschino cherry.

TIDAL WAVE

1 3/4 oz. Melon Liqueur
1 oz. Pineapple Juice
1 oz. Orange Juice
1/2 oz. Coconut Syrup
3/4 oz. Superfine Sugar (or
Simple Syrup)
3/4 oz. Lemon Juice
1/2 oz. Light Rum

Combine all ingredients in
blender with 1 cup of
crushed ice and blend until
smooth. Pour into parfait
glass. Garnish with a lime
wheel and a maraschino
cherry.

TIDBIT

1 oz. Gin
1 scoop Vanilla Ice Cream
1 dash Dry Sherry

Blend ingredients in blender at low speed and pour into highball glass.

TROLLEY CAR

1¼ oz. Amaretto
2 oz. Fresh Strawberries
2 scoops Vanilla Ice Cream

Combine all ingredients in blender until smooth. Pour into parfait glass and garnish with a fresh strawberry.

HOT DRINKS

$\mathbf{H}$ ot Toddies, simple mixtures of hot water, sugar or
honey, and a single spirit—usually Bourbon, but
any whiskey, rum, brandy, or even gin could be
used—are remembered by many as old-fashioned cold reme-
dies, especially by people who remember the first edition of
this book. While it was thought that the spirit made you feel
better, it was really the heat combined with the spirit that
did the trick. Indeed, Toddies are one of those classic com-
forts that we are loath to abandon even today. That's because
hot drinks are both comforting and stimulating. You don't
need a fireplace to feel the warmth of the hot drinks found
on the following pages—though, if you have a fireplace, all
the better—from the classic Irish Coffee to the ethereal Hot
Buttered Rum.

Many hot drinks employ coffee as their base, laced with
either whiskey, rum, brandy, or liqueurs, or a combination of several of these. However, virtually any heated beverage can make a
great hot drink, and in this section you'll find recipes made with
hot chocolate, tea, cider, steamed milk, and even orange juice.

Whichever you choose, remember that the best hot drinks are made with high-quality ingredients: piping hot, freshly-brewed coffee or tea, old-fashioned hot-chocolate made with real cocoa and milk instead of a mix, cream you've whipped yourself, and fresh spices.

Lastly, heed the temperature of these drinks, take your time with them, and prolong the pleasure they bring.

AMARETTO TEA

6 oz. Hot Tea
2 oz. Amaretto

Pour hot tea into parfait glass, putting a spoon in the glass to prevent cracking. Add Amaretto, but do not stir. Top with whipped cream.

AMERICAN GROG

1 cube Sugar
¾ oz. Lemon Juice
1½ oz. Light Rum

Pour ingredients into hot mug and fill with hot water. Stir.

APRIHOT

3 oz. Apricot-flavored Brandy
3 oz. Boiling Water

Combine in coffee mug with a dash of cinnamon, and garnish with an orange or lemon slice.

BLACK GOLD

¼ oz. Triple Sec
¼ oz. Amaretto
¼ oz. Irish Cream Liqueur
¼ oz. Hazelnut Liqueur
4 oz. Hot Coffee
1 dash Cinnamon Schnapps

Pour first four ingredients into Irish coffee glass. Add coffee and schnapps and stir. Top with whipped cream and shaved chocolate. Serve with a cinnamon stick as stirrer.

BLUE BLAZER

2½ oz. Blended Whiskey
2½ oz. Boiling Water
1 tsp. Sugar

Use two large, silver-plated mugs with handles. Put the whiskey into one mug and the boiling water into the other. Ignite the whiskey and, while it is flaming, mix both ingredients by pouring them four or five times from one mug to the other. If done well, this will have the appearance of a continuous stream of liquid fire. Sweeten with sugar and serve with a twist of lemon peel. Serve in 4-oz. punch cup.

BOSTON CARIBBEAN COFFEE

1 oz. Crème de Cacao (Brown)
1 oz. Dark Rum
Hot Coffee

Pour liqueur and rum into sugar-rimmed Irish coffee glass. Fill with freshly brewed coffee. Top with whipped cream and sprinkle with cinnamon. Garnish with a cinnamon stick as a stirrer.

BRANDY BLAZER

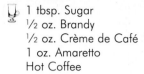

1 cube Sugar
1 piece Orange Peel
2 oz. Brandy

Combine all ingredients in old-fashioned glass. Light the liquid with match, stir with long spoon for a few seconds, and strain into hot punch cup.

CAFFÈ DI AMARETTO

1 oz. Amaretto
1 cup Hot Coffee

Add Amaretto to a cup of hot black coffee, then transfer to an Irish coffee glass. Top with whipped cream.

CAFÉ L'ORANGE

1/2 oz. Cognac
1/2 oz. Triple Sec
1 oz. Mandarine Napoléon
4 oz. Hot Coffee

Pour cognac and liqueurs into Irish coffee glass. Add coffee. Top with whipped cream and garnish with finely chopped orange rind.

CAPRICCIO

1 tbsp. Sugar
1/2 oz. Brandy
1/2 oz. Crème de Café
1 oz. Amaretto
Hot Coffee

Put sugar in bottom of Irish coffee glass rimmed with cinnamon-sugar. Add brandy and liqueurs. Fill 3/4 full with coffee. Top with whipped cream, toasted almond slices, and a maraschino cherry.

CHOCOLATE COFFEE KISS

3/4 oz. Coffee Liqueur
3/4 oz. Irish Cream Liqueur
1 splash Crème de Cocoa (Brown)
1 splash Mandarine Napoléon
1 1/2 oz. Chocolate Syrup
Hot Coffee

Combine first five ingredients in Irish coffee glass, and then fill with coffee. Top with whipped cream and garnish with shaved chocolate and a maraschino cherry.

HOT BRICK TODDY • 193

COFFEE NUDGE (AKA KIOKE COFFEE)

½ oz. Brandy
½ oz. Coffee Liqueur
½ oz. Crème de Cacao (dark)
5 oz. Hot Coffee

In a pre-warmed coffee mug, add the brandy, coffee liqueur, and crème de cacao. Pour in the coffee. Top with a dollop of whipped cream. Optional: Sprinkle grated chocolate as a garnish. Serve with cocktail straws.

DOUBLEMINT

1 oz. Spearmint Schnapps
Hot Coffee
1 dash Crème de Menthe (Green)

Pour schnapps into Irish coffee glass and then fill with coffee. Top with whipped cream. Add crème de menthe for color.

GIN TODDY (HOT)

1 cube Sugar
Boiling Water
2 oz. Gin

Put sugar into punch cup and fill two-thirds full with boiling water. Add gin. Stir and garnish with a slice of lemon. Garnish with fresh-grated nutmeg on top.

HANDICAPPER'S CHOICE

1 oz. Irish Whiskey
1 oz. Amaretto
5 oz. Hot Coffee

Pour whiskey and Amaretto into Irish coffee glass and fill with hot coffee. Top with whipped cream.

HOT BRANDY ALEXANDER

¾ oz. Brandy
¾ oz. Crème de Cacao (Brown)
4 oz. Steamed Milk

Pour ingredients into heated mug. Top with whipped cream and chocolate shavings.

HOT BRANDY TODDY

1 cube Sugar
Boiling Water
2 oz. Brandy

Put sugar in coffee mug and fill two-thirds with boiling water. Add brandy and stir. Garnish with a slice of lemon and fresh-grated nutmeg.

HOT BRICK TODDY

1 tsp. Butter
1 tsp. Powdered Sugar
3 pinches Cinnamon
1 oz. Whiskey
1 oz. Hot Water

Put first three ingredients into punch cup. Dissolve thoroughly. Add whiskey, fill with boiling water, and stir.

HOT BUTTERED RUM

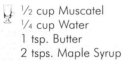

1 tsp. Brown Sugar
Boiling Water
1 tbsp. Butter
2 oz. Dark Rum

Put sugar into punch cup and fill two-thirds with boiling water. Add butter and rum. Stir and garnish with fresh-grated nutmeg on top.

HOT BUTTERED WINE

½ cup Muscatel
¼ cup Water
1 tsp. Butter
2 tsps. Maple Syrup

Heat wine and water just to simmering—do not boil. Pre-heat Irish coffee glass with boiling water. Pour heated wine mixture into glass and add butter and maple syrup. Stir and garnish with fresh-grated nutmeg on top.

HOT CINNAMON ROLL

Hot Apple Cider
1½ oz. Cinnamon
Schnapps

Pour hot cider into Irish coffee glass. Add schnapps. Top with whipped cream. Add a cinnamon stick as a stirrer.

HOT GOLD

6 oz. Very Warm Orange
Juice
3 oz. Amaretto

Pour orange juice into red-wine glass or mug. Add Amaretto and garnish with cinnamon stick as stirrer.

HOT KISS

6 oz. Hot Coffee
½ oz. Crème de Menthe
(White)
1 oz. Irish Whiskey
½ oz. Crème de Cacao
(White)

Pour liqueurs and whiskey into Irish coffee glass. Add coffee and stir. Top with whipped cream and garnish with a chocolate-covered mint.

INDIAN SUMMER

2 oz. Apple Schnapps
Hot Apple Cider

Wet rim of sour glass and dip in cinnamon. Add schnapps and top off with cider. Add a cinnamon stick, if desired.

IRISH COFFEE

1½ oz. Irish Whiskey
Hot Coffee
Sugar to taste

Into Irish coffee glass rimmed with sugar, pour Irish whiskey. Fill to within ½ inch of top with coffee. Add sugar, if desired. Cover surface to brim with whipped cream.

HOT DRINKS

ITALIAN COFFEE

½ oz. Amaretto
Hot Coffee
1½ tbsps. Coffee Ice
  Cream

Pour Amaretto into Irish coffee glass. Fill with hot coffee. Top with coffee ice cream and sprinkle with ground coriander.

JAMAICA COFFEE

1 oz. Coffee-flavored
  Brandy
¾ oz. Light Rum
Hot Coffee

Pour brandy and rum into coffee mug. Fill with hot coffee. Sweeten to taste. Top with whipped cream and fresh-grated nutmeg.

MEXICAN COFFEE

1 oz. Coffee Liqueur
½ oz. Tequila
5 oz. Hot Coffee

Stir coffee liqueur and tequila in coffee cup, add coffee, and top with whipped cream.

MEXITALY COFFEE

¾ oz. Coffee Liqueur
¾ oz. Amaretto
Hot Coffee

Dip rim of Irish coffee glass in maraschino cherry juice, then in cinnamon-sugar. Pour liqueurs into glass and add coffee. Top with whipped cream and shaved chocolate.

MULLED CLARET

1 cube Sugar
1 oz. Lemon Juice
1 dash Bitters
1 tsp. Mixed Cinnamon
  and Nutmeg
5 oz. Claret or Red Wine

Put all ingredients into a metal mug. Heat poker red-hot and hold in liquid until boiling and serve—or just warm on a stove.

RAZZMATAZZ

1 oz. Black Raspberry
  Liqueur
½ oz. Crème de Cassis
½ oz. Coffee Liqueur
Hot Coffee

Pour liqueurs into Irish coffee glass. Add coffee. Top with whipped cream and garnish with berries in season.

RUEDESHEIM KAFFE

3 cubes Sugar
1½ oz. Brandy
Hot Coffee

Place sugar cubes in heat-proof coffee cup. Add brandy and set aflame. Allow to burn for a good minute, and then fill with coffee. Top with whipped cream and sprinkle with grated chocolate.

RUM TODDY (HOT)

1 cube Sugar
Boiling Water
2 oz. Light or Dark Rum

Put sugar into Irish coffee cup and fill ⅔ full with boiling water. Add rum and stir. Garnish with a slice of lemon and fresh-grated nutmeg.

RUSSIAN COFFEE

½ oz. Coffee Liqueur
½ oz. Hazelnut Liqueur
¼ oz. Vodka
Hot Coffee

Pour liqueurs and vodka into Irish coffee glass. Add coffee. Top with whipped cream.

SNOW BUNNY

1½ oz. Triple Sec
Hot Chocolate

Pour triple sec into a heavy mug. Fill with hot chocolate. Garnish with a stick of cinnamon for flavoring and to use as a stirrer.

SPANISH COFFEE

1 oz. Spanish Brandy
Hot Coffee

Add coffee to brandy in mug and top with whipped cream.

STEAMING PEACH

2 oz. Peach Schnapps
4 oz. Hot Water

Pour schnapps into snifter. Add hot water and stir. Float an orange slice as a garnish.

WHISKEY TODDY (HOT)

1 cube Sugar
Boiling Water
2 oz. Blended Whiskey

Put sugar into Irish coffee glass and fill ⅔ full with boiling water. Add whiskey and stir. Garnish with a slice of lemon and fresh-grated nutmeg.

► Lover's Kiss and Pousse Café

► Limoncello Sunrise

▶ Angel's Kiss and Sex on the Beach

► Cranberry Cooler and Frozen Cappuccino

▶ Hot Buttered Rum

▶ Ambassador's Morning Lift

▶ Champagne Punch

▶ Kir Royale

▶ Sunshine Splash

EGGNOGS AND PUNCHES

Eggnog first became popular during colonial times, when rum was the favorite spirit of the early Americans, who mixed it with milk, eggs, and sugar. Over the years, whiskey and brandy have been used as substitutes for rum, depending on personal preference. Today, eggnog is all but a holiday drink enjoyed during the colder months, if at all, which is a colossal shame. This is probably the result of the proliferation of pasteurized prepared eggnogs, which are seldom as good as homemade (but a heck of a lot easier to serve), coupled with concerns over salmonella poisoning associated with raw eggs.

Fortunately, there are three solutions to the raw egg problem: One, use a prepared mix such as Mr. Boston Egg Nog. Two, use pasteurized eggs, which can be found next to the regular eggs at good supermarkets. Three, if using regular eggs that have not been pasteurized, cook the egg mixture very slowly to 160° Fahrenheit, at which point the mixture thickens enough to coat a spoon, and then refrigerate immediately. Also, if a recipe calls for folding raw, beaten egg whites into the eggnog, you can use either pasteurized egg whites (separated by hand from the yolks) or pre-packaged egg whites found in the supermarket, which have already been pasteurized. Hopefully, you'll feel inspired—and safe enough—to make your own homemade eggnog (see page 200) before transforming it into one of the following recipes.

Punches are an ideal way to serve a large number of guests without making individual drinks. Since they are usually made with only a single spirit, punches are also a great budget-conscious party beverage. Punch can be made with virtually any spirit, as well as wine, Champagne, and even beer. Cold punches are popular any time of year, while hot punches are especially appropriate for winter get-togethers. Recipes for both can be found under separate headings within this section, serving anywhere from 6 guests to more than 40. Also included are several nonalcoholic punch recipes.

While cold punches in smaller quantities can be mixed in and served from a pitcher, larger recipes are usually served in a punch bowl from which guests can help themselves. Use a block of ice, not ice cubes, to keep punch chilled. Ice blocks can be elaborately decorative, frozen in gelatin molds with embedded fruits, or made simply by freezing water in a plastic freezer container.

EGGNOGS

AMBASSADOR'S MORNING LIFT

32 oz. Eggnog
6 oz. Cognac
3 oz. Jamaica Rum
3 oz. Crème de Cacao
(Brown)

Combine all ingredients in large punch bowl and serve. Sprinkle fresh-grated nutmeg on top of each serving. Brandy or Bourbon may be substituted for Cognac.
(Makes 10 to 12 servings.)

BALTIMORE EGGNOG

32 oz. Eggnog
5 oz. Brandy
5 oz. Jamaica Rum
5 oz. Madeira Wine

Combine all ingredients in large punch bowl and serve. Sprinkle fresh-grated nutmeg on top of each serving.
(Makes 10 to 12 servings.)

BRANDY EGGNOG

32 oz. Eggnog
12 oz. Brandy

Combine all ingredients in large punch bowl and serve. Sprinkle fresh-grated nutmeg on top of each serving.
(Makes 10 to 12 servings.)

BREAKFAST EGGNOG

32 oz. Eggnog
10 oz. Apricot-flavored
Brandy
2½ oz. Triple Sec

Combine all ingredients in large punch bowl and serve. Sprinkle fresh-grated nutmeg on top of each serving.
(Makes 10 to 12 servings.)

CHRISTMAS YULE EGGNOG

32 oz. Eggnog
12 oz. Whiskey
1½ oz. Light Rum

Combine all ingredients in large punch bowl and serve. Sprinkle fresh-grated nutmeg on top of each serving.
(Makes 10 to 12 servings.)

EGG CRUSHER

8 oz. Eggnog
1 oz. Light Rum
1 oz. Coffee Liqueur

Stir with ice and strain into oversized snifter. Sprinkle with fresh-grated nutmeg.

EGGNOG (HOMEMADE)

6 Eggs
1 cup Sugar
$1/2$ tsp. Salt
1 cup Golden Rum
1 pint Half-and-Half
1 pint Milk

In a large bowl, beat eggs until light and foamy. Add sugar and salt, beating until thick and lemon colored. Stir in rum, cream, and milk. Chill at least 3 hours. Garnish with a sprinkle of fresh-grated nutmeg.

FROSTY NOG

$1/2$ cup Eggnog
2 tbsps. Sugar

Combine eggnog and sugar in blender. Slowly add up to 3 cups of ice, blending at medium speed, until smooth. Pour into parfait glass. Garnish with almond slivers and fresh-grated nutmeg.

IMPERIAL EGGNOG

32 oz. Eggnog
10 oz. Brandy
2 oz. Apricot-flavored Brandy

Combine all ingredients in large punch bowl and serve. Sprinkle fresh-grated nutmeg on top of each serving. (Makes 10 to 12 servings.)

MAPLE EGGNOG

32 oz. Eggnog
$1/2$ cup Maple Syrup

Combine all ingredients in large pitcher and chill. Stir before serving. Garnish with fresh-grated nutmeg, if desired. (Makes 8 servings.)

NASHVILLE EGGNOG

32 oz. Eggnog
6 oz. Whiskey (Bourbon)
3 oz. Brandy
3 oz. Jamaica Rum

Combine all ingredients in large punch bowl and serve. Sprinkle fresh-grated nutmeg on top of each serving. (Makes 10 to 12 servings.)

NOG DE CACAO

$1 1/2$ oz. Crème de Cacao
$1 1/2$ oz. Eggnog

Pour over ice in old-fashioned glass and stir.

PORT WINE EGGNOG

32 oz. Eggnog
18 oz. Port Wine

Combine all ingredients in large punch bowl and serve. Sprinkle fresh-grated nutmeg on top of each serving. (Makes 10 to 12 servings.)

RUM EGGNOG

32 oz. Eggnog
12 oz. Light Rum

Combine all ingredients in large punch bowl and serve. Sprinkle fresh-grated nutmeg on top of each serving. (Makes 10 to 12 servings.)

RUSSIAN NOG

1 oz. Vodka
1 oz. Coffee Liqueur
1 oz. Eggnog

Pour over ice in old-fashioned glass and stir.

SHERRY EGGNOG

32 oz. Eggnog
18 oz. Cream Sherry

Combine all ingredients in large punch bowl and serve. Sprinkle fresh-grated nutmeg on top of each serving. (Makes 10 to 12 servings.)

WHISKEY EGGNOG

32 oz. Eggnog
12 oz. Blended Whiskey

Combine all ingredients in large punch bowl and serve. Sprinkle fresh-grated nutmeg on top of each serving. (Makes 10 to 12 servings.)

COLD PUNCHES

APRICOT ORANGE FIZZ

1 1/2 cups Orange Juice
1/2 cup Light Rum
1/4 cup Apricot-flavored Brandy
2 tbsps. Lime Juice
Club Soda

Combine first three ingredients in pitcher and stir. Pour into ice-filled collins glasses about 2/3 full. Top with club soda. Stir and garnish with lime slices. (Makes 6 servings.)

BOMBAY PUNCH

3 cups Lemon Juice
Superfine Sugar (or Simple Syrup)
32 oz. Brandy
32 oz. Dry Sherry
1/2 cup Maraschino Liqueur
1/2 cup Triple Sec
4 bottles (750-ml) Champagne, Chilled
64 oz. Chilled Club Soda

Add enough sugar/syrup to sweeten lemon juice. Pour over a large block of ice in punch bowl and stir. Then add remaining ingredients. Stir well and garnish with fruits in season. Serve in punch cups. (Makes 60 servings.)

EGGNOGS AND PUNCHES

BOOM BOOM PUNCH

64 oz. Light Rum
32 oz. Orange Juice
1 bottle (750-ml) Sweet
   Vermouth
1 bottle (750-ml) Cham-
   pagne, Chilled

Pour all ingredients except
Champagne into punch bowl
over large block of ice. Stir.
Top with Champagne. Gar-
nish with sliced bananas.
(Makes 36 servings.)

BRANDY PUNCH

3 cups Lemon Juice
2 cups Orange Juice
Superfine Sugar (or Simple
   Syrup)
1 cup Grenadine
32 oz. Club Soda
1 cup Triple Sec
1.75 liters Brandy
2 cups Tea (optional)

In pitcher add enough
sugar/syrup to sweeten
lemon and orange juice and
mix with grenadine and club
soda. Pour over large block of
ice in punch bowl and stir
well. Then add triple sec,
brandy, and tea, if desired.
Stir well and garnish with
fruits in season. (Makes 32
servings.)

BRUNCH PUNCH

3 qts. Chilled Tomato Juice
1 liter Light or Dark Rum
2½ tsps. Worcestershire
   Sauce
5 oz. Lemon or Lime Juice
Salt and Pepper to taste

Combine all ingredients in
large container and stir. Pour
over block of ice in punch
bowl and garnish with thinly
sliced lemons or limes.
(Makes 40 servings.)

CAPE CODDER PUNCH

3 bottles (32-oz.) Cranberry-
   apple Drink
3 cups Vodka
2 cups Orange Juice
⅔ cup Lemon Juice
½ cup Sugar
1 bottle (28-oz.) Mineral
   Water, chilled

Combine first five ingredients, stirring until sugar dissolves and chill. Stir in
mineral water just before
serving. (Makes 40 servings.)

CARDINAL PUNCH

3 cups Lemon Juice
Superfine Sugar (or Simple
    Syrup)
16 oz. Brandy
16 oz. Light Rum
1 split Champagne, Chilled
64 oz. Red Wine
32 oz. Club Soda
8 oz. Sweet Vermouth
16 oz. Strong Tea
    (optional)

Add enough sugar/syrup to
sweeten lemon juice. Pour
over large block of ice in
punch bowl and stir well.
Then add remaining ingredients. Stir well and garnish
with fruits in season. (Makes
42 servings.)

CHAMPAGNE CUP

4 tsps. Superfine Sugar (or
    Simple Syrup)
6 oz. Club Soda
1 oz. Triple Sec
2 oz. Brandy
16 oz. Champagne,
    Chilled

Fill large glass pitcher with
cubes of ice and all ingredients except Champagne. Stir
well, then add Champagne.
Stir well and garnish with
fruits in season and rind of
cucumber inserted on each
side of pitcher. Top with a
small bunch of mint. Serve in
red-wine glasses. (Makes 6
servings.)

CHAMPAGNE PUNCH

3 cups Lemon Juice
Superfine Sugar (or Simple
    Syrup)
1 cup Maraschino Liqueur
1 cup Triple Sec
16 oz. Brandy
2 bottles (750-ml) Cham-
    pagne, Chilled
16 oz. Club Soda
16 oz. Strong Tea
    (optional)

Add enough sugar/syrup to
sweeten lemon juice. Pour
over large block of ice in
punch bowl and stir well.
Then add remaining ingredients. Stir well and garnish
with fruits in season. (Makes
32 servings.)

CHAMPAGNE SHERBET PUNCH

3 cups Chilled Pineapple
    Juice
1/4 cup Lemon Juice
1 qt. Pineapple Sherbet
1 bottle (750-ml) Cham-
    pagne, Chilled

In a punch bowl combine
juices. Just before serving,
scoop sherbet into punch
bowl, then add Champagne.
Stir gently. (Makes 20 servings.)

CIDER CUP

4 tsps. Superfine Sugar (or
   Simple Syrup)
6 oz. Club Soda
1 oz. Triple Sec
2 oz. Brandy
16 oz. Apple Cider

Fill large glass pitcher with
ice. Stir in the ingredients
and garnish with fruits in
season and a rind of
cucumber inserted on each
side of pitcher. Top with a
small bunch of mint. Serve in
red-wine glasses. (Makes 6
servings.)

CLARET CUP

4 tsps. Superfine Sugar (or
   Simple Syrup)
6 oz. Club Soda
1 oz. Triple Sec
2 oz. Brandy
16 oz. Red Wine

Fill large glass pitcher with
ice. Stir in the ingredients
and garnish with fruits in
season and a rind of
cucumber inserted on each
side of pitcher. Top with a
small bunch of mint. Serve in
red-wine glasses. (Makes 6
servings.)

CITRUS-BEER PUNCH

6 Lemons
2 cups Sugar
2 cups Water
1 cup Chilled Grapefruit
   Juice
2 cans (12-oz.) Light Beer,
   chilled

Remove peel from lemons
and set aside. Juice lemons
(about 2 cups juice). In large
saucepan, stir together sugar
and water. Bring to boiling
and add reserved lemon peel.
Remove from heat. Cover
and let stand 5 minutes.
Remove and discard peel.
Add lemon juice and grapefruit juice to sugar mixture.
Transfer mixture to a 3-quart
pitcher; cover and chill. Just
before serving, add beer. Pour
into glass mugs over ice and
garnish with lemon slices.
(Makes 8 servings.)

CLARET PUNCH

3 cups Lemon Juice
Superfine Sugar (or Simple
   Syrup)
1 cup Triple Sec
16 oz. Brandy
3 bottles (750-ml) Red
   Wine
32 oz. Club Soda
32 oz. Strong Tea
   (optional)

Add enough sugar/syrup to
sweeten lemon juice. Pour
over large block of ice in
punch bowl and stir well.
Then add remaining ingredients. Stir and garnish with
fruits in season. (Makes 40
servings.)

EGGNOGS AND PUNCHES

EXTRA-KICK PUNCH

2 qts. Water
1 cup Brown Sugar
2 cups Dark Rum
1 cup Brandy
1 cup Lemon Juice
1 cup Pineapple Juice
¼ cup Peach Brandy

Combine water and brown sugar, stirring until sugar dissolves. Add remaining ingredients; chill. Pour over block of ice in punch bowl. (Makes 28 servings.)

FISH HOUSE PUNCH

3 cups Lemon Juice
Superfine Sugar (or Simple Syrup)
1½ liters Brandy
1 liter Peach-flavored Brandy
16 oz. Light Rum
32 oz. Club Soda
16 oz. Strong Tea (optional)

Add enough sugar/syrup to sweeten lemon juice. Pour over large block of ice in punch bowl and stir well. Then add remaining ingredients. Stir well and garnish with fruits in season. (Makes 40 servings.)

KENTUCKY PUNCH

12 oz. Frozen Orange Juice Concentrate, thawed and undiluted
12 oz. Frozen Lemonade Concentrate, thawed and undiluted
1 cup Lemon Juice
1 liter Whiskey (Bourbon)
1 bottle (2-liter) Lemon-lime Soda

Combine all ingredients except soda in large container and chill. Pour into punch bowl over large block of ice and stir in soda. (Makes 32 servings.)

LOVING CUP

4 tsps. Superfine Sugar (or Simple Syrup)
6 oz. Club Soda
1 oz. Triple Sec
2 oz. Brandy
16 oz. Red Wine

Fill large glass pitcher with ice and stir in the ingredients. Garnish with fruits in season and a rind of cucumber inserted on each side of the pitcher. Top with a small bunch of mint sprigs. (Makes 6 servings.)

MINT JULEP PUNCH

1 cup Mint Jelly
4 cups Water
3¼ cups Whiskey
   (Bourbon)
6 cups Pineapple Juice
½ cup Lime Juice
7 cups Lemon-lime Soda

Combine mint jelly and 2
cups of water in saucepan,
stirring over low heat until
jelly melts. Cool. Add
Bourbon, pineapple juice,
remaining water, and lime
juice; chill. To serve, pour
mixture over a block of ice in
punch bowl. Slowly pour in
soda, stirring gently. Garnish
with lime slices and fresh
mint leaves, if desired.
(Makes 44 servings.)

RHINE WINE CUP

4 tsps. Superfine Sugar (or
   Simple Syrup)
6 oz. Club Soda
1 oz. Triple Sec
2 oz. Brandy
16 oz. White Wine

Mix ingredients and pour
into large glass pitcher over
cubes of ice. Stir and garnish
with fruits in season. Insert a
rind of cucumber on each
side of pitcher. Top with mint
sprigs. Serve in red-wine
glasses. (Makes 6 servings.)

SANGRIA

¼ cup Superfine Sugar (or
   Simple Syrup)
1 cup Water
1 Thinly Sliced Orange
1 Thinly Sliced Lime
1 bottle (750-ml) Red or
   Rosé Wine
6 oz. Sparkling Water
Assorted Seasonal Fruits
   (bananas, strawberries,
   etc.)

Dissolve sugar/syrup in water
in large pitcher. Add fruit and
wine and 12 or more ice
cubes. Stir until cold. Add
sparkling water. Serve in red-
wine glasses, putting some
fruit in each glass. (Makes 10
servings.)

WHITE WINE CUP

4 tsps. Superfine Sugar (or
   Simple Syrup)
6 oz. Club Soda
1 tbsp. Triple Sec
1 tbsp. Curaçao
2 oz. Brandy
16 oz. White Wine

Put all ingredients in large
glass pitcher with ice. Stir
and garnish with fruits in
season and a rind of
cucumber inserted on each
side of pitcher. Top with a
small bunch of mint sprigs.
Serve in white-wine glasses.
(Makes 6 servings.)

TEQUILA PUNCH

1 liter Chilled Tequila
1 bottle (750-ml) Cham-
pagne, Chilled
4 bottles (750-ml) White
Wine
64 oz. Fresh Fruits (cubes
or balls)

Put all ingredients in large
punch bowl and sweeten to
taste with simple syrup. Add
ice cubes just before serving.
(Makes 40 servings.)

WEST INDIAN PUNCH

64 oz. Light Rum
1 bottle (750-ml) Crème de
Banana
32 oz. Pineapple Juice
32 oz. Orange Juice
32 oz. Lemon Juice
¾ cup Superfine Sugar (or
Simple Syrup)
1 tsp. Grated Nutmeg
1 tsp. Cinnamon
½ tsp. Grated Cloves
6 oz. Club Soda

Dissolve sugar/syrup and
spices in club soda. Pour into
large punch bowl over a
block of ice and add rum,
crème de banana, and juices.
Stir and garnish with sliced
bananas. (Makes 48 serv-
ings.)

WHISKEY SOUR PUNCH

3 cans (6-oz) Frozen
Lemonade Concentrate
thawed and undiluted
4 cups Whiskey (Bourbon)
3 cups Orange Juice
1 bottle (2-liter) Chilled
Club Soda

Combine all ingredients over
block of ice in punch bowl.
Stir gently. Garnish with
orange slices. (Makes 32
servings.)

EGGNOGS AND PUNCHES

HOT PUNCHES

HOT APPLE BRANDY

6 cups Apple Juice
1 1/2 cups Apricot-flavored
   Brandy
3 Cinnamon Sticks
1/2 tsp. Ground Cloves

Simmer all ingredients over
low heat for 30 minutes.
Serve warm in brandy
snifters. (Makes 6 to 8 servings.)

HOT BURGUNDY PUNCH

1/4 cup Sugar
1 1/2 cups Boiling Water
Peel of 1/2 Lemon
1 3-inch Cinnamon Stick
5 Whole Cloves
1/2 tsp. Ground Allspice
1 cup Apple Juice
1 bottle (750-ml) Red Burgundy Wine (or Pinot
   Noir)

In large saucepan, dissolve
sugar in boiling water. Add
lemon peel, cinnamon,
cloves, allspice, and apple
juice. Cook over moderately
high heat for 15 minutes.
Strain into another saucepan
and add wine. Simmer over
low heat but do not boil.
Serve hot in heat-proof cups
with a sprinkle of fresh-grated
nutmeg. (Makes 16 servings.)

HOT RUMMED CIDER

1 1/2 qts. Apple Cider
6 tbsps. Brown Sugar
3 tbsps. Butter
1 1/2 cups Light Rum

Bring cider and sugar to a
boil in large saucepan.
Reduce heat and add butter.
When butter is melted, add
rum. Serve in heat-proof
punch bowl or pitcher.
(Makes 6 to 8 servings.)

SMUGGLER'S BREW

1 1/2 cups Dark Rum
1 qt. Tea
3 tbsps. Butter
1/2 cup Sugar
1/2 tsp. Nutmeg
1/2 cup Brandy

Heat all ingredients except
brandy in large saucepan
until boiling. Heat brandy in
small saucepan until barely
warm and add to rum mix-
ture. Pour into heat-proof
container to serve. (Makes 8
servings.)

WINTER CIDER

1½ cups Rum
1 cup Peach-flavored
    Brandy
¾ cup Peach Schnapps
6 Cinnamon Sticks
1 gal. Apple Cider

In large saucepan, bring cider and cinnamon to a full boil over medium heat. Reduce heat and add rum, brandy, and schnapps, stirring until heated through. Serve in Irish coffee glasses, garnished with a cinnamon stick and an apple slice. (Makes 18 to 20 servings.)

NONALCOHOLIC PUNCHES

BANANA PUNCH

1½ qts. Water
3 cups Sugar
12 oz. Frozen Orange
    Juice Concentrate,
    thawed and undiluted
46 oz. Pineapple Grapefruit
    Juice
4 Bananas, Mashed
Club Soda

Mix water and sugar. Add juices and bananas. Pour into quart-size freezer containers and freeze overnight. About 1 hour before serving, remove from freezer and place mixture in punch bowl. Add 1 liter of club soda per 2 quarts of mix and stir gently. (Makes 40 servings.)

DOUBLE BERRY PUNCH

2 qts. Cranberry Juice
3 cups Raspberry-flavored
    Soda, Chilled
10 oz. Frozen Raspberries,
    Thawed
1 qt. Raspberry Sherbet

Chill cranberry juice in punch bowl. Just before serving, slowly pour in soda and stir gently. Serve over small scoops of sherbet in punch cups and garnish with raspberries. (Makes 25 to 30 servings.)

FUNSHINE FIZZ

2 cups Orange Juice
2 cups Pineapple Juice
1 pint Orange Sherbet
1 cup Club Soda

Combine first three ingredients in blender, blending until smooth. Pour mixture into pitcher and stir in club soda. Serve in collins glasses. (Makes 6 to 8 servings.)

TROPICAL CREAM PUNCH

14 oz. Sweetened Condensed Milk
6 oz. Frozen Orange Juice Concentrate, thawed and undiluted
6 oz. Frozen Pineapple Juice Concentrate, thawed and undiluted
1 bottle (2-liter) Chilled Club Soda

In punch bowl, combine sweetened condensed milk and juice concentrates; mix well. Add club soda, and stir gently. Add block of ice and garnish with orange slices. (Makes 22 servings.)

WINE IN MIXED DRINKS

I t's true that there aren't many cocktails that employ classic varietal wines like Chardonnay, Cabernet, or Merlot (we do list a couple in the following pages), but wine is a broad term for several subcategories less familiar to classic wine drinkers until you say their names—many of which are proprietary. Do Fernet Branca, Dubonnet, and Lillet sound familiar? How about bitters or vermouth? All of these are wines that are aromatized, meaning they are wines whose basic grape flavor has been augmented with the addition of flavorings such as spices, herbs, flowers, nuts, honey, or even, as in the case of the Greek wine Retsina, pine resin.

Proprietary aromatics are often sipped solo in Europe either before or after a meal, whereas here in the United States they more often show up in cocktails. Vermouth, on the other hand, is familiar to anyone who drinks Martinis or Manhattans, as the Martini calls for the smallest drop of dry vermouth, while the Manhattan begs for just a kiss of sweet vermouth. Vermouth is wine infused with herbs, alcohol, sugar, caramel, and water according to specific recipes crafted in France and Italy. There are three types of Vermouth: **Dry,** which is white, usually 18 percent alcohol (36-proof), and contains at most 5 percent residual sugar; **Sweet,** which can be white (bianco) or red (rosso), and is usually 15 percent to 16 percent alcohol (30–32-proof) with up to 15 percent sugar; **Half-Sweet** vermouth is the least well known and least used of the three.

Sparkling wine and/or Champagne is used in many cocktails, often splashed on top of a drink to add a touch of fizz. In the classic Champagne Cocktail, of course, the bubbly is the main ingredient, as it should be. Unless specified, use a dry Brut style of Champagne or sparkling wine.

Lastly, the term Claret in some of the following begs description, as its inclusion in recipes like the Claret Cobbler and Claret Lemonade hearken back to the very first edition of this book. Claret was a British term used to describe what was originally a rosé wine from Bordeaux—*clairet* in French—but, by the advent of the cocktail, it had simply come to mean red Bordeaux wine, which is a blend of Cabernet Sauvignon and Merlot grapes (along with three lesser known grapes). Therefore, feel free to use whatever red wine you like in recipes calling for Claret.

1815

2 oz. Ramazzotti Amaro
½ oz. Lemon Juice
½ oz Lime Juice
Ginger Ale

Shake with ice and strain into ice-filled collins glass. Top with ginger ale and garnish with a lemon and lime wedge.

AMERICANO

2 oz. Sweet Vermouth
2 oz. Campari
Club Soda

Pour sweet vermouth and Campari into ice-filled highball glass. Fill with club soda and stir. Add a twist of lemon peel.

ANDALUSIA

1½ oz. Dry Sherry
½ oz. Brandy
½ oz. Light Rum

Stir well with ice and strain into chilled cocktail glass.

BISHOP

¾ oz. Lemon Juice
1 oz. Orange Juice
1 tsp. Superfine Sugar (or Simple Syrup)
Red Burgundy

Shake with ice and strain into chilled highball glass. Add two ice cubes, fill with Burgundy, and stir well. Garnish with seasonal fruits.

BRAZIL COCKTAIL

1½ oz. Dry Vermouth
1½ oz. Dry Sherry
1 dash Bitters
¼ tsp. Anisette

Stir with ice and strain into chilled cocktail glass.

BROKEN SPUR COCKTAIL

¾ oz. Sweet Vermouth
1½ oz. Port
¼ tsp. Triple Sec

Stir with ice and strain into chilled cocktail glass.

CHAMPAGNE COCKTAIL

1 cube Sugar
2 dashes Bitters
Champagne, Chilled

Place sugar and bitters in
chilled Champagne flute and
fill with Champagne. Add a
twist of lemon peel.

CHRYSANTHEMUM COCKTAIL

1½ oz. Dry Vermouth
¾ oz. Benedictine
3 dashes Pastis (Pernod or
Other Absinthe Substi-
tute)

Stir with ice and strain into
chilled cocktail glass. Garnish
with a twist of orange.

CLARET COBBLER

1 tsp. Superfine Sugar (or
Simple Syrup)
2 oz. Club Soda
3 oz. Claret or Red Wine

Dissolve sugar/syrup in club
soda and then add claret. Fill
red-wine glass with ice and
stir. Garnish with fruits in
season. Serve with straws.

DEATH IN THE AFTERNOON

1 oz. Pastis (Pernod or
Other Absinthe Substi-
tute)
5 oz. Champagne, Chilled

Pour Pastis into a Cham-
pagne flute. Top with Champagne.

DIPLOMAT

1½ oz. Dry Vermouth
½ oz. Sweet Vermouth
2 dashes Bitters
½ tsp. Maraschino Liqueur

Stir with ice and strain into
chilled cocktail glass. Serve
with a half-slice of lemon and
a maraschino cherry.

FALLING LEAVES

2 oz. Reisling (Alsatian)
1 oz. Pear Eau De Vie
½ oz. Honey Syrup*
½ oz. Orange Curaçao
1 dash Peychaud's Bitters

Shake all ingredients with ice
and strain into a chilled
cocktail glass. Garnish with
star anise.

*To make honey syrup: Mix equal
parts of honey and warm water. Stir
until dissolved, and then chill.

WINE IN MIXED DRINKS

KIR ROYALE

6 oz. Champagne, Chilled
1 splash Crème de Cassis

Pour into large Champagne flute or white-wine glass.

LEMONADE (CLARET)

2 tsps. Superfine Sugar (or Simple Syrup)
2 oz. Lemon Juice
2 oz. Claret or Red Wine

Dissolve sugar/syrup and lemon juice in collins glass. Add ice and enough water to fill glass, leaving room to float wine. Garnish with slices of orange and lemon, and a maraschino cherry. Serve with straws.

LEMONADE (MODERN)

1 Lemon
2 tsps. Superfine Sugar (or Simple Syrup)
1½ oz. Dry Sherry
1 oz. Sloe Gin
Club Soda

Cut lemon into quarters and muddle well with sugar/syrup. Add sherry and sloe gin. Shake with ice and strain into chilled collins glass. Fill glass with club soda.

LONDON SPECIAL

1 cube Sugar
2 dashes Bitters
Champagne, Chilled

Put a large twist of orange peel into Champagne flute. Add sugar and bitters. Fill with Champagne and stir.

PIMM'S CUP

2 oz. Pimm's Number One
3 oz. Ginger Ale or Lemon-Lime Soda

Pour Pimm's into pint glass; fill with ice. Top with chilled ginger ale. Garnish with a slice of lemon and a slice of cucumber.

PORT WINE COCKTAIL

2½ oz. Port
½ tsp. Brandy

Stir with ice and strain into chilled cocktail glass.

PORT WINE SANGAREE

½ tsp. Superfine Sugar (or Simple Syrup)
1 tsp. Water
2 oz. Port
Club Soda
1 tbsp. Brandy

Dissolve sugar/syrup in water in highball glass. Add Port and ice cubes. Fill with club soda to nearly top of glass and stir. Float brandy on top and sprinkle with fresh-grated nutmeg.

TRIDENT

1 oz. Dry Sherry
1 oz. Cynar
1 oz. Aquavit
2 dashes Peach Bitters

Stir with ice and strain into chilled cocktail glass. Garnish with a twist of lemon peel.

NON-
ALCOHOLIC
DRINKS

There's a very good chance that, among your circle of friends and acquaintances, there are those who do not consume alcohol at all. While it's certainly important that you respect their personal choice not to drink, there's no reason why nondrinkers cannot raise their glasses in a toast with a libation that's prepared with the care and creativity with which all mixed drinks and cocktails are made.

Most everyone has heard of a Virgin Mary and Shirley Temple, and recipes for these old standards are included here. But there are also nonalcoholic versions of other popular cocktails, such as the Unfuzzy Navel and Punchless Piña Colada. From the frosty Summertime Barbarian to the refreshingly tangy

Yellowjacket, you'll find quaffs to offer nondrinkers that are a giant step above plain old soft drinks.

Who knows? Perhaps you may even make one for yourself when you're the designated driver, or order one when you're at a business meal or important meeting. Feel free to be creative and experiment with omitting the alcohol in some of the standard cocktail recipes throughout this book, especially those made with a variety of fresh fruit juices. And, of course, don't forget that presentation is just as important with these drinks as with any other.

BEACH BLANKET BINGO

3 oz. Cranberry Juice
3 oz. Varietal Grape Juice
(Chenin Blanc, etc.)
Club Soda

Pour juices into ice-filled
highball glass. Top with club
soda and stir. Garnish with a
lime wedge.

BUBBLETART

3 oz. Cranberry Juice
1 oz. Lime Juice
3 oz. Mineral Water

Shake juices with ice and
strain into chilled highball
glass. Fill with mineral water.
Garnish with a lime wheel.

BUBBLY ORANGEADE

4 tsps. Orange Juice Con-
centrate, thawed and
undiluted
3/4 cup Club Soda

Stir together in collins glass
and then add ice. Garnish
with an orange slice.

COFFEE ALMOND FLOAT

1/4 cup Instant Coffee
2 tbsps. Water
4 cups Milk
2 tbsps. Brown Sugar
1/4 tsp. Almond Extract
Chocolate Ice Cream

Dissolve coffee in water in a
pitcher. Add milk, brown
sugar, and almond extract.
Stir well and pour over ice
cubes into parfait glasses. Top
with a scoop of ice cream.
(Makes 4 to 6 servings.)

COFFEE-COLA COOLER

2 cups Cold Coffee
1 tbsp. Maple Syrup
12 oz. Chilled Cola

Combine coffee and maple
syrup. Slowly stir in cola.
Serve in ice-filled collins
glasses. Garnish with lemon
slices. (Makes 3 to 4 servings.)

CRANBERRY COOLER

2 oz. Cranberry Juice
1/2 tbsp. Lime Juice
Club Soda

Add juices to ice-filled collins
glass. Top with club soda and
stir. Garnish with a twist of
lime.

CREAMY CREAMSICLE

8 oz. Orange Juice
2 scoops Vanilla Ice Cream

Combine all ingredients in
blender on low speed. Pour
into highball glass and garnish with an orange slice.

CROW'S NEST

4 oz. Orange Juice
1 oz. Cranberry Juice
1/2 tsp. Grenadine

Shake with ice and strain into
ice-filled old-fashioned glass.
Garnish with a lime slice.

FLAMINGO

4 oz. Cranberry Juice
2 oz. Pineapple Juice
1/2 oz. Lemon Juice
2 oz. Club Soda

Shake juices with ice and strain into highball glass. Top with club soda and stir. Garnish with a lime wedge.

FRUIT SMOOTHIE

8 oz. Chilled Orange Juice
1 Banana, peeled and sliced
1/2 cup Ripe Strawberries, Blueberries, or Raspberries

Combine all ingredients in blender on low speed. Pour into highball glass and garnish with assorted fruits.

FUZZY LEMON FIZZ

6 oz. Peach Nectar
4 oz. Lemon-lime Soda

Pour ingredients into ice-filled highball glass. Garnish with a twist of lemon peel.

GRAPEBERRY

3 oz. Cranberry Juice
3 oz. Grapefruit Juice

Combine juices in large ice-filled red-wine glass. Garnish with a wedge of lime and serve with a short straw.

ICED MOCHA

2 cups Milk
1/3 cup Chocolate Syrup
1 tbsp. Instant Coffee

Combine milk, chocolate syrup, and coffee, and mix well. Pour into ice-filled collins glasses. Top with whipped cream and chocolate shavings. (Makes 3 to 4 servings.)

INNOCENT PASSION

4 oz. Passion Fruit Juice
1 dash Cranberry Juice
1 dash Lemon Juice
Club Soda

Combine juices in ice-filled highball glass. Top with club soda, and stir. Add a maraschino cherry and a long straw.

LAVA FLOW

4 oz. Light Cream
1/2 oz. Coconut Cream
3 oz. Pineapple Juice
1/2 Banana
1/2 cup Strawberries, sliced

Combine all ingredients except strawberries in blender with 1 cup ice and blend until smooth. Put strawberries at the bottom of a parfait glass, then quickly pour in blended mixture for a starburst effect.

LEMON SQUASH

1 Lemon, peeled and quartered
2 tsps. Superfine Sugar (or Simple Syrup)
Club Soda

Muddle lemon and sugar/syrup well in collins glass until juice is well extracted. Then fill glass with ice. Add club soda and stir. Garnish with fruits.

LEMONADE (CARBONATED)

2 tsps. Superfine Sugar (or Simple Syrup)
1 oz. Lemon Juice
Club Soda

Dissolve sugar/syrup and lemon juice in collins glass. Add ice and enough club soda to fill glass, and then stir. Garnish with slices of orange and lemon, and a maraschino cherry. Serve with straws.

LEMONADE (FRUIT)

1 oz. Lemon Juice
2 tsps. Superfine Sugar (or Simple Syrup)
1 oz. Raspberry Syrup
Water

Combine in collins glass. Add ice cubes and enough water to fill glass, and then stir. Garnish with slices of orange and lemon, and a maraschino cherry. Serve with straws.

LEMONADE (PLAIN)

2 tsps. Superfine Sugar (or Simple Syrup)
1 oz. Lemon Juice
Water

Stir sugar/syrup and lemon juice in collins glass. Fill glass with ice. Fill with water and stir well. Garnish with slices of orange and lemon, and a maraschino cherry.

LIME COLA

½ oz. Lime Juice
Cola

Add juice to ice-filled collins glass. Fill with cola. Stir and add a long twist of lime.

LIME COOLER

1 tbsp. Lime Juice
Tonic Water

Add lime juice to ice-filled collins glass. Top with tonic water. Garnish with a lime wedge.

LIMEADE

3 oz. Lime Juice
3 tsps. Superfine Sugar (or Simple Syrup)
Water

Combine in collins glass, then add ice and enough water to fill glass. Stir, and add a wedge of lime and a maraschino cherry. Serve with straws.

LITTLE ENGINEER

4 oz. Pineapple Juice
4 oz. Orange Juice
½ oz. Grenadine

Pour over ice in parfait glass. Garnish with a paper flag.

ORANGE AND TONIC

6 oz. Orange Juice
4 oz. Tonic Water

Pour ingredients over ice into highball glass. Garnish with a lime wedge.

ORANGEADE

6 oz. Orange Juice
1 tsp. Superfine Sugar (or Simple Syrup)

Mix in collins glass. Add ice cubes and enough water to fill glass, and stir. Garnish with slices of orange and lemon, and two maraschino cherries. Serve with straws.

PASSION FRUIT SPRITZER

4 oz. Passion Fruit Juice
Club Soda

Pour juice into Champagne flute and fill with club soda. Garnish with a lime wedge.

PEACH MELBA

8 oz. Peach Nectar
2 scoops Vanilla Ice Cream
½ Whole Sliced Peach
3 oz. Ripe Raspberries

Combine all ingredients in blender on low speed. Pour into highball glass and garnish with raspberries.

PUNCHLESS PIÑA COLADA

1 oz. Cream of Coconut
1 oz. Pineapple Juice
1 tsp. Lime Juice

Combine all ingredients in blender with 1 cup of crushed ice. Pour into collins glass. Garnish with a slice of pineapple and a maraschino cherry.

RUMLESS RICKEY

1 oz. Lime Juice
1 dash Grenadine
1 dash Bitters
Club Soda

Add juice, grenadine, and bitters to ice-filled old-fashioned glass. Top with club soda. Stir. Garnish with a long twist of lime.

RUNNER'S MARK

4 oz. V-8 Vegetable Juice
2 drops Tabasco Sauce
2 drops Lemon Juice
1 dash Worcestershire Sauce

Combine all ingredients in ice-filled old-fashioned glass. Stir, and garnish with a celery stalk or scallion.

SHIRLEY TEMPLE

Ginger Ale
1 dash Grenadine

Add grenadine to ice-filled collins glass; top with ginger ale. Garnish with an orange slice and a maraschino cherry. .

STRAWBERRY WONDERLAND

1 oz. Coconut Cream
2 oz. Frozen Strawberries
3 oz. Pineapple Juice
1/2 oz. Superfine Sugar (or Simple Syrup)
1/2 oz. Lemon Juice

Combine all ingredients in blender with 1 cup ice and blend until smooth. Pour into snifter. Top with whipped cream and garnish with a strawberry.

SUMMERTIME BARBARIAN

1/2 cup Fresh Strawberries
1/2 cup Fresh Pineapple
1/2 cup Grapefruit Juice

Combine all ingredients in blender with 1 cup ice and blend until smooth. Pour into collins glasses. Garnish with kiwi fruit wheels. (Makes 2 servings.)

SUNSHINE SPLASH

3 oz. Pineapple Juice
3 oz. Orange Juice
1/2 oz. Superfine Sugar (or Simple Syrup)
1/2 oz. Lemon Juice
1/2 oz. Grenadine
2 oz. Lemon-lime Soda

Pour into ice-filled parfait glass and stir. Garnish with a pineapple slice.

TOMATO COOLER

8 oz. Tomato Juice
2 tbsps. Lemon or Lime Juice
Tonic Water

Combine tomato and lemon juices in ice-filled highball glass and top with tonic water. Garnish with a wedge of lime, a sprig of dill, and a cucumber slice.

UNFUZZY NAVEL

3 oz. Peach Nectar
1 tbsp. Lemon Juice
3 oz. Orange Juice
1 dash Grenadine

Combine all ingredients in shaker with ice. Strain into chilled red-wine glass. Garnish with an orange slice.

VIRGIN MARY

4 oz. Tomato Juice
1 dash Lemon Juice
1/2 tsp. Worcestershire Sauce
2 drops Tabasco Sauce
Salt and Pepper to taste

Fill a large wine glass with ice. Add tomato juice, then remainder of ingredients. Stir and garnish with a wedge of lime.

WAVEBENDER

1 oz. Orange Juice
½ oz. Lemon Juice
1 tsp. Grenadine
5 oz. Ginger Ale

Shake juices and grenadine with ice and strain into ice-filled highball glass. Top with ginger ale and stir.

YELLOWJACKET

2 oz. Pineapple Juice
2 oz. Orange Juice
½ oz. Lemon Juice

Shake with ice and strain into ice-filled old-fashioned glass. Garnish with a lemon slice.

INDEX